The Astounding UFO Secrets of James W. Moseley

A Special Tribute To The Editor of Saucer Smear And The Court Jester Of UFOlogy

Includes The Full Text Of "UFO Crash Secrets At Wright-Patterson Air Force Base"

ISBN:1606111442

ISBN 13: 9781606111444

Copyright © 2013 by Timothy Green Beckley

dba Global Communications/Inner Light

Box 753 · New Brunswick, NJ 08903

Cover graphic © Luca Oleastri/Dreamstime.com

Cover Design by William Kern

Staff Members

Timothy Green Beckley, Publisher

Carol Anne Rodriguez, Assistant to the Publisher

Sean Casteel, General Associate Editor

Tim R. Swartz, Graphics and Editorial Consultant

William Kern, Layout, Formatting and Art Consultant

Credit Card Order Hotline: 1-732-602-3407

PayPal: Mr UFO8@hotmail.com

CONTENTS

THIS BOOK IS DEDICATED TO JIM MOSELEY'S DAUGHTER

BETTY MOSELEY

FOR THE COMMANDER IN CHIEF WHO LIVED A DREAM – A POEM BY EDGAR ALLAN POE

A DREAM WITHIN A DREAM

Take this kiss upon the brow!
And, in parting from you now,
Thus much let me avow-
You are not wrong, who deem
That my days have been a dream;
Yet if hope has flown away
In a night, or in a day,
In a vision, or in none,
Is it therefore the less gone?
All that we see or seem
Is but a dream within a dream.

I stand amid the roar
Of a surf-tormented shore,
And I hold within my hand
Grains of the golden sand-
How few! yet how they creep
Through my fingers to the deep,
While I weep- while I weep!
O God! can I not grasp
Them with a tighter clasp?
O God! can I not save
One from the pitiless wave?
Is all that we see or seem
But a dream within a dream?

Edgar Allan Poe

Jim Moseley and his daughter, Betty, to whom this book is sincerely dedicated.
Photo by Antonio Huneeus

Caption—A photo of the author taken in the late 1960s standing next to the famous late-night radio talk show host, Long John Nebel.

**Somewhere within the perimeter of Wright-Patterson Air Force Base
is said to exist "Hangar 18," where crashed UFOs
and Alien Bodies may still be stored!**

Photos by James W. Moseley

INTRODUCTION

WEIRD HAPPENINGS AT WRIGHT-PATTERSON

When a UFO crashed outside the town of Roswell, New Mexico in July, 1947, rumor spread that the wreckage—as well as the remains of several alien beings who had been onboard the ill-fated craft—was quickly gathered up by the military, put on the back of a flatbed truck and hauled away. Within hours—at the most several days—the ship and the badly-burned aliens were flown to Wright Patterson Air Force Base for scientific analysis and research purposes.

Speculation that a mysterious building known as "Hangar 18" might contain the remains of these small, gray-colored, extraterrestrials and their vehicle has remained constant over the years. Supposedly, there have been other crash landings in addition to the one at Roswell, and whatever was found—wreckage and bodies—ended up stored in this facility near Dayton, Ohio.

Such accounts have been fueled by the fact that the Air Force's various UFO projects (including Project Blue Book, its most famous) have been headquartered at this base. In addition, there have been many bizarre tales told by various retired military personnel who, while stationed at Wright Patterson, insist they "stumbled" upon the "truth" when they saw with their own eyes what they couldn't at first believe, and which they were later told to shut up about by their superior officers.

Furthermore, it remains a curious fact that even the likes of Senator Barry Goldwater has not been allowed inside this highly restricted area even though he is a retired Major in the Air Force and possesses a Top Secret security clearance. Goldwater, over the years, has written several letters to various researchers verifying this. Thus, it remains a puzzle why—if Hangar 18 doesn't contain something very unusual—he would not have been granted the right to inspect the inside of this facility.

Those who have followed UFOs will instantly recognize the name James W. Moseley, for Jim has a reputation in the field for being "older than dirt," in that he has been trying to track down these elusive disks as far back as the early 1950s. A veteran researcher who, until recently, made his home in Key West, Florida, Moseley was the former editor and publisher of SAUCER NEWS (a magazine that in its heyday had nearly 10,000 subscribers), and he once put on the largest indoor UFO convention of all time, attracting 15,000 to the three day event held at New York's Hotel Commodore in 1967. Moseley—as those who know him can testify—is a no nonsense sort of guy when it comes to UFOs. Though he'll give just about anyone the benefit of the doubt, he's always questioning, probing, trying to get to the heart of the matter regardless of the outcome or what repercussions it may have.

Way back in 1954, Jim tried to get onto Wright-PattersonAir Force Base and was turned away."I happened to be passing through Dayton," Moseley recalls "and decided to telephone the base. I managed to get through to the officer then in charge of the UFO project. However, I was told that no one except accredited newsmen were allowed on the base, and that was the end of it!"

Over the years, Jim would drop in periodically at the Pentagon in Washington to interview whoever was in charge of releasing UFO information to the public. Several times he tried to get the okay to visit Wright-Patterson Air Force Base. Finally, on March 28, 1962 he was admitted to the facility—no cameras were to be permitted and he was asked not to name the exact building where he was taken.

"I had no opportunity to see any rooms other than the one in which my host, Col. Friend, worked. But in the halls were signs reading, approximately, 'This is a Security Area.'" For the most part, Moseley's trip to the base was uneventful—certainly he was not shown the contents of Hangar 18. But he did learn something about the way UFO reports were handled.

"At Wright Field, all cases are accurately filed both according to date and location.. . .Then, after Wright-Patterson's complete analysis has been done, approximately 2% of the cases are re-investigated personally either by Col. Friend or any of four other officers at his disposal, who are sent out from the base to the area,wherever it may be, that the sighting took place....In analyzing and solving UFO reports, Wright Field has at its disposal equipment which could not be duplicated by civilian researchers without the expenditure of many thousands of dollars—or perhaps millions. Col. Friend has, when necessary,the use of photographic, chemical and aeronautical laboratories. By simple phone calls, he can consult with aircraft project chiefs concerning experimental aircraft flights, or with personnel who have complete data about missile, satellite and balloon launchings."

While at the base, Jim says he only saw or heard one thing which seems pretty peculiar—if not downright mysterious. "There was a blackboard in Col. Friend's office with peculiar writing on it. This writing was peculiar because it obviously was not in our alphabet. I asked Friend about it, and he said (as nearly as I can recall) that it was a motto or saying, in ancient Syrian, which he had copied out of a book and which he had left up on the blackboard for the past week just to attract questions from visitors to his office. He told me what the motto was, but I unfortunately have forgotten it, as I did not write it down at the time. It was something nearly as commonplace as 'Never put off till tomorrow what you can do today.' But why put mottos in strange languages on the blackboard of an office devoted to serious intelligence work?"

Despite the fact that Jim might not have learned anything particularly earthshaking on his "official" visit to the base, it did not stop him from digging deeper and uncovering some potentially damaging evidence that the Air Force, the U.S. government, and the military, know a hell of a lot more about UFOs and aliens than they are letting any of us know about. This book should provide even further evidence that there is possibly something "not of Earth" inside Hangar 18!

The Publisher

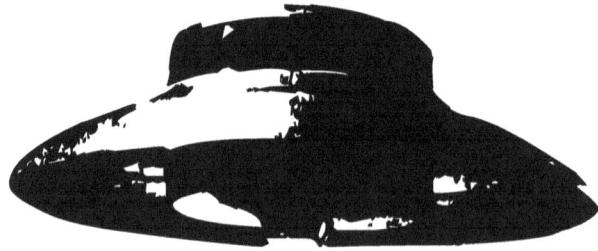

GLOBAL COMMUNICATIONS
EX LIBRIS
POST OFFICE BOX 753
NEW BRUNSWICK, NJ 08903

THE ASTOUNDING UFO SECRETS OF JAMES W. MOSELEY

Memories Are Made Of This —

A Personal Look Back At Jim Moseley

By Timothy Green Beckley

As Told To Sean Casteel

This is the book the author swore to the day he died that he never wrote! Jim Moseley insisted that his beer-drinking buddy, Gray Barker, a long time UFO researcher like himself, wrote the manuscript you are holding during a series of late night, alcohol-fueled sessions, pounding away on a manual typewriter into the wee hours of the morning.

The work was originally published by Barker's Saucerian Press back in the 1970s and I obtained the rights from Jim by paying him a one time "buy out" fee while on a visit to Moseley's one-room museum in Key West, Florida. But before I went forward with my plans, I did a little research of my own, as I was uncertain as to why Barker would spend so much time starting from scratch to pen a book that he knew would probably only go through a very small press run of maybe a thousand or fifteen hundred copies at best.

Thumbing through this volume I immediately recognized most of the material in its reincarnated form. What Barker had done was to take Moseley's earliest writings that had appeared in the pages of "Saucer News" when the magazine was still called "Nexus." This would have been the period around 1953 — 1955. These were the articles Moseley had planned to use in a book he hoped to write following his travels around the United States in search of the true meaning of the mysterious craft then most popularly known as flying saucers.

The wording was mostly Jim's with a bit of "transforming" by publisher Barker.

1

THE ASTOUNDING UFO SECRETS OF JAMES W. MOSELEY

But by no means was this a case of "ghostwriting." Hell, all of contactee George Adamski's books were ghostwritten by the likes of Charlotte Blob and Little Listening Post publisher Clara John; and hadn't Ray Palmer said he had rewritten almost all of Richard Shaver's prose? Hardly a punishable crime by any literary standards – even in this field where the picky sometimes get overly sticky.

What Barker had done to make Moseley's book "unique" was to put it in a "timeline" format, as if these were the subjects being covered on a Long John Nebel Party Line broadcast over radio station WOR in New York that Jim was appearing as a guest on. It never happened in this manner, but it is a clever twist, and Barker was a master of the English idiom, more so than anyone else in the UFO field . . . certainly more than my friend Jimbo.

My first recollections of meeting Jim Moseley go back to the early to mid-1960s. I was a fan of the aforementioned Long John Nebel radio talk show. Now, Long John of course was broadcasting long before Art Bell and George Noory, and he had regular shows on the paranormal, though he heavily specialized in flying saucers. His regulars included some of the most famous contactees of the era, like George Adamski, George Van Tassel, Orfeo Angelucci.

Let it be known, Long John was not a big believer in UFOs, and he certainly didn't profess to believe in some of these far out tales where the contactees claimed that they had actually met a Venuisian in the desert or traveled inside cigar-shaped ships to other planets. In some cases, their stories got even wilder. However, he did give everyone the free opportunity to discuss these subjects, which were pretty taboo in those days.

Among Long John's regular panelists were science fiction writers like Arthur C. Clarke. Even Jackie Gleason would be on the show from time to time. Jackie had one of the largest private libraries on psychic phenomena in the world. Also appearing at that time, on a regular basis, was Jim Moseley.

Jim was the publisher of a magazine called "Saucer News," which had previously been called "Nexus." His publication was pretty widely read. Like Long John, Jim didn't find himself swallowing some of the more hysterical elements in the UFO field. He certainly was not a believer in George Adamski, who he pretty much exposed in an early issue of his publication. So I got to know Jim as a guest on the Long John Show, and I would regularly attend monthly UFO meetings that he hosted around the rather seamy Time Square area of Manhattan. I was only 14 or 15 at the time, so my brother-in-law Carl would take me on a bus over to the Port Authority. Moseley's meetings were quite eventful. It didn't matter if he believed your story or not, he gave everyone a platform (which is more than his critics would ever do!) It was nice to hang out as a teenager with some of the luminaries in the field, and it inspired me later to organize my own conferences, seminars and exposes. After Jim folded his tent, I even founded the New York School of Occult Arts and Sciences, branching out from just a platform for flying saucer speakers.

A MAN OF MANY MOODS

Little by little, I got to know Jim very well. He was pretty gracious about sharing his information and data with people who were serious about the subject, and that included me.

I had my own organization that I had started around 1962. It was called "The Interplanetary News Service," and I put out kind of a hefty little publication. We started out with 50 subscribers and ended up with a circulation of probably about fifteen hundred. We had as many subscribers as APRO had members, actually. The magazine grew to about 40 pages. In those days, there were no quick copy places like Kinko's, so if you put out a UFO-zine you had to print them yourself. We purchased a little mimeograph machine. It was messy, but it did the job.

It got to be too much for me to do. Jim was taking over the circulation of other magazines just so he could build up his own subscription list. He agreed to take over my subscriptions. I was tired of staying at home and just printing every day instead of going out and doing what other teenagers did. We combined my circulation with "Saucer News," and he probably ended up with around 12,000 subscribers. Part of the deal was that he hired me as managing editor of the publication. I started coming in to Manhattan every day and it was a regular job. I sought out advertisers, wrote some short articles and did some of the mail order chores. So the job Jim gave me at "Saucer News" got me started in the publishing business. "Saucer News" was the first of about 30 magazines that I edited or helped to edit over the years. That's how I got to know Jim and he and I were close friends ever since. . . Not that we agreed on everything in or out of "Ufoology," as he liked to call the field. Jim was just sort of liberal and let you go your way – if you let him go his! He did have his mood swings, slept late and drank a lot, but expected his staff to be in the office by 10:30 or 11. I guess he was up burning the midnight oil, drinking a shot or two of Van 69 and cooking up a hoax or two with Gray Barker on the telephone when the rates were lowest (no flat rates in those days).

In 1967, Jim rented out the Hotel Commodore, which had one of the largest indoor lecture facilities. The auditorium held about 2000 people and was right next to Grand Central Station. Jim got some of the top UFOlogical talent of the day and put together a weekend-long convention. He probably drew around 10,000 people over those three days. I was instrumental in running the telephone room because we were getting an average of 100 phone calls an hour. People wanted to know how to get to the convention and how much it was going to cost. We sold out the hall and it was quite a spectacular event. Mainly due to the help of Long John

Nebel, who interviewed each of the guest speakers on his show for the entire week leading up to the convention.

FROM VENUS TO CENTRAL PARK

Long John was also responsible for a very unusual woman named Vivenus showing up for the conference. Vivenus had apparently walked into Long John's office right off the street one day and told his secretary that she was from the Planet Venus. At first, the secretary felt like throwing her out because Vivenus was clearly crazy, but the secretary realized after speaking with her briefly that Vivenus seemed to be an educated and very intelligent woman. So the secretary told Long John that this Venusian woman wanted to come on the air. He put her on and liked her so much that he had her on several nights in a row. She agreed to come to Jim Moseley's conference and to give a talk there, and people were just spellbound by what she said.

She actually claimed that she had landed in a spaceship in Central Park and had taken over the body of a young woman here who was very suicidal and wanted to change her life, so she went off to Venus. I figured they kind of switched bodies or switched souls or whatever you do if you're a walk-in. People came from all over the Tri-State area and probably even further away to hear Vivenus tell her story. She was very popular. Of course, Jim was very skeptical about her story, but as a rule, like I mentioned he always allowed people to have their say whether he believed in their presentation or not.

In the audience was Professor Edward Condon of the infamous Condon Report. He was taking notes and interviewing people and acting "respectable," pretending like he was taking this seriously. Although later on, when he wrote his finished project report, we know he didn't accept any of this type of material, not even the straight-laced reports, never mind the contactees.

Also in attendance was Roy Thinnes, who was the star of the weekly TV show "The Invaders," which was probably one of the most popular science fiction programs ever broadcast. I got to meet people like Howard Menger, who said UFOs were landing on his property in High Bridge, New Jersey, and he was having regular conversations with these individuals.

And for the first time I met someone who has become a lifelong friend of mine, Brad Steiger. Brad was just getting started in the UFO field, and he had just written his first book on UFOs. He was there to meet everybody and take notes. So it was a spectacular program to say the least. They even had a fellow named Louis Abolafia, who was the nudist candidate for president at the time. His motto was, "What have I got to hide?" He was kind of a counterculture personality during the hippy era. He was well known around New York. It wasn't just a UFO conference.

THE ASTOUNDING UFO SECRETS OF JAMES W. MOSELEY

It was also a counterculture, kind of hip thing to do during that particular summer. Everybody that was anybody in the UFO field showed up there. It was a wonderful conference and it's never been repeated again and I damn well know it never will be!

TAKING IT ON THE ROAD

Over the years, Jim and I also did a bit of traveling to investigate some cases. We went down and hooked up with icon Bishop Allen Greenfield of Atlanta to see if we could observe the Brown Mountain Lights in North Carolina. This was a popular phenomenon – "spook lights" we called them. These mysterious glowing orbs would show up on a regular basis and were seen on the tops of the mountains and down into the valleys below. We did see a strange light off to the side of the road, but we didn't think it was really one of the Brown Mountain Lights. Over the course of a couple of days, we talked to quite a few witnesses there. They had even built an observation tower. People felt these lights were under intelligent control. They weren't just swamp gas or marsh gas. People would approach them, then the lights would disappear and show up in back of them, like a mischievous kind of game. It was quite a phenomenon and of course it's been written about over the years.

We also went looking for a ghost in North Carolina. The ghost of a railroad conductor is repeatedly seen there waving a lantern back and forth. Apparently, he had been beheaded in the 19th century in some kind of railroading accident. His ghost is seen along these tracks outside the tiny town of Macon, North Carolina, the phantom railroad conductor. We didn't have any real luck there with seeing it, but we did talk to other people who said they had seen his light and so forth. There were other cases that Jim and I investigated together, but most of my recollections are lost in the fog of time.

Jim, in the early years, right after he had left college, traveled around the country interviewing people. In fact, he was planning to write a book about the early years of UFOs. He traveled along the East Coast and the West Coast and met up with anybody who was anybody of that period, including George Adamski, Orfeo Angelucci and of course George Van Tassel out there at the Giant Rock Airport. But his job as editor and publisher of "Saucer News" was more what I'd call "office-oriented" than actually being on the road.

Of course, he also spent a lot of time in Peru, where he was technically robbing graves, I guess you could say. In his other life, he was a treasure hunter. The thing was, it was illegal to dig up the graves looking for gold artifacts in Peru, but you could bring the gold here into this country legally without any problem. Later on, he had enough artifacts that he even opened up a little museum of his own down in Key West, Florida. He had a couple of spectacular items that I know were of some value. So he did that for a long while until it got impossible to deal in pre Columbian antiquities.

A MAN-IN-BLACK SHOWS UP

Then there was the time that Jim and I encountered a Man-In-Black. Jack Robinson, who was the assistant editor at "Saucer News," had talked to these teenagers in New Jersey who had had a sighting in New Jersey. It was 1967, and there had been a big flap of UFO sightings along the East Coast that included a lot of sightings of humanoids and creatures.

So Jack was talking to these teenagers who had observed a landed craft of some kind and they were out in this field where the sighting had taken place. And parked across the street and down the block was this black car. You know, the Men-In-Black are notorious for coming in black Cadillacs and black Lincolns. Anyway, it appeared as if the men in the car had the window rolled down and were looking or staring in their direction while Jack talked to the witnesses.

Shortly after that day, Jack reported that he was having problems with his telephone and apparently his files were broken into. His wife, Mary, said that whenever she would go to do the errands early in the morning and Jack was on his way to work, she would see this individual dressed in black – a black suit and black hat – standing in the doorway right next to where they lived, apparently watching everybody going in and out of the apartment building.

She called three or four times to tell Jim and me this story. She seemed a little perturbed by what had happened, as if she and Jack were made the target of either some prankster or someone who was really out to do them harm. We didn't know whether to believe Mary or not. It seemed like a pretty farfetched story. But we gave her the benefit of the doubt, and without telling her or Jack what we were going to do, we got into Jim's car at around 8 o'clock in the morning and took the Lincoln Tunnel over to Jersey City. We figured if there was somebody there lurking about, maybe we could see them. If the story was made up, obviously no one would be there. We went to test the waters and see if there was anything going on at all.

Anyway, when we got there, sure enough there was a black car parked at the curb. Now this was rush hour, and the traffic was really packed in. But there was a black car parked there and there was someone lurking in the doorway that fit the general description of one of these MIBs. We decided to go around the block and see if we could find a place to park. One of us was going to confront this individual and see exactly what he was doing there. We went around the block, which took a few minutes. Jim handed me his camera and I took a few photographs of the car and one of the person standing in the doorway. We couldn't find a parking space so we went around the block again. When we got back, the gentleman was gone and the car was gone.

I always told Jim I think this is the only case where UFO investigators actually scared off the Men-In-Black instead of the Men-In-Black scaring off the UFO investigators. He got a chuckle from that. Of course I've told this story over the years and I've published the photographs and been on the television program "UFO Hunters" to discuss this. Now Jim, being his usual skeptical self, said he was not certain that this was an actual Man-In-Black. He thought perhaps it might be a pall bearer, but there was no funeral home around there. Then he figured it might have been a member of the mob or a gangster or something. Well, that's not even plausible. What would he be doing out there at that time of the morning? So I've always believed there was a good possibility that in fact he was some sort of Man-In-Black, a UFO Silencer, whatever you want to call it.

Jim was a little more skeptical about it, but then Jim was skeptical about a lot of things, a little bit more than I was. Jim was of course very skeptical of the contactees. He even published an expose issue of "Saucer News" on George Adamski, and Jim probably lost a lot of readers because Adamski had quite a following. Jim wanted the truth, and he could see there were a lot of elements of the contactees' stories that just did not hold up under close scrutiny. So he published this expose issue, which is still quoted to this day.

There were some people who despised Jim because he was either a member of the silence group or a member of the CIA. Kind of pathetic. But the thing was, Jim had inherited quite a bit of money when he turned 21, so he was – I wouldn't say well-to-do, because he certainly went through the money over the course of his life – but aside from running "Saucer News" and selling those Columbian antiquities, he never really had a regular job. So people who are prone to believe that say, "Oh, he's a member of the silence group" or "He's getting a regular paycheck from the CIA," which is absolutely preposterous. His family had owned stock in the Barber Steamship Line, and when he was old enough he inherited what I heard was a million dollars. Even in those days, a million dollars wasn't a lot of money and it isn't going to last you a lifetime.

Knowing Jim socially, he was a smoker and a drinker and also used other substances. He was a very funny person. He was the type of person you either loved or hated. And of course he had many feuds in his time, some of which were legitimate and some of which were just kind of ridiculous.

FUN AND GAMES WITH GRAY BARKER

For years, there was this big "pretend" feud that he had with his buddy Gray Barker. Gray Barker was a good friend to both of us. He's been deceased now for quite a number of years. If it wasn't for Gray, I'd probably never have become a

THE ASTOUNDING UFO SECRETS OF JAMES W. MOSELEY

UFO publisher. He put out my first three books (and helped write parts of this one!)

Jim and Gray were buddies, and they used to drink together and carry on (not in that way, even though just about everyone realizes Gray was gay during a period when this was certainly not socially permissible – certainly not down south in West Virginia where Gray ran a theatrical booking business along with his modest UFO publishing enterprise).

In fact, they were responsible for creating a number of hoaxes in the UFO field, including the Straith letter. Apparently they had gotten hold of some State Department stationary and pretended to be a person named Straith who worked for the Cultural Exchange Committee. "He" wrote a letter to Adamski confirming UFOs and said Adamski's UFOs were real. And of course Adamski, utilizing anything for the purposes of publicity, used the letter to support his UFO contactee claims. Jim and Gray chuckled about this for many, many years. They would also get drunk together and call people in the middle of the night and make outrageous claims, pretending to be other people who they weren't. They had a good time with this, but to the public, they had this feud going. They would try to attack each other in their various publications figuring it would build circulation.

Jim was truly upset when Gray passed away, and he often spoke of him. Now, Jim always claimed that Gray was totally skeptical and a nonbeliever and just liked to promote the subject to have a good time with it. But I new Gray fairly well too, though certainly not as well as Jim did. And I always thought that at the heart of the matter Gray was probably even a little bit more serious-minded than Jim was. But that's open to question. Jim would have refuted that idea.

People ask me, "What did Jim Moseley really think about UFOs?" And that's kind of hard to say, because he did change his opinions from time to time. In the beginning, I guess like most of us, he felt that UFOs came from outer space. But then he got disillusioned about that possible point of origin fairly early on. He had become firmly established with some of the spokespersons there at Project Blue Book and at Wright-Patterson Air Force Base. So he would believe almost anything they told him. Probably Jim's biggest fault, as far as I was concerned: if somebody told him something, even a skeptic, he wouldn't investigate it himself. If he liked that person, or trusted that person, he would just believe what that individual had to say at face value and not look into it himself. I think that was why people would not consider him a serious researcher toward the end.

But everybody doesn't have to be the same in this field. We have room for a court jester, and Jim was certainly that. But he was also serious about the subject to a large degree. In fact, he did have at least one UFO sighting of his own. He was lying on a beach in Florida looking up at the sky at night when he decided to play a game. Mentally, he told the "stars" up above to move, thinking they might actually be UFOs hiding out in the heavens. Three of them, Jim told me, moved about as if they were intelligently controlled and were responding to his command. Obviously he wouldn't have stayed with the subject for 50 or 60 years, up until the time of his passing away, unless he felt there was something to all this. But he did see the humorous side to it, and certainly the field does have its moments of burlesque. So Jim went into this with a great deal of gusto and he called the shots as he saw them. If some people didn't like the way he called the shots, he didn't give a damn, to be honest with you. So he did have some natural-born enemies, such as the late Budd Hopkins.

THE MOSELEY - HOPKINS FEUD

Jim and Budd did not speak for many, many years. And I was kind of the reason for that, to some degree. Budd had investigated this sighting by a fellow who owned a liquor store over here in Manhattan named George O'Barski. He once claimed that he had seen a saucer, complete with tripod landing gear, and little men get out and dig up some soil samples and then go back inside the craft. This was over in North Hudson Park in New Jersey. There was another sighting there as well. It wasn't the only one. But it was the O'Barski one that Hopkins had made famous. He wrote it up in "The Village Voice" and also later on for "Cosmopolitan Magazine."

Well, I was the publicist for a talk show in Chicago hosted by Warren Freiberg. He was one of the first of these kind of right wing, conservative talk show hosts. But his wife Libby was a psychic and a medium, so he had her on his program and they were characters to say the least. Warren had hired me as his publicist and was a client of mine. I ran a little public relations company at the time.

We decided we were going to take Warren and his wife Libby over to the park where the supposed encounter and sighting had taken place. Libby was going to go into a trance to see if she couldn't contact the ultra-terrestrials behind the sighting. Somehow word of this coming experiment leaked out to the press and there was a front page article about it in the "Newark Star Ledger," which in those days had a circulation of probably a million. So we got to the park and there were six or seven hundred people there waiting for us. It was a night to remember. It was almost like a mini UFO circus. There was an individual dressed in tinfoil carrying sparklers through the crowd. There were people selling UFO-shaped balloons. And people who were just curious came out.

Anyway, Libby and Warren did try to have the séance, but the crowd was disappointed because the aliens didn't show up. And the crowd got a little rowdy, so Jim and I and a small group headed for the Freibergs' car, which the crowd, being crazy, almost tipped over. Then we went to the nearby Stonehenge Apartments building there, which is near where the security guards had seen some weird lights in the sky when the O'Barski encounter had taken place. We tried to have the séance on the roof there and it was actually broadcast on the radio. My clients received quite a bit of publicity.

Budd Hopkins was furious about what had transpired, including quite a bit of media attention, because Jim was hosting a party at his place in Fort Lee after the earlier public display of hoopla. I guess Budd didn't think that Jim was taking this all seriously enough. I'm not sure that we were either, obviously. But to us it was a seemingly credible incident that had taken place there, but Budd got a little bit out of control about it. I mean, it's a UFO sighting, it's a UFO encounter. It's not the end of the world. So if Jim wanted to have a party to celebrate the more bizarre aspects of this – well, Jim had some pretty bizarre parties anyway. So we had another party and Budd got all bent out of shape about it. I don't know if they ever talked after that. For over 30 years, I don't think they ever had a civil word to say about each other.

And there were others who felt the same way about Jim. Myself, I figure we're all in this together, whatever we believe. There's something that always unites us in the end, and UFOs are kind of just a symbol for all this and you've got to see beyond a personal belief system. That's the way I've always felt about it.

But people always asked me, "How can you deal with Jim Moseley if you're serious about this?" Well, you can't be serious all the time. Jim did have his moments of being serious, and he did have his moments of being perhaps a little more frivolous than I would be, but that doesn't mean that I can't respect his approach to this. He certainly did a bang-up job of putting out "Saucer Smear," and I think he kept everybody in line, because you knew if you got just a little bit beyond the norm, he was going to take you to task. And a lot of these guys certainly deserved it.

But an era always has to come to an end. Jim and his outrageous shenanigans certainly had a monumental impact on my life. So I say – Long live the name of Jim Moseley! May he always be remembered! And a toast to him wherever he might be! And the best to his daughter Betty Moseley, who I remember from the time she was still an infant. She had a very unusual father. He was one of a kind, and you can bet your Roswellian saucer wreckage pieces on that fact, my good flying saucer friends.

THE ASTOUNDING UFO SECRETS OF JAMES W. MOSELEY

IN MEMORY OF JAMES W. MOSELEY-Expanded Version

By Antonio Huneeus

On November 18, <u>cryptozoologist Loren Coleman wrote</u>: 'Fortean friend, ufology humorist, and writer James W. Moseley, 81, died Friday night, November 16, 2012. He passed away at a Key West, Florida, hospital, several months after being diagnosed with cancer of the esophagus. Upon hearing of the death of Moseley, Anomalist Books publisher and editor Patrick Huyghe said: "He was one of the <u>last</u> remaining old timers from the golden age of flying saucers. Goodbye, Jim."'

Remembering Jim Moseley (1931-2012), the Voltaire of American Ufology

Friday, November 23, 2012

By Antonio Huneeus

Jim Moseley the way he would want to be remembered: somewhat mysterious and somewhat funny. (Credit: Antonio Huneeus)

Just as I returned from a two-week trip to Chile I found the sad news that my old friend, the "Supreme Commander" James W. Moseley, better known as Jim Moseley, had passed away from cancer on Friday November 16 in Key West, Florida, where he lived for the last few decades. Fortunately, I spoke on the phone with Jim right before my trip; he was still alert and interested in all sorts of ufological gossip, even as he was getting ready to go to the hospital for a complicated cancer surgery. I'll write a more formal biographical profile of Jim in the next issue of Open Minds magazine, of which he was a fan, keeping this piece more personal and informal, which is the way Jim liked to do things, including his relentless but at the same time hilarious critique of American ufology and ufologists.

Jim Moseley was born in 1931, the third son of Major General George Van Horn Moseley, who was a prominent U.S. Army officer but also a notorious right wing and anti-Semitic figure during the FDR era. Jim didn't get along with his father and so became a rebel, quitting Princeton University after a couple of years and pursuing a number of independent activities which included real estate deals, antiquarian pursuits in South America and of course ufology.

Until the last few years, when his age and health slowed him down, Jim was a permanent fixture at all major American UFO conferences. You could always find him at the bar drinking martinis and collecting gossip, which would then appear in his longstanding newsletter "Saucer Smear." This was the only American UFO publication devoted not to UFO cases per se but to the discussion of the personalities of ufologists. It was technically "non-scheduled" and free, although Jim was glad to receive donations, which he called "love offerings." In the last few years it became his main intellectual activity since he always had a lot of fun editing it and making fun of people.

Jim Moseley having some fun with arch-debunker Philip Klass at the MUFON Symposium in Albuquerque, NM, in 1992. (Photo: A. Huneeus)

Many in the UFO community considered Moseley a skeptic because he was always reluctant to accept the validity of some of the more famous incidents like the Roswell crash, the abduction cases researched by Budd Hopkins and others, and the ET theory in general. But Jim was also equally skeptical and sarcastic with the debunkers, making fun of many of the explanations proposed by the late Philip Klass and maintaining a long standing feud with the magician James the Amazing Randi. He could also keep a good friendship with some witnesses and researchers, even though he didn't believe in their cases, as it happened with Ed Walters of the Gulf Breeze, Florida, UFO saga in the late eighties and early nineties. That's why someone (I don't remember who) called him once the Voltaire of ufology in the letter section of "Saucer Smear." Like the famous 18th century wit, who used his pen to ridicule the Catholic Church, the French monarchy and everything else in the society of his time, Moseley was critical and sarcastic regarding just about everything and everybody in ufology. Yet Jim did believe a core of the UFO phenomenon was real and truly unexplained after filtering out all the hoaxes, conspiracy theories, misidentifications and just plain nonsense that pervades much of the field. Philosophically he was closer to Jacques Vallee and Col. John Alexander, about whom he expressed admiration in some of our last phone conversations.

Moseley, the time machine

Moseley shaking hands with President Harry Truman at a press conference in Clarksburg, West Virginia, in 1962. (Photo: Gray Barker/ James W. Moseley)

Moseley's investigation of UFOs began in 1953, when he traveled throughout the USA trying to elucidate what was then the new mystery of flying saucers. He visited the Project Blue Book facilities at Wright-Patterson Air Force Base in Dayton, Ohio, meeting Col. Bob Friend. He attended the famous "Giant Rock" contactee convention and interviewed many witnesses, researchers and officials. He even met former President Harry Truman at his office in Independence, Missouri, and asked him about flying saucers. In what became one of Moseley's favorite anecdotes, Truman responded, "I've never seen a purple cow, I never hope to see one." This was the serious period of Moseley's career, when he published "Saucer News," which was a critical publication devoted to real cases and investigations and not just gossip.

One of "Saucer News'" most famous issues was an exposé of the colorful contactee George Adamski, who was then at the peak of his fame. Later, Moseley produced a famous hoax with his compadre Gray Barker (an open promoter of ufology who was not shy of "inventing" cases when needed), the so-called "Straith letter" mailed to Adamski by an alleged official from the "Cultural Exchange Committee" of the U.S. Department of State, which confirmed and encouraged Adamski's claims of contact with benign blondes from Venus and elsewhere in the solar system. Adamski was delighted and paraded the "Straith letter" as proof of his claims, which led to an FBI investigation. Only after Barker's death in 1984 did Jim Moseley publish the full inside story of how he and Barker created the letter using real U.S. government stationary that Barker had obtained from a friend.

THE ASTOUNDING UFO SECRETS OF JAMES W. MOSELEY

Jim Moseley in his "Indiana Jones" period in Peru in 1954. (Photo: James W. Moseley)

I don't remember exactly the year I first met Jim Moseley, although it must have been around 1978 or 1979, but I do recall the circumstances. It was at a party in the Manhattan apartment of his close friend Tim Beckley, the well known publisher of many paranormal and UFO-related books, whom I had met recently and who was publishing some of my early UFO articles. Jim and I struck up a good friendship immediately, as he was very knowledgeable of the field and had a great sense of humor. We also had a common interest for all things South American, as one of Jim's most cherished periods was the few years in the late fifties when he went back and forth to Peru and to a lesser extent Ecuador and northern Chile, purchasing and digging up pre-Columbian antiquities. Moseley was unabashed about his grave-robbing activities, his adventurous days as a huaquero (from the Quechua word 'huaco' for pottery, found frequently in tombs) as they are called in the Andean countries.

One of Jim's funniest anecdotes he told me personally many years ago was when the Peruvian Ambassador to the UN in that period came to dinner at Moseley's apartment in Gutenberg, New Jersey (he owned the building back then). To avoid any possible legal problems in Peru (the black market antiquities trade is now enforced strictly in South America but back then was a different story) Jim gave the Ambassador a $2,000 bribe in cash inside a paper bag. When Moseley moved to Key West, Florida, sometime in the eighties, he opened a pre-Columbian art gallery. His prized collection (which I once saw at his Gutenberg apartment in a locked glass cabinet) was eventually donated to the Graves Museum of Archaeology and Natural History in Dante, Florida, near Fort Lauderdale.

Cover of Moseley's UFO memoirs, coauthored with Karl Pflock, Shockingly Close to the Truth!, published in 2002. (Photo: PrometheusBooks)

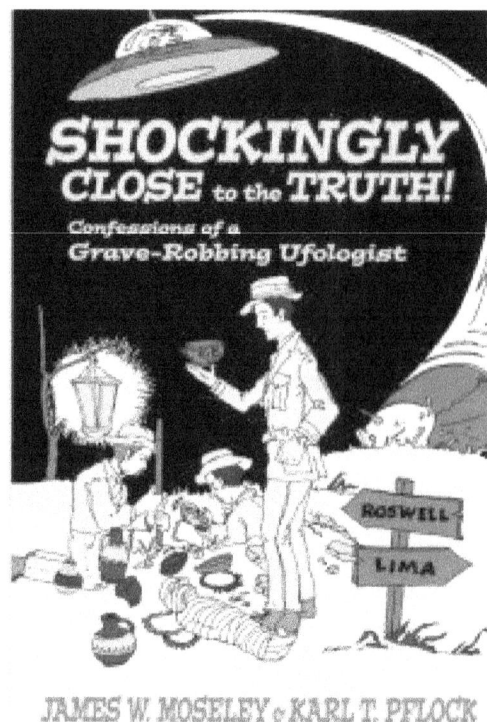

It would take a whole book to narrate all the

funny, sometimes insightful, sometimes banal and occasionally outrageous, anecdotes of Jim Moseley's unique pursuit of ufology. He kept complete diaries of his early investigations in the fifties with the intention of publishing a book someday, but he needed a partner to sort them out. This finally happened in the late nineties when he teamed up with the late Karl Pflock. Karl had an interesting background which included a professional career in the CIA and the Department of Defense and also a longstanding interest in UFOs (he had been a member of NICAP). After his retirement from government service, Pflock became a Roswell researcher (he started out believing in its ET origin but in the end accepted the government's official explanation of the Mogul balloon). Pflock and Moseley thought alike about most ufological topics and they struck up a great partnership. Pflock had called Moseley "a time machine" because of the huge number of UFO personalities and stories he had seen or investigated first-hand. The result was the 2002 book, "Shockingly Close to the Truth! –Confessions of a Grave-Robbing Ufologist." Jim was very proud of this book, as opposed to his earlier "The Wright Field Story," which was a hack job produced by Barker (it was later reprinted by Tim Beckley as "UFO Crash Secrets at Wright-Patterson Air Force Base").

Moseley and friends attending a Conference in 2001 at the Gray Barker Collection, housed at the Clarksburg-Harrison Public Library in West Virginia, where historical records are kept. (Left to right): Tom Benson, Jim Moseley, Antonio Huneeus and librarian David Houchin, curator of the Barker Collection. (Photo: A. Huneeus)

Moseley also played an important role in organizing UFO conferences in the period between the sixties and mid-nineties. He put together an outfit called the National UFO Conference (NUFOC), which was not a formal members' organization but basically a vehicle to put on an annual conference in different parts of the country. His most famous conference was a huge one with well over a thousand attendees in 1967 at the Commodore Hotel in New York City, at the peak of the flying saucer controversy in the sixties. He put on another one in New York in 1980 which I attended as a journalist. One of NUFOC's highlights was the "Ufologist of the Year" award given to a researcher every year. I was honored to receive that award at the NUFOC Conference in Miami Beach in 1990.

Antonio Huneeus receives the "Ufologist of the Year award" at the National UFO Conference in Miami Beach in 1990. (Photo: Huneeus Collection)

There can be little doubt that the "Supreme Commander" (as stated on the masthead of "Saucer Smear") Jim Moseley was a unique personality that will never be replaced. He played the role of the joker, making a permanent social commentary about the state of ufology in America. He was an equal-opportunity cynic as the debunkers and skeptics were certainly not immune from his barbs. But underneath it all he was a good guy and he was also truly fascinated and baffled by the inside core of unexplained UFO incidents. His iconoclast style will certainly be missed and let's hope that he doesn't team up with Gray Barker again and begin to produce hoaxes from "the other side."

Following his move to Key West, Moseley would still visit the New York area often to meet old friends and local ufologists. (Left to right): Tim Beckley, Moseley, Harold Salkin, John Keel and Carol Rodriguez. (Photo: A. Huneeus)

Jim Moseley and his daughter Betty in 1993. (Photo: A. Huneeus)

2012-11-23 23:05:58

Source: http://www.openminds.tv/remembering-jim-moseley-1931-2012-the-voltaire-of-american-ufology/

Antonio Huneeus has had a long and illustrious career writing about UFOs and the paranormal and is an editor at "Open Minds Magazine."

THE ASTOUNDING UFO SECRETS OF JAMES W. MOSELEY

James W. Moseley as Trickster

By George P. Hansen

It is "not how men think in myths, but how myths operate in men's minds without their being aware of the fact."

—Claude Lévi-Strauss

Jim Moseley has been called the Clown Prince and the Court Jester of UFOlogy. The appellations are entirely fitting—Moseley was indeed a trickster. He perpetrated some amusing hoaxes, exposed others, mocked and antagonized UFOlogy's "establishment," and often referred to the field as "UFOOLogy."

During the eight years I spent writing *The Trickster and the Paranormal*, I often pondered Jim's life and work. His zine, *Saucer Smear,* provided invaluable information—information critical to judicious assessments of UFO cases, witnesses, and researchers. But for me, Moseley was more than that; he himself was one of the trickster exemplars that I used in my thinking.

Here I want to express my appreciation for Jim Moseley, comment from the perspective of trickster theory, and explain why he remains an important figure. Moseley, UFO phenomena, and the field of UFOlogy generally share some abstract qualities that can be illuminated by recourse to certain scholarly works on the trickster. Those works help clarify several major predicaments of UFOlogy. But before I say much about Moseley and UFOlogy, I will need to explain a few concepts.

THE ASTOUNDING UFO SECRETS OF JAMES W. MOSELEY

What Is "The Trickster"?

The trickster is a character type found worldwide in mythology and folklore, and trickster tales must number in the thousands. The trickster is something of an irrational being. He—the trickster is typically male—can be seen as a personification of a cluster of abstract qualities that often manifest together. These include deception, disruption, abnormal sexuality, boundary crossing, taboo breaking, supernatural/paranormal powers, marginality, and outsider-hood. When a few of these characteristics are found in a person, group, or situation, one should be alert for others.

The trickster is an irrational figure; he cannot be captured by a crisp, precise definition; there is necessarily some blurriness and ambiguity. Though there is considerable academic analysis of the trickster in anthropology, literary theory, Jungian psychology and folklore, that work is appreciated by few people in our culture today.

UFOs, Myth, Ritual, and the Trickster

In the 1960s and 1970s, John Keel and Jacques Vallee pointed out that reports of UFO occupants are strikingly similar to entities described in myths and folklore. During those same decades, anthropologists made significant advances in understanding myth and ritual. That scholarship can be applied to UFO phenomena. However, most scientists, including most UFOlogists, shun the topics of myth and ritual. Those are often thought to be remnants of superstition and hence have no place in science. Yet myths have survived for thousands of years; it is hubris to dismiss them.

The most illuminating theoretical work on the trickster utilizes analyses of myth and ritual—particularly the structural study of myth (which focuses on binary oppositions) and the analyses of ritual that generated the concept of *liminality*. Earlier cultures used myth to understand supernatural forces and ritual to channel and control them. It is under liminal conditions, and around liminal people, that paranormal (i.e., supernatural) events are more likely to be reported.

I find it impossible to give a succinct, comprehensible, and comprehensive explanation of liminality. But briefly, it involves change, transition, transformation, flux, ambiguity, instability, blurred boundaries, and uncertainty—these apply both to persons (e.g., James Moseley) and to groups (e.g., the field of UFOlogy). Some synonyms include betwixt and between, interstitial, and anti-structure. Marginality and outsider-hood are types of liminality. Paranormal organizations and phenomena display properties of liminality. The trickster exemplifies the concept.[1]

Most people probably associate the trickster with deception, and that provides an obvious connection to UFOlogy. The field is plagued by frauds, hoaxes, con artists, and government disinformation, even though the vast majority of UFO reports are made by honest people. Deception is one of UFOlogy's greatest challenges. But there are many other aspects of UFOlogy that can be addressed within the framework of trickster theory. I will describe only a couple of applications here—anti-structure and the betwixt and between.

Anti-structure

Anti-structure is a synonym of liminality. It primarily refers to conditions of instability in social relations, including those within and between institutions. Strong manifestations of anti-structure are incompatible with hierarchical institutions. Groups and organizations that seek to directly study paranormal phenomena using rational, scientific methods frequently encounter infighting, schisms, and dissolution. UFOlogy has never established viable, long-lasting, well-recognized, widely-trusted institutions that study and comment authoritatively on the phenomena. No university departments are devoted to the study of UFOs. College courses on the topic are rarely offered for academic credit.

UFOs generate massive popular interest. UFO movies have grossed hundreds of millions of dollars. In contrast, the more serious interest by MUFON, CUFOS, and other organizations gains meager support. Most research is done by individuals and small groups, who operate independently of larger institutions. This state of affairs illustrates the anti-structural nature of the field.

Moseley's style was highly compatible with anti-structure. His UFO activities were not undertaken as an employee or representative of any organization, and he proudly proclaimed his low rank within the UFO field by appending "J.S." to his name on the masthead of *Smear* (*J.S.* standing for *Journal Subscriber* of the *MUFON UFO Journal*).

Moseley did head NUFOC (National UFO Conference), but it was a small group that only occasionally helped him to organize conferences. A few colleagues assisted him with *Smear*. For instance, Vince Ditchkus provided him with information from the Internet, but *Smear* was essentially Moseley's product. His newsletter appeared for 59 years. It was produced by an individual, not an organization, thus reflecting the anti-structural nature of UFOlogy.

Betwixt and Between

A concept closely related to liminality is the *betwixt and between*. Among other things, it refers to a social position between two larger or more powerful groups.

Moseley held a spot betwixt and between aggressive proponents and sneering debunkers. He was not part of UFOlogy's "establishment," but neither was he

THE ASTOUNDING UFO SECRETS OF JAMES W. MOSELEY

a fan of the Committee for Skeptical Inquiry (CSI, formerly CSICOP). Moseley accepted the reality of UFOs, even though *Shockingly Close to the Truth* was published by Prometheus Books, whose founder co-founded CSICOP.

Moseley maintained open, even friendly, relations with individual skeptics and debunkers. He has described Philip Klass as a personal friend, and Klass's comments frequently appeared in *Smear*. Also, Moseley published remarks from Michael Dennett, Martin Gardner, James Oberg, Gary Posner, Tim Printy, James Randi, and Robert Sheaffer. Shortly after Moseley's death, Lance Moody reported that, "Jim and I had long conversations about once a month for 20 years. I loved talking to him, hearing all of his stories and discussing UFOs and the paranormal. We never had a single cross word even though he knew I was a hard core skeptic."[2]

While Moseley was friends with individual proponents and skeptics of UFOs, his relations with "the establishment" of UFOlogy were not so warm. Members of that establishment were not shy in saying what they thought of him.

Jerry Clark, author of many books on UFOs and longtime editor of *International UFO Reporter* of the Center for UFO Studies (CUFOS), wrote to Moseley: "Though you have nothing of consequence to say about the UFO phenomenon as such anymore (if you ever did, after you exposed Adamski), you are still the Greatest Living Authority on the history of saucer fandom and the funniest writer around." (Posted above the masthead of *Saucer Smear*, October 5th, 2002).

Michael Swords, a now-retired professor, a stalwart member of CUFOS, and former editor of its *Journal of UFO Studies*, wrote the following: "Moseley, however nice a guy he may or may not be, has spent a life fouling the waters of UFOlogy with hoaxes, misrepresentations, rumors, misplaced 'humor' ... it has been an almost wholly unhelpful 'career' to the field." (ellipses in original).[3]

Richard Hall was perhaps the epitome of establishment UFOlogy. He worked for NICAP, served as a board member of MUFON, wrote a column for *UFO Magazine*, and was dubbed the "dean of UFOlogy." His feelings toward Moseley were those of revulsion. In an online roast that celebrated Moseley's 50 years of saucering, Hall responded to a commentator who wrote, "Love him or hate him, there's no denying Jim Moseley, for better or worse, has been and remains a Presence in UFOlogy." Hall replied, "Yes, like a steaming turd on the living room carpet. This sort of silly crap explains why you and your idol, who constantly treat the whole subject as a joke, might just as well be on the Government payroll for UFO debunkers."[4]

Clark, Swords, and Hall served in official capacities within major organizations of UFOlogy. They spent decades of their lives contributing to the field and attempting to gain mainstream acceptance for it.[5] Moseley, on the other hand, had little concern for such acceptance; he not only accepted his marginality, he reveled in it.

Tricksters are often looked upon with suspicion, especially by those who aspire to respectability. Tricksters today are frequently seen as amusing or annoying, but also as rather inconsequential characters, not serious, and not worthy of much attention.

Centuries ago, court jesters were held in esteem; they were often highly intelligent and were allowed to say what others were not. Earlier cultures honored them and understood their importance.

Moseley's Significance

Shortly after Moseley died, Lance Moody reported, "We spoke about two weeks ago and had an excellent and upbeat conversation. He faced his illness soberly. He also wondered if his life with UFO's had any value—in the end I think he concluded that he had fun and that maybe that was enough."[6]

Grandiosity is an occupational hazard of UFO research, but Jim avoided it. I never found him to be pompous, pretentious, or self-important. Consequently, he seems not to have recognized his own substantial contributions to the field. They were masked by humor, and it is easy for many (including himself) to overlook or dismiss them. Yet in more than two decades of non-subscribing to *Smear*, I found sharp intellectual engagement, impressive critical judgment, and commentary far more credible and insightful than that produced by the major UFO organizations.

My own view of Moseley's *Saucer Smear* was expressed by the late psychic Ingo Swann, who was an official non-subscriber. (Swann trained many of the U.S. government's psychic spies, and he reported a number of bizarre UFO encounters himself.) Swann wrote: "Although many of its readers might view 'Saucer Smear' merely as a droll UFOlogy gossip rag, in the larger picture it is rather more accurately a profound 'window' opening up onto the sociology of UFOlogy. Therefore its cumulative issues constitute a precious historical archive." (See *Saucer Smear*, January 5, 1995, page 1).

If UFOlogy sees substantial intellectual advances in the years to come, I am confident that Moseley's work will be much more appreciated than it is today. Jim exemplified the liminal, anti-structural, marginal, trickster nature of UFOlogy and of UFO phenomena. Both his writings and his life are worthy of contemplation.

Endnotes:

1. The most advanced theoretical work on the trickster was done by Barbara

Babcock in 1975. That work has been largely ignored by white male members of the academic establishment. Black scholars, American Indian scholars, and some women have recognized its importance. Those who have been in positions of significant marginality often have some appreciation for the trickster. See: Babcock-Abrahams, Barbara. (1975). "A Tolerated Margin of Mess": The Trickster and His Tales Reconsidered. *Journal of the Folklore Institute*, Vol. 11, pp. 147-186. An early, noteworthy application of liminality to the topic of UFOs is Peter Rogerson's 1986 paper "Taken to the Limits." As far as I am aware, it is the earliest work that provides significant discussion of liminality in relation to the paranormal. See: Rogerson, Peter. (1986). Taken to the Limits. *Magonia*, No. 23, July, pp. 3-12. Available at: http://magonia.haaan.com/2009/limits-1/ and http://magonia.haaan.com/2009/limits-2/

2. For Moseley's acknowledgment of his friendship with Klass, see the video prepared by Lance Moody on YouTube at http://www.youtube.com/watch?v=lOokh3re0G8. For Moody's brief account of his contact with Moseley, see Moody's post on Kevin Randle's blog on November 18, 2012 at http://kevinrandle.blogspot.com/2012/11/jim-moseley-is-dead.html.

3. See Michael Swords' blog post of July 18, 2012 at http://thebiggeststudy.blogspot.com/2012_07_01_archive.html.

4. For background information on Richard Hall, see Rojas, Rick. (2009, August 23). 'Dean' of UFO Studies Devoted Life to Seeking Others Beyond Earth. *Washington Post*, at http://articles.washingtonpost.com/2009-08-23/news/36812967_1. For Hall's comment on Moseley, see http://www.martiansgohome.com/moseley_roast/memories.html.

5. I submit that their failure to gain such mainstream recognition had little to do with any personal character flaws, rather the liminal nature of UFO phenomena themselves precludes acceptance by establishment institutions of science.

6. See Moody's post on Kevin Randle's blog on November 18, 2012 at http://kevinrandle.blogspot.com/2012/11/jim-moseley-is-dead.html.

George P. Hansen was an official non-subscriber to *Saucer Smear* for more than two decades. For eight years he was employed full time in parapsychology laboratories. He is author of *The Trickster and the Paranormal*.

PUBLISHER'S NOTE: Referencing Michael Swords' comments — at least Moseley did what he did openly with no attempt to conceal his approach; while others do the same in a condescending way behind everyone else's backs. Mr. Swords seems awfully naive for someone associated with the field for such a long time. Same with Jerry Clark, who flip flops back and forth in his beliefs and takes the easiest approach to the field and its solution. Talk about thinking INSIDE the box.

THE ASTOUNDING UFO SECRETS OF JAMES W. MOSELEY

THE SILVER AGE OF THE FLYING DISCS IS OVER

By Tim Brigham

The silver age of the Saucers, the Flying Discs, has ended. I mark the end as having occurred in November of 2012 with the death of my friend, Jim Moseley (aka James W. Moseley), editor of the longest running UFO magazine in the known universe. Loved, hated, but ever-present in the world of the UFO, or the 'Saucer' as he called it, was Jim.

Jim has been referred to as "the court jester of ufology," as well as "a boil on the ass of" the same (by John Keel), an insult Jim proudly printed in the masthead of his 'zine "Saucer Smear," as it was called during its later years. But others have taken on the task of sharing Jim's history, and detailing his better known escapades. Special thanks are due to Tim Beckley, whose reissue of the book you now hold in your hands helps assure that at least some record of Jim's adventures live on.

It is the honor I had of being close friends with Jim for over 20 years before he passed from this realm at the age of 81 to which my thoughts now turn. My own strange story intertwined with his when I met him at the impressionable age of 14. Having grown up during the "Gulf Breeze UFO flap," which gained national media coverage, I read UFO books from the library in my bed late at night with a clear view of the skies in which the UFOs were allegedly zipping around routinely. Soon I stumbled into one of the first UFO conventions held in Gulf Breeze, where I met the UFO gurus and celebs, from Budd Hopkins to Phil Klass. And then there was Jim Moseley, who seemed oddly immune to, yet fascinated by, the strange and powerful social dynamics at work in this curious "Saucer scene." A world in which, when voicing skepticism of even some of the wilder claims – the abductions, the super top secret government cover-ups, etc – one might quickly in response observe the wide smile of a gentle New-Ager quickly disappear, as I saw it do the first evening I conversed with Jim when he snapped a photo of Budd Hopkins during a cocktail party, to which Budd responded by giving Jim "the finger."

"Did you see that?!" Jim asked me, purely due to my spatial proximity at the moment. "He gave me the finger! Ha ha!"

Later, I wandered over to the hotel bar and the semi-mysterious man who had taken the picture. Sitting at the bar, smoking Winston cigarettes and having a rum and Coke, was the guy everyone seemed to whisper about snidely, all the while sneaking photos of him and excitedly commenting in still barely audible tones, "Hey, that's Jim Moseley!"

He loved every moment.

Jim was the first person I met who maintained a non-dogmatic yet genuinely curious view of this strange UFO enigma, and thus I was immediately drawn to him. Perhaps just as amazing to me at the time, Jim was BOLD about it. He said and wrote what he thought, with no fear of giving his opinion on a topic or person if asked, and even if not! Jim didn't know all the answers, and he was not afraid to tell you that neither did anyone else. He could laugh along with anyone over a drink, whether he thought they were genuine or, as he often did, thought they were full of shit. As many can attest, Jim was also an amazing story teller, and he had many stories to tell. He knew all the original guys, he mentioned names like Hynek and Adamski as if they were sitting in a room next door. He talked of shrunken heads from Peru.

A bottle of "Old Smuggler" brand rum was for many years both a gift and inside joke in reference to Jim's (later well known)… "amateur archeology" work. "Grave-robbing," that would be to you and me, as it was to Jim. As detailed in the time capsule you now hold in your hands, it was during one of his Peruvian expeditions that he made note of something that would become another aspect of the saucer mythos that he would, depending on your point of view, either popularize or create. The smart answer is probably both. It was en route via airplane to a Peruvian expedition site that he passed over the Nazca Lines, noting the oddness of them being only interpretable from the air. Decades later, I obtained an original copy of the "Fate Magazine" in which Jim had written, with impressive authority, informing the Saucer world of the now (in)famous connection between the Nazca Lines and UFOs. He would gain another measure of fame (or infamy – perhaps it was the same to Jim) by being the only American to ever dig upon the Nazca Lines. Whether this honor is official or, like many of Jim's other expeditions, occurred under "questionable legal and archeological" circumstances is a question I neither know nor care to know the answer to. It was a hell of a story! I can picture my old friend, at a midnight dig in Peru, with only his money and his wits keeping him alive.

Jim never shied from the fact that he, like his best friend Gray Barker, whose death preceded Jim's by over two decades, approached the Saucer enigma with a mindset of wonder and FUN. He was a hunter of, and simultaneously, a creator of, modern mythology. Similarly, Jim deserves credit for his role in popularizing the idea of "The Men-in-Black," with his friend Barker.

Jim's approach in "Saucer Smear" was perhaps best summed up when he was referred to as "The Hunter S. Thompson of UFOs." Gonzo journalism was the only way to capture the high weirdness and strangeness of both the Saucer story and the characters involved in it. Jim, like all great storytellers, embellished some aspects of the mythos, yet the UFOs represented to him a genuine mystery, a fact he reiterated often yet which seemed to go unheard by those wishing to pigeon-hole him as a skeptic or hoaxer. Jim would talk deeply, not just about the characters, but the Saucers themselves. He thought understanding the Saucers required an element of what he could only call "4D" thinking. Saucers were something "real," but truly reaching an understanding of what they were would require a lengthy scientific quest, to be done by guys like me (Jim often tried to invigorate my interest in Saucers, sometimes playing to my ego). In return, I reminded him of the genuine impact he had on my life, both as a mentor in the wild world of The Saucers, and also as a good friend.

For about 10 years we met regularly, often in his travels to Gulf Breeze, sometimes at other UFO conferences he encouraged me to attend. We spoke weekly on the phone for most of the years of our friendship. As I attended graduate school (in part because of Jim's encouragement) I withdrew from "the field," Jim sometimes being my only contact with the saucers at all.-
Our greatest moment never to occur was the 2001 National UFO Conference (which had run annually for something like 30 years). I had been appointed by Jim as one of the members of the "permanent organizing committee," a position for which I got no pay but admittedly did no work. It was a sign of love from Jim. This particular NUFOC event was to be held by SMiles Lewis in Austin, Texas, at the Alamo Drafthouse. We had even booked Robert Anton Wilson to come and receive the "lifetime achievement award." I stare at a postcard in which Jim pitched the idea that "Bob" (who suffered from post polio syndrome and spent most of his time in a wheelchair at that point) should receive the award and suddenly rise from his chair, exclaiming, "I can walk! Hallelujah!" Big plans were playing out. I was to be on an evening panel and help present the award to RAW at what would surely be the coolest UFO convention to never take place. I held my boarding pass and turned on the radio. My flight was to leave at 11am on September 11th, 2001. Perhaps it could never have lived up to the possibility.

THE ASTOUNDING UFO SECRETS OF JAMES W. MOSELEY

In later years, Jim didn't travel as much, for a variety of reasons. I never made it to Key West, but our friendship continued. I have perhaps hundreds of his signature postcards stamped "Burn before reading!" with a personal message on the other side. As the years passed since we had last seen each other, he suddenly promoted me to "Contributing Editor" of "Saucer Smear" (a move he later told me was to draw me back in - which worked!). Jim kept writing "Saucer Smear," on a typewriter, and mailing it out about every 6 weeks up until his death. The final issue of "Saucer Smear" had been sent to the printer just prior to Jim being admitted to the hospital from which he would step off this plane to join Gray Barker and Karl Pflock. I did what I felt was my duty to my friend by (with the help of many) releasing his final issue after his death. As Contributing Editor (Retired), I can only advise as Jim so often did: Watch the skies!

Tim Brigham was a personal friend of Jim Moseley and a contributing editor to "Saucer Smear."

THE ASTOUNDING UFO SECRETS OF JAMES W. MOSELEY

The Passing Parade in the UFO Field

By Gene Steinberg

As I write this issue, I'm still thinking about all the years I knew Jim Moseley, who passed away early this year, 2013, at the ripe old age of 81. My friend Jim was both writer and court jester, the gadfly of the UFO field. But he was, alas, only one of the elder statesmen who left us in recent years.

Since The Paracast debuted in 2006, we have broadcast special shows honoring the memories of such veteran researchers as John Keel, Richard Hall, and Lucius Farish.

Except for Hall, with whom I had some bad run-ins during the 1960s, they were all good friends, and I only regret they never appeared on the show. In contrast, we featured Moseley as a guest on 16 different episodes, including the very first one, in 2006, which also included Brad Steiger in a separate segment. The special episode to honor Moseley aired soon after his passing.

I think it's fair to suggest that we have one of the larger online archives featuring the voice of Jim Moseley. The Paracast's staff announcer, Bob Zanotti, also has a number of analog recordings of Jim that were recorded in the 1960s, when he was a guest on Bob's "Coffee Klatch" radio show. That show was broadcast from a college station in East Orange, NJ, and had a surprisingly large following throughout the New York area.

In the larger scheme of things, however, as the so-called "old guard" of Ufology passes, it's fitting to examine their legacy, their influence on the field, and how they may have helped us make progress towards finding a solution to the ever-elusive enigma.

THE ASTOUNDING UFO SECRETS OF JAMES W. MOSELEY

When it comes to Jim, aside from the phony feuds and silly hoaxes he and his pal Gray Barker were engaged in during the early years, he was also a chronicler of the UFO subculture. To him, it was very much about the sometimes eccentric people who got heavily involved in chasing after mysterious flying objects. It has always been fascinating to attempt to understand what attracts people to devote sometimes most of their working lives to the subject, even though there are rarely any large financial rewards.

Yes, when it comes to money, don't expect to earn much of a living from writing about flying saucers, although a few lecturers, including Jim, managed to make a decent living as a visiting expert over the years. When it comes to books, authors are lucky to get an advance against royalties, and when they do, it's rarely more than a few thousand dollars. That may seem to be decent pay, except when you consider that it may have taken a few years to write those books.

Yes, it's true that a few authors of UFO books have written best sellers, such as Leslie Kean, Budd Hopkins, Whitley Strieber, and even Major Donald E. Keyhoe, to name a few of the more successful scribes.

But Jim once admitted to me that he and co-author Karl Pflock shared approximately $4,000 in advances from their publisher for their efforts in writing "Shockingly Close to the Truth." Several thousand copies were printed, and Moseley said he heard that some 1,500 were left unsold at the publisher's warehouse a decade after the book's publication.

Could it be that the sum of 50 years of Moseley's life was worth no more than a pittance to a major book publisher? Hardly, as anyone who became a "non-subscriber" to "Saucer Smear," and eagerly read each and every issue, will attest.

As for Lucius Farish, who died earlier this year, he helped keep the subject alive by providing a UFO news clipping service to subscribers over the years, and as a sponsor of regular conventions covering the paranormal. Indeed, whenever I would begin to think that fewer people were seeing the saucers over the years, I'd soon get an envelope from Farish with lots of cases to chew over.

Richard Hall, who died in 2009, was a straight-ahead UFO researcher, serving once as assistant to Major Keyhoe at the legendary UFO club, NICAP. He was responsible for two volumes of "The UFO Evidence," which extensively chronicled sightings over the years, and made a compelling case for the possibility that we were being visited by extraterrestrials.

I had my unpleasant encounter with Hall in the 1960s, when, upon visiting NICAP headquarters with several friends in the field, was unceremoniously shown the door. That unfriendly reaction stemmed in large part from the fact that I was working as Managing Editor for Moseley's original "Saucer News." It seems that Jim and Hall were decidedly at odds with one another in those days

There was one episode, in fact, when Moseley called NICAP headquarters to ask about a matter, probably a sighting, only to have Hall accuse him of recording the conversation. As anyone who knew Moseley over the years can testify, he was decidedly un-technical. I don't think he even owned a tape recorder, ever. And, even though "Saucer Smear" was eventually offered online, the actual version Jim wrote and edited was all done on an aging portable electric typewriter, printed on regular paper, and mailed via the U.S. Postal Service in regular envelopes. Jim not only never used or owned a personal computer, he also didn't have a fax machine or an answering machine. Plus, his two telephone lines didn't even include Caller ID.

A decade after this unfortunate episode at NICAP headquarters, Hall and I shook hands and made up. Years later, he was too ill to participate when I invited him to appear as a guest on The Paracast.

John Keel, who also left us in 2009, was an intriguing contrast to the usual run of UFO authors. He usually focused on the negative – some say possibly the demonic side – of the UFO enigma. The cases he described in great detail in his books and occasional lecture appearances were all about paranormal side effects, strange phone calls in the night, and visits by the Men-In-Black. To him, we were all the victims of deception and misinformation, and woe to the person who got too heavily involved with the subject.

Sure, it was also fair to suggest that the level of scholarship in Keel's books was seriously lacking, and they often read more like pulp mystery novels than serious compendiums of facts and theories.

But it's also true that Keel helped us to think out of the box, to consider possibilities, even though potentially frightening, which may have not occurred to us had we accepted what passes for conventional wisdom in the UFO field.

There are others who were among us over the years who also made sometimes significant contributions to advancing the UFO field. As more of us enter our twilight years, it's fitting that we remember what came before, and learn from their wisdom, and, yes, their mistakes, as we continue to strive to understand the great mystery that we continue to confront.

Gene Steinberg is the host of "The Paracast" at paracast.com

THE ASTOUNDING UFO SECRETS OF JAMES W. MOSELEY

Smear On, Jim!

By Allen Greenfield

In the 50th Anniversary Roast I commented,

I began reading "Saucer News" in 1961 or 62, first corresponded with Jim about then, met him at the FIRST National UFO Conference in Cleveland in June of 1964; we chatted in my room after the big public session until Jim was too smashed to talk, and I have considered him a friend ever since. We visited Ray Palmer together in '65, chased the Brown Mountain Lights together, ghosts on the Georgia Coast, etc., in the late '60s. And at his GIANT SAUCER SHOW at the Commodore Hotel in NYC I chaired his delegate sessions, went on The Amazing Randi's show with Tim Beckley, and - uhm - we'll skip the '70s. But I lived for awhile in Key West after Jim "retired" there and we hung out a lot. I've known him since my teens, and I consider him one of the funniest, most intelligent, most complex and worthwhile people I have had the pleasure to know. I once owned something like a complete set of "Saucer News," back to NEXUS "Book One Tome One" (whatever that means). And I do hope to see him at least once more in this present incarnation. I really wish someone would post the picture here of Moseley and the late Georgia governor Lester Maddox, as Maddox pretended to read what he called "Sausage News," telling JW how much he loved sausage. Take that however you want. Smear on Jim!

(**posted:** Fri Jul 23 03:38:28 2004) The Wikipedia piece on him is almost as off

THE ASTOUNDING UFO SECRETS OF JAMES W. MOSELEY

point as the entry on me, so I won't send you there. Look it up, but grains of salt. "The Key West Citizen's" online Obit is fairly accurate and quite respectful.

Thursday, November 22, 2012

JAMES MOSELEY

James Moseley, known as Jim, was born Aug. 4, 1931, in Brooklyn, N.Y. He was the only child of the famous General Van Moseley and Florence Barber, one of the heirs to the Barber Steamship Lines of New York City. Jim loved travel most of all. His fondest memories were of his youthful days in Peru and the excavating of various Incan pottery and gold.

He loved the excitement, danger, and his girlfriend Josephine, and the Spanish culture and language. He returned to the U.S. to New York City and started "Saucer News" magazine after getting involved with the offbeat crowd in Greenwich Village. It was there that he met his wife, Sandra.

He then established the National UFO Conference and managed the first N.Y.C. convention. He had one child, Elizabeth, in 1963. He later became a landlord, which he hated, saying "everyone hates the landlord."

He moved to Key West in 1983 with his girlfriend Anna and her son, Patrick, and owned Rose Lane Gardens, a motel behind Fat Tuesdays, in downtown Key West. He had an antique gallery with some remaining antiques from Peru. He owned an apartment building, also on Duval Street.

Jim was a Key West character who was an original. He made a lot of jokes about life and death, and the unknown.

He was a pioneer in the UFO field of investigation. He did radio and TV interviews, and some film. He continued to lecture on the existence of UFOs. He thought both sides of the story were fascinating. He was interested in the serious investigation, or even if it was a fake, but more importantly, he put a humorous twist to it. That was clear in the "Saucer Smear" magazine he published for many years until his death.

He had his daughter, Elizabeth, by his side at the hospital. He spoke of his love for her and his seven grandchildren. He also had his friends Nick and Bob there. His cat was named Lucky, which says it all. He was proud, on his last day, of his loved ones.

He died at 81 years old on Friday, Nov. 16, 2012, at 5 p.m.

Allen Greenfield is the author of "Secret Cypher of the UFOnauts and "Secret Rituals of the Men-In-Black," an occultist, ceremonial magician and UFOlogist.

THE ASTOUNDING UFO SECRETS OF JAMES W. MOSELEY

Rick Hilberg On "The Moseley Years" Of *Saucer News*

Back in 1953, young James W. Moseley set out on a cross-country auto tour to interview UFO witnesses and "flying saucer personalities" with the intention of writing a book. The book, however, would not be published until 2002, when Jim and the late Karl Pflock came out with *Shockingly Close to the Truth: Confessions of a Grave-Robbing Ufologist,* which used a fair amount of material from the original 130-page 1950s manuscript.

Happily, however, Jim's trip prompted him to begin publishing a "saucer-zine" entitled *Nexus* in 1954. *Nexus* became *Saucer News* a year later and would be published with Jim as the editor until early in 1968, when the late Gray Barker took over the publication. Barker produced a number of issues before it ceased to be published in 1970. During the "Moseley years," *Saucer News* evolved into the premier UFO publication – bar none. It was breezy and at the same time filled with all sorts of timely reports of the elusive platters, not to mention informative articles by some of the most respected UFO writers and researchers of the day. Most people today remember Jim for his delightfully irreverent *Saucer Smear*, a little newsletter that he began publishing in the early 1970s and would continue with up until literally weeks before his untimely death. Although Jim was very active in the UFO scene after selling *Saucer News* to Gray, he just couldn't resist publishing a saucer-zine. People nowadays have literally no idea how important and influential *Saucer News* was back in the day, and that is indeed unfortunate.

Back in 2007 I did a small anthology of articles from the glory years of *Saucer News* entitled *Jim Moseley and The Saucer News Years* and I asked Jim just why he started it and what its greatest accomplishments were. Here is what Jim had to say: "My purpose with *Saucer News* was to entertain the readership and also, of course, to find an answer to the flying saucer mystery. I had no idea that now, more than fifty years later, I would still be looking for that answer.

"Along the way, I came up with what I called the 'Earth Theory,' which proved to be extremely unpopular. This was the idea that all 'real' flying saucers were made by the U. S. or some other earthly government. That leaves no room for spaceships, which most of my readers desperately wanted to believe in.

"Then, based on the 'little men' sightings of the late 1940s and early 1950s, I decided that UFOs came from the Planet Mars. In those days some scientists apparently still believed in the 'canals' on Mars, not realizing that they are merely optical illusions.

"Later, I became convinced, as I am now, that the saucer mystery involves genuine unknown phenomena, but (for complicated reasons) no spaceships from other planets. The saucers, which definitely have a paranormal aspect, are somehow a permanent part of the Earth's environment. In some way or other, they are related to *US!* Hopefully, some day in the future, science will find the answer."

I knew Jim for more than fifty years and considered him to be one of my mentors in the UFO field. He was one of the last of the first generation of saucerers, and certainly one of the most unique. I will miss him and our frequent conversations in recent years where we would exchange gossip and the latest news.

Rick Hilberg

Editor and Publisher of *Flying Saucer Digest*

THE ASTOUNDING UFO SECRETS OF JAMES W. MOSELEY

ED BIEBEL

AND THE THANKSGIVING SWIMMING POOL SAGA

EDITOR'S NOTE: Ed is originally from Cleveland and was involved in organizing the Congress of Scientific UFOlogists which had several of its earliest yearly functions in that city and where he met JWM for the first time, probably around 1965.

One of my fondest memories of Jim was when he made the trip to my home in Arizona for Thanksgiving. He rented a car in Phoenix and drove down to my Mother's house in Nogales. Jim checked into a motel in town and asked them if they had a swimming pool. They said, "Yes." (At this time Jim still lived in Fort Lee in the apartment house he owned, so for him swimming outdoors in November was a treat.).

Jim got ready for his swim and discovered there was no water in the pool! He went to the front desk and asked what was going on. In Spanish, the staff consulted and said, "What do we tell the Gringo?" Little did they know that Jim Moseley of the pasty face, dark suits and glasses understood and spoke excellent Spanish. (Jim went to secondary school in Tucson and spent years in Peru "stealing" Incan artifacts.).

He quickly checked out of that motel and into another one across the street. Jim came to my Mother's house for Thanksgiving Dinner in the afternoon. That evening he got hungry and went to the motel's restaurant. They were closed for a "private party," so he went to the nearest mini-mart and bought sandwich meat, bread, etc. and had a fine meal.

The next day Jim came by with his rental car and I took him for a tour of the nearby Patagonia Mountains and his old haunts in Patagonia. You see, while being

THE ASTOUNDING UFO SECRETS OF JAMES W. MOSELEY

a student at a school in Tucson (his Mother was an heiress and his Father an Army General) he lived in a house with a housekeeper/maid while all the other students were locals. Thus, during vacations, he was on his own in Tucson. He spent some time at the Circle Z Guest Ranch (dude ranch) outside of Patagonia, AZ, and re-members riding into town and tying up his horse on the main street. There are still some hitching posts around town, but there probably haven't been many horses using them.

Jim and I drove into the Patagonia Mountains and went to Lochiel, which was a border crossing station (soon to be permanently closed). It was basically a one-man station. We posed for photos which have unfortunately disappeared. We then drove north through the mountains and into Patagonia.

Jim was "vetting" me for the 1983 National UFO Conference to be held in Tucson. He knew, based on my early May dates, that he would be unable to attend and suggested as the main speaker Tim Beckley. As owner of that apartment building in Fort Lee, Jim told me that he had to be there on "rent day" or the tenants would not pay their rent!

There are many other stories about Jim, to include various National UFO Conferences/Congress of Scientific Ufologists meetings, visiting him in Key West and going to see J. Allen Hynek at the Northwestern University Observatory in Evanston, Illinois. But I will save them for my autobiography about my life in Ufology which I hope everyone will want when it is eventually published!

THE ASTOUNDING UFO SECRETS OF JAMES W. MOSELEY

Poetic License And The Legendary Jim Moseley

By Greg Bishop

In early 1994, I wrote to Jim Moseley to ask him for an interview. He was a legendary and (to me) almost unapproachable figure in the UFO community. We talked on the phone and Jim suggested that we meet at the National UFO Conference in San Diego that summer. I heard from someone that he liked whisky, so I brought along a bottle of Johnny Walker Black Label and on a whim, I stopped off at a Toys-R-Us to buy a pair of "Groucho glasses" on the off-chance that I could get a picture of UFOlogy's jester in appropriate attire.

I was amazed that Jim was so patient and kind with my stupid questions. It took most of two hours to cajole him into wearing the glasses while I took a few photos. It was during this interview that he read and showed me the now famous "UFO Is A Bucket of Shit" poem by his friend Gray Barker. The historical significance of this was awe-inspiring. He also brought along some correspondence and hand-made, flying saucer-themed Christmas cards that Barker had sent him over the years.

In the years that followed, Jim became a good friend and continued to shape my opinions (actually "non-opinions" would be more accurate) on the UFO subject. We spoke often on the phone and exchanged letters, all of which I saved, tucked into my copy of *Jim Moseley's Book Of Saucer News*. Unfortunately, I never asked him about the letterhead he occasionally used, which I assumed was for his old Incan grave-robbing business. The name, "Ancient Hallucinations," was a custom logo in stylized letters. I always wondered whether Jim had taken the sacred Ayahuasca or any other number of South American hallucinogens in his travels there in the 1950s. I certainly hope so.

A few years ago he asked me to locate a woman in the Los Angeles area whom he knew from his Peruvian travels. He provided an address and a name (Josephine.)

37

THE ASTOUNDING UFO SECRETS OF JAMES W. MOSELEY

After some cajoling, she came out of her cat-filled home to talk with my wife and I. We got Jim on the phone and Josephine talked to him for the first time in perhaps 20 years. Later, her face lit up as she told us, "He was such a handsome man when we met." I never pried about this relationship, but I made up some story for my own amusement that they had carried on a passionate affair while Jim smuggled Incan artifacts and that she had later followed him to the U.S. He apparently wanted to put her in his will, so perhaps the flame never really died.

From his expose on George Adamski to his hoax on George Adamski to his friendship with a gay man (Gray Barker - in far less enlightened times) to his appearances on the Long John Nebel show to his pot smoking to his constantly evolving views of the UFO phenomenon, Jim Moseley was always far ahead of his time. He was perhaps more accurately "to the side" of his time, as he seemed to inhabit his own, more refined, uncategorizable realm.

He was also one of the main influences on me, and the hundreds (?) of non-subcribers on the "Saucer Smear" mailing list. I think he thought of himself as outside of the "real" field of saucer research, but his attitudes and philosophy left a deep impression on many, even those who would claim to dislike him. The best research really comes from those who tend not to take themselves and the subject so deadly seriously.

One of my favorite quotes from Jim came from that first interview: "Yeah, I've seen things I can't explain, but so what?" If the UFO research field adopted this attitude (and also kept in mind that UFO Is A Bucket Of Shit) there is a very good chance that we would be much closer to an understanding of the phenomenon.

> UFO Is A Bucket Of Shit
> By Gray Barker
> UFO is a bucket of shit
> Its followers: perverts, monomaniacs, dipsomaniacs
> Artists of the fast buck
> True believers, objective believers, new age believers
> Keyhoe believers
> Shushed by the three men
> Or masturbated by space men
> UFO is a bucket of shit
> The A.F. investigated UFOs
> And issued a report
> Couched in polite language
> Which translated, means:
> "UFO is a bucket of shit"
> Meade Layne is a bucket of shit

THE ASTOUNDING UFO SECRETS OF JAMES W. MOSELEY

Lex Mebane is a bucket of shit
James W. Moseley is a bucket of shit
Richard Ogden is a bucket of shit
Ray Palmer is a bucket of shit
And I sit here writing
While the shit drips down my face
In great rivulets

Greg Bishop is the author of "The Excluded Middle" and the host of "Radio Mysterioso."

THE ASTOUNDING UFO SECRETS OF JAMES W. MOSELEY

My Memories of Jim

By T. N. Hackney

My memories of Jim Moseley begin in New York City about forty years ago, though I don't recall the specific UFO venue. I was little more than a wide-eyed, and staring (I'm sure) teenager with an interest in extraterrestrials but no credentials. Jim was a tall, good looking, confident man, usually in a suit (though the tie was usually off), someone who seemed to know what both he and UFOs were all about. He possessed an enviable speaking voice, and an even more enviable wit. What's more, he had money, something most of the people that hovered around him didn't. The UFO conferences, parties and events I was attending were more than likely sponsored and promoted by him.

About fifteen years later a wealthy real estate client of mine that owned a large collection of pre-Columbian artifacts invited me to a dinner meeting of the New York chapter of the Explorer's Club. I knew that Jim was also an avid collector and excavator of these items, so I asked him to attend the meeting with me so that he could meet and maybe do some business with my client while experiencing an award dinner at the fabled club. He gladly accepted. It sealed the notion of my worthiness in his mind, and from that evening forward I became the guy who got him into the ultra-selective club. One does what one can to get noticed, especially by someone who had been publishing UFO publications since before I was born, and that went back a bit.

I remember the appalled reaction of those of us friends upon learning that Jim was leaving New York and moving to Key West, Florida. After that, his almost annual visits to the city became a major social event. Word would go out and Jim, Tim, Harold, maybe Antonio, one or two of the girls, myself and a few of the others would all meet for dinner on the second floor of Mrs. K's deli on E. 30th street. Over salad plates made of plastic we all reconnected to celebrate the man with the easy smile, the dark suit and trenchcoat.

I never saw a copy of "Saucer News," which he co-founded in 1954, but I knew about its reincarnation — "the longest running newsletter in the UFO field" — "Saucer Smear." This lively and often side-splittingly funny, members-only periodical, contributed to by all the big names, was a welcome stuffer of my mailbox for a number of years. I later advertised in "Smear" on several occasions.

Call it the giggle factor or "the fear," people in the field know all too well the inherent vulnerability of wanting like crazy to know the underlying truth of things, to plumb beneath the consensually prosaic explanation of the world. Nobody's fool, Jim had an incisive, get-to-the-quick mind, which his always handy wit worked well for. But his friends knew the latter for a ruse, that it covered up a deep curiosity or yearning for hard proof of something, *anything*, truly "other." He was someone you learned to listen to very carefully because beneath the joker facade was a serious and extremely likable investigator of the unknown.

* * * * *

With a longtime interest in the paranormal, Tom Hackney was a member of the New York Fortean Society before the passing of its founder John Keel. Tom is also the author of "The ETiGrail." He has appeared on Coast to Coast.

THE ASTOUNDING UFO SECRETS OF JAMES W. MOSELEY

A DOOBIE WITH MR. MOSELEY

By Kenn Thomas

Most of my encounters with Jim Moseley were in print, in issues of "Saucer Smear." Thirteen years ago, in the year 2000, I pointed out to him recent research that corroborated the Cutler-Twining memo, a document in the National Archives that refers to the Special Studies subgroup of MJ12. The corroboration had been found in the files of British diplomat Lew Douglas by Jim Martin for his book "Wilhelm Reich and the Cold War." I became a semi-regular *"Saucer Smear"* correspondent after that, mostly discussing internecine scheduling conflicts at various UFO gatherings. That seemed to be more what Jim Moseley was about than actually studying UFOs. I met him in person only once at a Crash Retrieval conference in Las Vegas. But he smoked a joint, although I understand he would be horrified to admit it. He was the last of an Old Guard, UFOlogists of the 50s, a very sociable and amiable man. You can't tell me that he'd never smoked dope before. A fond farewell to the marvelous Mr. Moseley.

Kenn Thomas

The editor of "Steamshovel Press" and a conspiracy theorist.

THE ASTOUNDING UFO SECRETS OF JAMES W. MOSELEY

JOKER & COMMANDER JIM MOSELEY

By Ed Komarek

I first came across and became friends with Jim Moseley in the 1980s. I had read a great deal of UFO literature and had already built my own local and national intelligence network to gather UFO/ET related data. This was all back before the Internet, when we kept up to date through various publications. I subscribed to Jim's "Saucer Smear," Walt Andrus's MUFON Journal, Bill Moore's magazine called "Focus," and Tim Beckley's "UFO Universe" to keep up on national and international developments.

Locally, I had built up an intelligence network, for which, when it was at its peak, I was receiving a couple of UFO reports every week. It was not enough for me to just study the literature and be an armchair investigator of UFO/ET. I knew it was important to have boots on the ground, so to speak, in order to compare my personal contacts and experiences with what I was studying in the literature. I started with letters to editors and when I got some cases I went to the local press and had articles written about UFOs along with my telephone number.

Pretty soon everybody within 50 miles of Cairo, Georgia, knew I had an interest in UFOs and when they experienced or heard about a sighting they would contact me. I eventually traced some of these sightings to individuals that I believed were having extraterrestrial contact. I even saw one of the craft myself when a contact took place in a swamp north of Cairo. Two of the craft followed me home to see where I lived that night. I know this because I saw two craft cruise over the corner of my property south of Cairo, just as I was arriving home.

I had been corresponding with Jim by snail mail and by phone while all this was going on. Jim needed a host for his National UFO Conference and he talked me into doing a conference in Tallahassee, Florida, about 20 miles south of where

THE ASTOUNDING UFO SECRETS OF JAMES W. MOSELEY

I lived. I had and still do live very frugally and so this was perhaps one of the most low budget conferences ever. Jim and I went into partnership with the conference and – "gasp" – we even made a small profit of 500 dollars, which we split between us.

We were able to do the conference on such a low budget because I used a Holiday Inn in Tallahassee that was under renovation for cheap rooms and a conference hall. Jim had national friends like Tim Beckley and contactee Frank Stranges and I had local contactees and also MUFON UFO investigator Don Ware, who lived only a several hours drive away in Ft. Walton Beach near Gulf Breeze. Gulf Breeze became a hotbed of UFO sightings around this time. I got to meet Jim personally at a Gulf Breeze conference, either before or after we hosted the National UFO Conference. Years later, I visited him at his home in Key West, journeying there in my sailboat.

Anyhow, we had an excellent regional UFO conference and a lot of fun. I had learned from my father that it was really good to have a barbeque and bonfire in the evening after a conference. This informal atmosphere really helped to cement and make new friendships. I had a particular treat for Jim because by that time I had learned how to fire-walk on about ten feet of hot coals. Jim had long ago given up on trying to figure out what UFOs were and instead concentrated on the UFO social scene. While he had his own UFO sightings, which he played down, he loved to play the skeptic just to annoy the believers.

Jim's favorite entertainment was to "needle" and tease those with an autocratic bent who took themselves too seriously. I made sure not to give him any slack and always took the offense on teasing to put him in his place, and he loved it. He would work up people like Walt Andrus and abductee researcher Budd Hopkins into a rage and sit back and enjoy the show. Jim's father was the general who kicked the veterans out of Washington DC when they demonstrated in the 1930s and he even met General MacArthur. He rebelled against his overly-dictatorial father and this carried over into his relations with autocrats in the UFO community.

With the fire-walk I had the opportunity to really poke fun at Jim's natural skepticism as he believed that fire-walking must be some kind of trick, like spoon bending. I got to know Uri Geller through Jim because Jim got right in the middle of a dispute between Uri and the skeptic Randi, which as usual he thoroughly enjoyed. A very skeptical Jim even went to one of Uri's performances to watch Uri bend spoons and, to Jim's utter amazement, Uri passed the spoon around, which continued to bend even while Jim was holding it. That proved to Jim that this was no trick.

THE ASTOUNDING UFO SECRETS OF JAMES W. MOSELEY

I really enjoyed hamming around with Jim before walking on the coals, getting him to look at the bottom of my feet before and after walking on the coals. That made quite an impression on Jim, and he would later send me photos of me walking on the coals. I laughingly tried to get him to follow me onto the coals, even walking the coals three times, but he was not about to try.

I was fortunate to meet and talk with Jim's lifelong friend Tim Beckley, who even allowed me recently to use a couple of his old articles from "UFO Universe" in my book "UFOs, Exopolitics and the New World Disorder." I also really liked meeting and talking with contactee Frank Stranges because by this time I had already begun specializing in extraterrestrial contact cases.

My book is full of the best contact cases that I am aware of from my over 40 years experience in the UFO/ET field. Those cases, along with the best whistleblower cases, provide the foundation for my exopolitical concepts outlined in the book. I really appreciate Jim, in spite of his skepticism, for making me aware of a lot of old contact cases. Jim and I both loved to tease each other, with him trying to make me out to be a deluded believer and me teasing him about being a blind skeptic. Some of this played out in "Saucer Smear."

Over the years we sort of went our separate ways, but we kept in touch on occasion by snail mail and by phone. I moved onto the Internet first, using email lists and later Facebook for my networking around the world, but Jim steadfastly refused to get on the new-fangled Internet, although he continued to put out his newsletter. Somebody then transferred "Saucer Smear" onto the Internet, where I read it on occasion. Jim was after me to re-subscribe and I would of course tease and annoy him, saying, "What for? I can read it on the Internet."

Another thing I learned from Jim were some unorthodox investigation techniques. Jim was a master of such techniques as "shake the tree and see what falls out," and "needle people till they get so angry that they spill the beans." I found that these were very productive means to get information out of people, especially those who did not have much of a sense of humor and took themselves too seriously. These people never learn and they fall for these techniques over and over again. Jim made this kind of interrogation an art.

I heard about Jim ending up in the hospital and his death over the Internet, of course, and even though we had not been in contact much the past few years, I certainly do miss him and his humorous outlook on life. Jim was a key character in the UFO field and he is being missed by many. He died about the same time as another colorful character, Gordon Novel, who I was fortunate to meet in person a couple of years ago.

I figure Jim, the skeptic, surely has been surprised once again, discovering that even though his body died, he still lives on. Not just his memories with us, but in an all-encompassing soul reality from which we come and go into the material world and learn through theater and acting. Jim certainly played his roles in life well, and I know I will see him again and again on stage and backstage over time.

Ed Komarek is the author of "UFOs, Exopolitics and the New World Disorder."

THE ASTOUNDING UFO SECRETS OF JAMES W. MOSELEY

Jim Moseley, The Lucid Partier

By Phyllis Galde

I first remember talking to Jim Moseley when I worked at Llewellyn Publications way back in the late 1980s. He had traveled to Minneapolis to give a talk at Dennis Stillings' Archaeus Project. Even though Moseley was a skeptic about much of UFOlogy, his presentation was fascinating. He was witty, urbane, well-spoken, and had great stories to tell. Many of those present would often convene later for a beer and more stories. I don't remember if I was included in that meeting, but I do remember hanging out at the Yacht Club with Jerry Clark, Dennis Stillings, and later, John Keel.

I was always a little in awe of Jim, believing he had so much more knowledge than I did. He was older and more confident.

A couple of years later, some friends and I went to Key West and stayed at his garden apartment. It was a great location, lovely private swimming pool, nice, neat apartment, and friendly stray cats who would come into our apartment for treats.

I went over to Jim's apartment one afternoon to visit and enjoyed it greatly. Of course I had to have a scotch and water to drink! His gold South American statues were ever present, as was the horrid smoke from his many cigarettes he chain smoked. He was a font of knowledge, and very opinionated.

In recent years, I would see Jim at various UFO conferences—one in Beverly Hills, where he would question Travis Walton's veracity regarding his abduction experience, and later in Hollywood at John Miller and Lisa Davis' UFO conference, where he was a speaker. I had to smile to myself, because all weekend it looked like he had the same light blue shirt on, same sport jacket, and the back of the shirt was always hanging out over his pants. Even though he was partying, his talk was coherent and lucid. Most impressive, even if you didn't agree with his conclusions.

I always read his *"Saucer Smear"* cover to cover, and was pleased when he mentioned *"FATE Magazine."* Jim wrote for "FATE" several times, and we will post his articles on our website, www.fatemag.com

Also, we had an agreement to reprint his recent issues of "Saucer Smear," so watch for those to become available on our website in the near future.

(I think Jim died exactly a month after my partner and managing editor, David Godwin, died. Synchronicity?)

He had a fine mind, a great wit, and we will miss him. I am sure he will find out the Truth in the spirit world.

Phyllis Galde

Editor-in-chief

"FATE Magazine"

www.fatemag.com

11:45

THE FORBIDDEN PLANET

August, 1959. A hot night. The 24th floor.

Microphones, and wires, and a room high above Times Square.

A blond man in a loud sports coat signaling, his long pointing finger reaching past those dials, into space, into the homes, into the automobiles, into the trucks. Then a strange electronic beeping that filled the studio.

If there were Martians, this is probably their kind of music, I thought, as I listened to the squealing sounds change pitch and rise to a crescendo.

The cacophony led into a beautiful melody. To a few people—buffs on remembering trivia—this music was, of course, David Rose's recording of Theme From the Forbidden Planet.

To those who twirled their radio dials at that hour, the electronic tonalities and the mystical, yet romantic theme, was now identified, however, with one single human voice.

"Good morning, neighbors. This is Long John." I tensed and squeezed tightly the object I held in my right hand, rolled up into a cylinder and crumpled. It was the latest issue of Saucer News, and it contained an article which would comprise the main agenda for discussion from midnight until 4:30 in the morning. It was the third time I had been on the Long John Show. As usual, I had stage fright. I looked over the table at Gray Barker, who appeared amazingly calm though he had armed himself with a small mountain of newspaper clippings, copious notes, and several copies of books which he, the popular West Virginia publisher, had brought out about UFOs.

He would be on the hot seat tonight. I would charge, as I had printed in Saucer

News, that Barker had dressed up three men in strange black suits and hired them to frighten Al K. Bender into an abrupt silence.

Rabbi Y. N. Ibn Aharon (shortened to just "Yonah" for ease of reference), would delve into a strange, other worldly book, titled **Oahspe**, sometimes termed a new Bible, its very title translated as "sky, earth and spirit."

He would charge that an anthropologist, named Dr. George Hunt Williamson, had set up a meeting by a man from outer space with Prof. George Adamski, and that somehow Barker had also been connected.

John Nebel wouldn't buy any of it—officially at least. As Long John introduced the guest of the morning and the panel who would question him, I wondered if he only pretended to be skeptical about the array of offbeat personalities who regularly appeared before the microphones of his all-night show.

"Now, neighbors, I don't buy this," he would say, "but. . ."

And across the airways went the voices of people such as Howard Menger, who claimed to have actually met with men from Venus. . .the Mystic Barber, who received telepathic beams from various planets. . .George Van Tassel, founder of the College of Universal Wisdom and designer of a rejuvenation machine.. .and, of course, Gray Barker, told fascinating tales of a Flatwoods Monster which had frightened seven of his neighbors out of reason on a bleak West Virginia hillside.

One of Barker's friends, Al K. Bender, had found out what the flying saucers actually were; others of his acquaintance had possessed pieces of the elusive discs, only to be silenced by threatening visitors, which some suggested to be none other than the space people themselves!

John believed some of it, I thought, else he wouldn't have so many offbeat guests on his show. Still the offbeat programming had been good radio box office, and upped his ratings.

But regardless of how much he believed, or how much Gray Barker believed, I knew one thing: that I hardly believed one word of the charges I would level at the guest of the morning. Although I couldn't talk about some of the things which had happened to me, and would have to put up a highly skeptical facade throughout the show, I knew in my heart that I believed more than Long John and Gray Barker put together. But I would play the game. Probably that was what made me so nervous.

Barker relieved the tension by passing a note to me which simply said, "STENDAK!"

Long John Nebel caressed the microphone, placing his hands around its pedestal, and began the monologue to set the stage for the show. To the listeners, John is presenting an absorbing synopsis of what has gone before; to a panel member in the studio, waiting to speak into his own microphone, it is fascinating.

John gets close to the microphone and seems to lose touch with those around him—the guests, the engineers, the producer and the people handing him commercials to read. Out of contact with the world, he speaks not to the microphone, for somehow in this brief period he is the microphone, the great mass of glowing tubes at the transmitter. Or to sum it up, at that moment he is radio.

Gray Barker, the author of a best-selling UFO book, **They Knew Too Much About Flying Saucers**, was up late and turning the radio dial when he heard John on one of his first radio shows. John was talking about flying saucers in a very skeptical manner. Barker angrily picked up the telephone and placed a long-distance call to the station. John had just installed one of the first so-called "beeper phones," whereby a telephone caller can speak over the air. He flipped a switch and Barker found himself on the radio for the first time. John told him that if he wanted to put his money where his saucer was he could buy an airplane ticket, fly to New York and be on the show any night and talk as loudly and long as he wanted to. Barker took the challenge and walked into the studio the following week. Expecting to receive a kind of microphonic third degree, Barker, to his surprise, immediately found that John was letting him talk as much as he pleased—as long as his flying saucer tales were interesting. So, taken by John's charm, he became a firm supporter of the fledgling show and shouted praises throughout the land, via his various publications.

< LONG JOHN NEBEL

Host of the famed all-night radio show on WNBC, New York. The author is especially indebted to Long John for allowing him to relate his experiences to the program's listeners, which number in the millions.

I caught myself wondering why I was there in the studio, staying up all night, and discussing a subject which to the majority of Americans still was considered ridiculous. Ostensibly it was to get publicity for my magazine. Subscriptions and inquiries always poured in after an appearance on the show.

But I knew secretly that I wasn't here for subscriptions, or money, or for publicity. It

went deeper than all that. And it all really started with *Krippine.*

When my mother died, early in my life, I had been thrown into the cold, outside world to fend for myself. Once in contact with that world of ordinary humanity, however, I found out for the first time that I was different. *For I was rich.*

Don't feel sorry for me. If you've never been rich, you should be. The wild tales of horror concerning the Rich Man, are mainly the inventions of the Rich to garner sympathy and toleration from the Poor.

At nineteen I began to Rebel Against Society.

I walked off the Princeton Campus in mid-semester and got hooked up with Ken Krippine.

That is how, in an incredible roundabout way, I got on the "Saucer Kick."

Ken Krippine was an explorer of sorts who financed his jungle adventures by taking on safari a huge supply of Canadian Club and other products which later appeared in jungle-setting magazine advertisements. He also supported his anthropological researches by taking along young adventurers. Young enthusiastic rich adventurers paid through the nose for these "dangerous" jungle treks.

Ken was in his Peruvian period when I laid out a thousand dollars to accompany him on a South American trip to search for a lost city. I don't think he quite promised to lead me to the Lost Cave of the Inca Treasures, but I was interested in adventure, and my appraisal of Ken's oral prospectus led me to believe I would be safe from jungle rot, poisonous snakes and wild tribesmen.

One rewarding part of the safari was a side trip which Krippine didn't sponsor. While flying from inland to the coast of Peru, my interest in viewing the countryside below had diminished as we left the verdant jungles and the sameness of the desert passed below. I picked up a newspaper to pass the time away while the secondhand DC-3 vibrated and groaned. The president of Peru had given a huge number of pesos to assist a family afflicted with tuberculosis. Marilyn Monroe had made the Latin press. Land reform had been suggested by certain officials. In other words, the usual dull daily news of Peru.

I yawned and once again looked out of the small window—I blinked and looked again.

We seemed to be passing over a huge complex of modern roads, or a city. A closer look disclosed that what I was seeing was actually a series of strange geometrical markings on the Peruvian desert.

I nudged the local businessman sitting next to me, who awakened from his afternoon siesta long enough to take a cursory look. "Senor, those are nothing much. They are nothing but the Nasca Lines."

Once on the coast, the subject of the Nasca Lines continued to intrigue me. I stopped into a local museum, hoping to obtain an explanation.

The part-time curator, the local parish priest, searched through a pile of documents and came up with a small booklet, that, translated, was titled *"Mystery On The Desert,"* and published in Peru by the British archeologist Maria Reiche.

"Only from an airplane," wrote Miss Reiche, "is it possible to appreciate the absolutely straight lines and borders of elongated surfaces, their great numbers, and the curious arrangement of stars, zigzags, and groups of parallels, and the strange network they form—as if traced on gigantic drawing boards. It is a strange fact that the ancient Indian designers probably never got a glimpse of the perfection of their own work, which can be seen well only from the air."

These lines, the curator Father Pacin explained to me, cover an area of more than 40 square miles, were made simply by overturning the reddish brown topsoil of the region to produce a pattern which from a distance looks something like white lines on a gigantic blackboard. Erosion is very slight in this region of Peru, and the lines and figures had survived the centuries with only a minimum of wear and tear.

In recent years treasure hunters had left their mark, particularly at the several points where the groups of lines intersect, their theory being that these points might have been the sites of temples or burial grounds.

So far, Father Pacin told me, nothing at all had been found in the diggings at the intersections.

I was intrigued by Miss Reiche's observations about the enormous amount of labor needed to produce the variety of large delineated surfaces and the wide lines.

"The absolutely straight lines and borders which sometimes cross considerable distances, cutting through valleys and passing over hills without ever swerving from their original direction, are a feat of engineering which must have been accomplished through the astoundingly keen eyesight of their designer... Stranger yet than the skill needed in tracing the lines and borders, is the technical accomplishment which was needed to solve the complicated problem of the transfer of the elaborate figures from models, which must have existed, to a scale at least a hundred times larger. It is hard to imagine how these ancient peoples with their limited knowledge could have projected these complicated patterns with such precision onto the desert." Miss Reiche goes on to say that even today, with modern skills and methods, the job of reproducing these figures would be fantastic.

THE ASTOUNDING UFO SECRETS OF JAMES W. MOSELEY

I thanked Father Pacin and made a small contribution to the upkeep of the museum by placing a few pesos on one of the large antique stones at the entrance of the museum. I made a mental note to ask Krippine his opinion of the Nasca Lines; this might make a good subject for a magazine article or even a book if enough research could be done.

"Naw!" Krippine concluded after reflecting a few minutes while he concentrated on the cigar smoke curling over his head. "Not fantastic enough." Then he straightened from his relaxed position as he apparently had a new thought. "Say, Kid"—that's what he always called me. "Did you ever think that those lines can be seen only from the air? Yet they were made centuries ago, before we had aircraft. What if the people in that area were in contact with these flying saucers, which people claim to see, saucers that were around in these early days."

I had read the saucer reports and had been mildly interested. I liked to read science fiction books, and I somehow had connected the saucers with SF.

"Oh yes," he continued. "The flying saucers were probably contacting these early peoples of Peru, and the people regarded them as gods. They, probably with the help of these space people, created the ground markings as landmarks for these hokey Martians." I could tell by his tone and facial expression that he did not believe a word he was saying. I had seen a book Ken had been reading. It was the now classic and familiar *Behind the Flying Saucers*, by Frank Scully.

"Look (I remember his exact words), if you want to write a book which will get published easily, here's a good thing," and he handed me Scully's book.

"But, Ken, I don't know anything about flying saucers."

"That's all for the better. You won't be prejudiced, so you probably could come up with a great book about them—with my help, guidance, and my usual financial share, of course."

I gathered that Ken's many books had been largely farmed out in similar ways. Though remarkably colorful, adventurous and talented in many ways, Ken wasn't the type who would follow the discipline of bending over a typewriter for long sessions.

"When you get back home, head for Los Angeles. It's the center of the flying saucer cult. Get yourself plenty of wild stories, when with my help we'll come up with an expose type of book which will be worth a few grand in paperback. I'll even let you put your own name on it if you'll do the actual work and handle everything through me."

"But why," I asked, "an exposé type book. Isn't there any truth to these flying saucer stories?"

54

"I doubt it. I think Frank got took." Again he referred to Scully's book which he picked from a table. "You never can tell," he added; "before I left New York, Holt told me they had just sent Scully a royalty check for twenty thousand—that's pretty large change, considering the book racket as it is today."

Ken outlined a plan whereby I would do the research and come up with a rough manuscript. He would read it and farm it out to a hack for a finished draft. I would get my name on the book as author, but would sign a contract to give him half the royalties.

I could hardly contain my enthusiasm. Half the royalties of an intangible but somehow immensely promising project seemed to me astronomical. I would probably get on the "Tonight" and "Today" shows to promote the book. I would be autographing copies that crowds of admirers would push toward me. I probably would be famous.

12:10

TWO MEN FROM VENUS

While packing for the trip to the green Ufological pastures of the West Coast to bait the "crackpots," a somewhat logical thought halted my impulsive rush.

In my haste to get on with the book project I had not realized that I knew practically nothing about the subject itself, nor did I have the first idea about whom to contact or interview after I arrived. I called up LA and had my hotel reservation set back a day, hoping this would give me some time for preparation.

As we talked about August C. Roberts and Dominick Lucchesi on the Long John Show, it seemed impossible that at one time I did not know this fantastic duo. Dom and Augie had figuratively pushed me off the diving board for my first plunge into the strange waters of Ufology.

I sat down in the middle of my living room, with my baggage all around me, for, strangely enough, it often seems that I do my best thinking when I am in disorganized situations. I had a little something to go on. In the back of my mind I remembered a New Jersey newspaper story about a local man who had witnessed and photographed a spectacular saucer. Though I had been only vaguely interested in the subject of flying saucers, I thought that I may have clipped out the item.

I suppose that psychologists would classify my youth as "a quiet reserved sort of kid." I had a habit of clipping out interesting stories and pasting them into scrapbooks—instead, I suppose, of the more acceptable social norm of going out and raising hell.

The only organization one could claim for these scrapbooks was that they were chronological. So, remembering that the story had appeared about a year back, I looked into the 1952 volumes.

THE ASTOUNDING UFO SECRETS OF JAMES W. MOSELEY

Things began to ring a bell as I got into the August dates, but it was not until I thumbed back to June that the subconscious memory link was explained. The man who photographed the saucer was August C. Roberts, of Jersey City.

Roberts was on a skywatch tower, the story related, when he and James Leyden spotted the incredible thing over the New York skyline. Roberts told reporters it looked like a huge shiny coin, tilted with its edge toward them. It hovered briefly, then vanished in a burst of tremendous speed.

Augie grabbed Leyden's Brownie camera and snapped two shots. Unfortunately the shutter was set on "timer" and he only got a blurred image on film; nevertheless the paper had run the two photos with a lengthy story.

The skywatcher's sighting had been accompanied with "a strange feeling, like nothing I ever felt before," and for no logical reason. Roberts felt certain that the object was an interplanetary spacecraft!

I decided Roberts might be the man who could give me some leads on saucer bugs. A check in the phone book disclosed no such person listed in Jersey City, so the next day I called his employer, mentioned in the story, found that Roberts was unmarried and boarded at his sister's house.

Once located by phone, however, he didn't sound like the crackpot I had expected. He said the paper had misquoted him, that he had no definite opinion as to what the object had been, and that he would gladly open his extensive UFO files, collected since this sighting, to me. He suggested that we meet that evening at the home of a gyroscope technician, also interested in saucers.

Dominick C. Lucchesi likely could give me a number of West Coast sources of information, for he had corresponded with saucer buffs out there.

But Dominick was frightened, he added, because of an incident involving a friend of his who had got hushed up, as Augie put it, and he would have to check with Dom. A few minutes later he called back and said they would be glad to meet with me, provided they could tape record the entire conversation!

Although the condition was odd, I quickly assented. As I thought about it I felt the beginnings of my own paranoia, which I have since discovered runs quite universally through the field; meanwhile I was wondering just what value a tape recording of my conversation would be to them, and what the frightening experience he mentioned had been.

Once inside Dom's book lined apartment, I was plunged into a bizarre promenade of various UFO theories and bits of information, and was certain what I was learning there would make the supposed West Coast saucer mecca anticlimactic.

THE ASTOUNDING UFO SECRETS OF JAMES W. MOSELEY

* * * * *

After Long John Nebel had finished setting the scene and I was called upon to talk, I referred to the Saucer News article by Lonzo Dove and commenced to assail Gray Barker.

Gray, I told John's listeners, had perpetrated a cruel hoax upon Albert K. Bender. He may have been one of the Men in Black himself! But, at the least, he had hired three men, possibly actors, possibly flying saucer enthusiasts of cynical attitudes, and they had visited Bender and scared the living saucers out of him. Barker had gone on the air knowing that it was just a radio show and that I didn't believe in the article, and he was all set, he promised, to make his rebuttal calmly.

But once on the air, the sincerity and belief which he finds difficult to admit to close friends, began to come across, as he angrily denounced the author who had quoted him out of context. John called a temporary halt to the program while producer, Dave Field, put a neck microphone on the angered West Virginian, who, forgetting he was on the air, persistently wandered off mike.

I still didn't know whether to believe Bender or not, though certainly Barker, who had written practically an entire book about the Bridgeport, Conn., saucerer, was sold on him. Once I had made my opening statement and Barker, Long John and the rest of the Panel had caught the controversial ball, my mind flashed back to my first meeting with Dom and Augie and my first encounter with the mystery of Al Bender and the three men in black suits.

August C. Roberts and Dominick C. Lucchesi had belonged to a sort of correspondence club which collected information about flying saucers. Albert K. Bender, the head of the organization, had by accident come across some accurate information about the origin and purpose of the discs, and had been told to stop— possibly by the government, my hosts thought.

The odd thing, though, was the black suits the three men, who visited Bender, had worn. Whoever they were, they had confirmed the secret information Bender had come by, then had severely threatened him. He was so frightened by the visit that he became physically ill. He wouldn't tell Augie and Dom who the men were, what agency they were from, or, of course, the secret they had sworn him to keep.

Dom had conjectured as to what the Bridgeport man had found out, and hoped he hadn't done anything wrong by sending Bender, his own engineering plans for an actual disc-shaped plane which would utilize jet power. Could that have been what the men were interested in? He doubted it. It had been his own idea, and he wasn't even sure it would work if it were actually built.

Dom and Augie were afraid they might also be visited and put under security regulations which would prevent their further research into the subject.

I thought they were overly anxious, though I was quite intrigued by the Bender mystery. After convincing them, though not entirely, that I was what I claimed to be—merely a prospective author—they opened up and soon had my head spinning with weird saucer data.

Besides giving me the names of many interesting personalities on the West Coast, they also freely gave local, and even interplanetary information! My notes from the session read in part:

(1) "Earth to tilt due to ice cap at South Pole and destroy civilization as it did 5,000 years ago. Saucers here to prevent this.

(2) "Lucchesi's friend in Pennsylvania had contact with female saucer occupant, was given strange black box which may be extremely dangerous. Box isolated in unpopulated area.

(3) "Saucers may come from inside the earth, where cave dwellers are alleged to pilot these craft.

(4) "Apposition of Mars and frequency of saucers.

(5) "Saucers historical. Get Charles Fort's book."

Dom got onto a chair and pulled a thick volume down from a high shelf of a huge bookcase. It was the classic Books of Charles Fort, a compilation of four different books written by a man who had enjoyed bedeviling scientists with accounts of phenomena they could not explain. Aside from his tongue-in-cheek proof that the world was flat and that the Moon was only 37 miles away, Fort immediately impressed me with his years of gathering unexplained data.

Tucked away among this voluminous material are hundreds of accounts of unidentified flying objects antedating by years and centuries the relatively recent reports which began in earnest during 1947 and reached a peak in 1952.

No doubt Fort impressed other UFO writers, for his books have provided filler and mileage for so many of their books. I mention him in passing, partly to express the misgivings I was beginning to feel. Although the reports I had heard from Dom and Augie certainly bordered on the fantastic, here was a writer who had spent a great deal of his lifetime scientifically gathering such data. He quoted from learned magazines and other scholarly sources.

Perhaps not all of the flying saucer reports could be dismissed as crackpot.

As I steered my Ford onto the New Jersey Turnpike which would lead to myriads of roads finally connecting with the wild freeways of Los Angeles, I reflected on my good fortune in finding the saucer photo in my scrapbook, and its leading me to Dom and Augie. They had not only filled me in on the UFO field but had given me a number of suggested contacts in LA.

And as the turnpike unwound before me I could not foresee other lucky breaks. It was impossible to predict how my visit to a relative in a movie studio would lead to a near-encounter with a man from Venus! Or how I would meet one of the most fascinating human personalities in the strange world of UFO research: Manon Darlaine.

I certainly won't embarrass my cousin by giving his identity here, for he's made quite a name for himself in a popular television series, and gained some stature as a solid Hollywood citizen of the type which film industry apologists often point to in a moment of civic pride. I doubt if he'd want it known that he has a relative who is a nut on saucers.

This was during his early, hard luck days, and he had just appeared in a number of ridiculous Class "D" movies. When I telephoned him to say hello, he suggested that I visit the movie set, where he was working in a minor role, the next day. He would introduce me to some stars, and generally entertain me.

I found the making of motion pictures one of the most boring procedures I had ever watched. The crew was shooting one scene, that of a soldier torturing some French peasants, over and over, with delays between shots.

My cousin's agent dropped by early in the day, shortly after the gosh-awful Hollywood work day began at 7:00 a.m., to take him off the set for a meeting with a producer, and I was left to fend for myself. I wandered around the set until lunch time, wondering how I could make an exit without offending my host, when I happened to speak to a woman who turned out not only to be a gold mine of saucer information, but a dear friend as well.

Manon Darlaine was a free-lance consultant retained by many studios on set decoration, particularly in her specialty, French provincial design.

Sensing that I was bored, Manon took the trouble to talk with me, asked if there was anything she could show me or explain to me. I confessed my lack of interest in what was going on there and invited her to lunch at the studio commissary.

When I happened to explain my mission in L.A., her eyes lighted up, and to my surprise, I became the recipient of a torrent of information about the very things I was looking for.

"Maybe I can take you along when I meet Venutio!" she said. She was tremendously excited. A man from Venus had volunteered information about himself to The Los Angeles Times, she informed me, and she was hot after a personal interview with him. She also did some reporting for a French newspaper syndicate, and all her papers were yelling for space information.

Only after many years of friendship with Manon Darlaine would I discover the wide and varied background she had enjoyed before becoming a United States citizen. She had worked with the French Underground during World War I, and possessed what she termed "seven safes" full of information that would "shake" not only the U.N. and the UFO field, but Hollywood itself! I remember the difference given to Manon on the set by a famous but aging film queen, who happened to be visiting a young actor, her current *bon amour*. I gather that Manon was no person to be lightly reckoned with, either by the space people or Hollywood stars!

Somehow it seems, in retrospect, that the great characters one meets while investigating saucers are as gratifying as the stories they provide. In this respect I shall always warmly remember people such as George Adamski, Orfeo Angelucci, Gray Barker, George Van Tassel (to name only a few), and, of course, Manon Darlaine.

Though of advancing age, probably in her 80's, she preserved a vivaciousness, poise and kind of beauty seldom approximated by the young starlets who walked through their scenes at the studios where she worked. Rumor has it, and in Hollywood rumor is more important than fact, that she was once a great beauty who toppled two French governments.

It was through Manon that I became personally enmeshed in one of the strangest saucer cases I have ever been involved with—that of "Venutio," or "Mr. Wheeler," the man who came from Venus to find out if Venusians could mate with L.A. women and produce offspring. This in itself—a male who evidently favored paternity cases—was enough to send any reporter, Ufological or otherwise, panting toward a typewriter!

Somehow Manon had managed to work her way into the action when a *Times* reporter who wrote under the pen name of Mortimer Bane let it leak out that two not-too-strange-looking, but nevertheless odd, men had visited his cubicle and announced they were from Venus and wanted to sell their story.

I perked up my ears at once, for this was one of the things Krippine had told me to look for. I assumed that the reporter had sensed that flying saucers was a good subject for the moment, probably planned to write a book, and had cooked up the story.

I don't know if Manon had mentioned the Seven Safes to Bane, or whether or not he gave her the information willingly, but he had promised her a meeting with "Venutio" so that she could write a story for the French syndicate.

Manon made the appointment and the two of us invaded Bane's cramped quarters. "I'm sure it's a hoax," he told us, "and that (he used curse words) is behind all this."

Then he told us how a year previous, this particular friend, a special effects man at one of the studios, had perpetrated a most remarkable hoax at his expense. An impeccably dressed Irishman had introduced himself, and in a remarkably matter-of-fact manner informed Bane he had won $10,000 on the Irish Sweepstakes, then had gravely handed him a cashier's check in that amount. That Bane had not bought a ticket, or even been approached, made no matter; in fact it had served io increase the believability when the man told him how a maiden aunt in Old Erin hid purchased it in his name. Bane fell for this, though he had been hoaxed more than once before—with the same man behind it all. Of course, the check proved to be a complete fabrication, a product of the studio printing department which produced various documents for on-camera closeups. Since that department had just forged the Magna Carta, for a historical film, Bane felt some small comfort in being taken in by experts. Even better than this one was the pitiful lady with the infant, which situation I won't go into here; nevertheless Bane admitted he had fallen for that one.

"But this time I have his number," he announced. "I have a laboratory analyzing how he did THIS."

Bane pulled out a photograph of a piece of metal which appeared to be an engraving plate.

I could sense that Bane genuinely liked Manon Darlaine—perhaps she affected other people that way too—so it seemed that in deference to her he repeated some of the story to me.

"Five weeks ago, this kook comes in here with another character. The one sits down there (he pointed to a chair) and the other just stands here glaring at me and finally says, 'I'm Mr. Wheeler, and I have come from Venus.'

" 'Sure,' I say; 'tell me all about it!' And he DOES. He's parked his space ship on the desert. You people probably don't know this, but on Venus, you see, due to the carbon dioxide in the atmosphere and all that strange jazz, it's pretty hot and dry. Just like the desert around here. So these kooks pick L.A. for it's more like their own planet.

"They want to sell me this story, like so many other nuts that sift in here through the woodwork, and of course I've got no budget, even though Jesus Christ himself would show up.

"Before I could throw him and this other weirdo out of here, Venutio—this Wheeler guy—says he can show me he's actually from way out from the fifth planet-

or whichever planet it is. He takes his thumbnail and with proper ceremony puts a deep scratch in the trim of the desk—here, look!"

There was a deep gash in the desk trim, but it didn't prove anything to me—though Madame Darlaine, sensing a good story, took copious notes.

"I figure the guy has a sharp piece of metal from the studio machine shop in his fist, and I go along with it, not wanting at that stage of the game to let on that I was hip."

I got the impression that Bane was a man who protested too much: He had found Venutio's story too credible for his own comfort, and was this blustery, though good-natured manner he employed in relating the account a part of CONVINCING HIMSELF it WAS a hoax?

This was more apparent as he continued the narrative. After he put the two strange men off by promising to speak to his editor about buying their story, they left, promising to return later.

One of them, Venutio, did return the following day, but had changed his mind about selling the story. He had decided he didn't want publicity about his work on Earth, but did need money to buy food. He asked Bane to secure a job for him.

"Whether or not it was a gag, I decided to keep going along," Bane told us. "So I called Hatch Graham—he's the deputy public defender—and told him, 'Hatch, I've got a man for you. He's from the planet Venus, but he needs a job and you were just asking me for a leg man last week.'

"'Sure, send him over!' Hatch has a really princely sense of humor. As to Venutio's fine record helping him track down witnesses, you'll have to talk with Hatch. He hired Venutio out of the fund he uses for occasional investigators and informers."

Bane then added a few more details about Venutio: He and the other man did not appear abnormal, just a bit strange. Their eyes, he thought, were wider apart than an average fellow's, and they had small ears, but not abnormally small. They were ruddy complexioned and their nostrils seemed a bit wide. "Just weird enough to make you a trifle uneasy, though you couldn't quite pin it down. My pal when he hired these extras must have really looked over a lot of people. He certainly didn't just pick them off the street. They didn't talk like bums; in fact their English was impeccable, except for an occasional misuse of a word. They were probably faking these misused words to go with their story of learning English back on their planet, listening to radio programs emanating from Earth."

"What about the interview with them? Is it set up yet?" Manon inquired. Bane's gruff tone changed and a look of genuine disappointment came over his face.

"You'll think I'm giving you the business. But you're a real nice girl, and this is the gospel. Venutio worked a few days for Hatch and disappeared. Neither of us has seen hide nor hair of him since. He's gone back to Venus ,or he's got enough money to bum it to some other town."

He picked up the phone and arranged for us to interview public defender Graham. Hatch Graham was much more serious about Venutio than Mortimer Bane had been.

"I only wish he hadn't vanished," he told us. He then related how Venutio had quickly found slippery witnesses and other sources of information important to the cases of poor clients his office was defending.

"Venutio claimed he found them in routine ways, such as looking up job records and the like, but he found people whom other investigators had failed to locate. It was almost as if he had occult powers."

"I kidded Bane that he was responsible for the disappearances," Hatch told us, and he smiled broadly. "I guess after talking to him you've found out how much this spaceman idea—whether or not it is a hoax—has bugged him. If somebody is pulling his leg, they really have him going!"

"Bane kept after me constantly the moment I hired Venutio. Did I believe it? Could we prove it was a hoax? I told him that to me it didn't matter as long as he was doing such an excellent job. I'm afraid I did pull his leg, myself. I was a trifle annoyed with his constant concern, so I made up a little thing or two about the remarkable accomplishments of Venutio the Venusian. But I really didn't have to exaggerate; this man was uncanny!

"Finally Bane came up with a really wild idea. I should have the police detain Venutio on suspicion, have him fingerprinted, and, most important, strip him down to see if certain details about his body, given to Bane by the spacemen, checked out.

"I didn't want to do this. Venutio, whether from Venus or Ventura, seemed to be an all-right guy, despite this queer line. I couldn't conscientiously have him held for interrogation. I put Bane off by telling him that Venutio probably had telepathic powers and seemed to know things that were going on behind his back. 'If you aren't careful,' I told Bane, 'he'll pick up your thoughts and go back to Venus, or some other city on Earth. Don't ask me to lose a good leg man!'

"I believe Bane took me seriously. He seemed satisfied and hung up. He didn't get a chance to bug me any more, for Venutio never showed up again.

"In fact," he added, "Now I almost believe my own story."

THE ASTOUNDING UFO SECRETS OF JAMES W. MOSELEY

The telephone interrupted Graham. He covered the mouthpiece after listening a minute or two, definitely exhibiting surprise. Then a smile played over his face and I could tell from certain references that he was talking to Bane.

"Well, Venutio has him going again," he told us. "You better get over there right away. I think he really has something for you."

Manon and I hurried back to the *TIMES* office. "You know what that creep friend of mine has done!" (Bane was still referring to the special effects man as he stood staring at a paper in his hand.) "He's bought off this whole damned laboratory!" His hand shook visibly as he handed us the document.

During Venutio's second visit to Bane's office the reporter had asked him to repeat the feat of scratching surfaces with his fingernail, only that time he offered him a steel engraving plate such as is used in special kinds of printing. Venutio had, with one stroke of his amazing thumbnail, made quite a dent in it.

I have recently read a magazine article which purports to cover the Venutio story accurately.

The account reports on an analysis by the Smith-Emery Company, a highly-reliable and respected testing laboratory. In the article the report states that metallic deposits, foreign to the usual composition of such a steel engraving plate, had been present: calcium, lead, strontium, cobalt, etc. But the lab report Bane offered to us did not say this.

I DID NOT MAKE AN EXACT TRANSCRIPT OF BANE'S LAB REPORT, BUT IT VERY SIMPLY STATED THAT THE LABORATORY HAD DUPLICATED THE SCRATCH ON THE SAME PIECE OF METAL, AND THAT THE LOAD REQUIRED TO MAKE THE INDENTION AMOUNTED TO 1700 POUNDS!

(In next issue: Another condensed chapter of Mr. Moseley's book, titled "The Missing Film". Learn how the confiscation of film footage of a flying saucer exposed the identity of the Silence Group and bankrupted a motion picture producer. These revelations never made public by Moseley prior to this time.)

12:45

THE MISSING FILM

Barker was winning the debate, and Long John had temporarily withdrawn from the discussion, sitting back from the microphone, enjoying our defeat. John usually takes the part of an underdog, and he was getting a visible kick out of seeing Barker defend himself so capably. The *Saucer News* article, accusing him of being one of the "Three Men In Black," seemed logical to me when I published it, but now it didn't seem to hold water as Barker countered it, point by point. About the only avenue of attack that Yonah and I saw open was to insist that Barker was making huge profits on the flying saucer books he published and sold. While indeed such a profit-making situation is acceptable to society nowadays, somehow it seemed that if you accuse a saucer book author of making money, you make him look bad.

This put Barker on the defensive. For a while it seemed the panel might be winning, but I still remember wishing that I was back in Los Angeles, working on my first saucer investigation, hearing for the first time the Venutio story and other incredible narratives.

My mind flashed back to the information Manon Darlaine had given me, along with her advice not to telephone a certain producer before I walked in on him at his office. He had made a flying saucer film with allegedly authentic footage of an actual space ship, which had been filmed in Alaska, according to her informant.

This producer shall be nameless here, for since my interview with him he happened to "hit" with a teenage picture cycle that made a million bucks. He has now been graduated to major film production.

I had always pictured a Hollywood film producer's office as a luxurious affair, in a plush section of town, with deep carpets and sexy receptionists. When I walked into the sleazy hotel and rode the ancient elevator up 15 flights and knocked on a door, I was entering the world of the film producer of the late 40's. It was the world of the quickie independent film production, which managed to survive in the movie-hungry market occasioned by the burgeoning of drive-in theatres.

Not realizing the money potential to be derived from renting their best films to the outdoor theatres, the major producers had hesitated to leave their "hardtopped" indoor theatre markets. Meanwhile the "passion pits", as the pious termed the drive-ins in those days, had put a new kind of producer into business: a fellow familiar with movie production who could scrape together a hundred thousand dollars to make a cheap, sensational type of film. Once the production was finished, processing laboratories would usually put up money for advertising and supply the film prints in return for a lucrative first mortgage on the picture. If the film did not do well in drive-in theatres, there was always the hungry infant, television, which at that time was still unable to obtain much major film footage and would buy practically anything.

I was about to interview such a mortgageer.

A bespectacled young man, with suspicion evident on his face, opened the door marked (I use a pseudonym) Stellar Productions. With the door open just enough to see through the crack, and not enough for a more aggressive caller to get his foot into, he inquired about my business.

It took a couple of minutes to convince the man that I was neither a process server nor a creditor. He admitted me after he was convinced that I was only a prospective writer wanting to know about the flying saucer film the company had shot.

He said that the producer (I'll call him Frank Miller) was due in any moment, and no doubt would be willing to talk with me. He offered me some trade papers to read, but I found these dull and, instead, pulled out some notes I had made while visiting the head of the Civilian Saucer Investigation, one of the earliest UFO investigative groups in the Nation.

In May of 1951, three technically trained men, Ed Sullivan, Werner Eichler and Victor Black, experienced a rather routine saucer sighting in the L.A. area, which, because of the background of the sighters, was given wide publicity—eventually appearing in Life magazine. As a result of the publicity, Sullivan decided to start a saucer investigation group, and invited the public to send in their sightings for analysis. The group grew to a dozen or so active members, and even attracted as an honorary member Dr. Walter Riedel, one of the country's leading rocket experts. Largely through the Life publicity, Sullivan and his co-workers received and analyzed more than a thousand sightings, hoping to find hidden within this mass of data some elements of consistency that would eventually tell them what saucers looked like, how and why they behaved as they did. Unlike most researchers, these men began with no preconceived notions. Perhaps that was why they failed to arrive at any definite conclusions beyond similarities of size, shape and performance.

Sullivan's group found that each sighting seemed to represent a law unto itself in regard to details, and finally they realized that by no amount of study could they hope to fit all genuine sightings into one or more specific category. In other words, they failed to solve the mystery, though it had gradually become apparent to the investigators that craft, probably from another planet, were responsible for the hard core of unexplained sightings.

"We're not "hushed up, " Sullivan assured me, "so don't help to spread this rumor that is going around. We just found we were not equipped to solve the mystery, with our limited facilities of equipment, money and time, and we gave up."

I removed the group's last publication, which Sullivan had given me, from my portfolio.

"Then you run into this sort of thing," Sullivan told me, pointing to a report in the publication headed *'1949 Sighting-One of the Most Interesting Reports Received by CSI.'*

The writer is a college graduate who has had several years graduate study as well. For five or six years I have been a cattle breeder on a farm a couple of miles from G. An article in *Life* magazine, which I read last week, has brought to mind again an experience which took place in 1949. I have debated with myself for some time as to writing about it. At the time it happened I mentioned it to my wife, and to my wife alone; I had not then, nor do I have any desire to be considered now an ass, so please do not publicize my name. However, on the chance that this information may be of use to you, here is what happened:

I had run an expectant cow into the barn lot for delivery, since she has always had trouble delivering without aid. That night, a clear, rather chilly fall evening, I had stayed up past one a.m., reading, until time to go make a check on her before retiring. Our house faces south and the barn is to the north and some distance away from the house. With a bucket of warm water, some soap and twine, I left the house and stopped to look at the stars, because it was such a clear evening, I suppose.

To the south, in the form of an equilateral triangle, I noted three lighted bodies which I knew in an instant were not stars. For a moment I thought them to be airplanes, but then they moved too rapidly for even jet planes. Suddenly one (the leading one) peeled off from the formation and seemed to be coming directly at me. I was frankly terrified. I threw myself onto the ground and remember thinking what a poor place to be if struck. I guess I was praying and shaking at the same time. Suddenly, I had a feeling that I had nothing to fear, and I guess my curiosity was very great so I rolled over.

There it was, a little to my left (east) seemingly stationary. It was a few hundred feet off the ground (my guess). I would also guess that it was between 300 and 400 feet in diameter. There appeared to be windows which seemed about twice as high as they were wide. These windows were evenly placed and were on the edge, where the over and the under curved surfaces came together. I noted that the other two had moved north, but had become stationary. This close one did not revolve. However, the longer I looked at it, the more I had a feeling of undulation. The thickness, I would guess to be a minimum of 75 feet and a maximum of 100 feet. It was absolutely without sound, but I had a very deep feeling that it embodied terrific energy.

The light coming from the windows, I would describe as being a blue-white, much as the color of a welding flame. Then I guess it was (after my feeling of undulation) that I became aware of (this is very hard to describe) a very, very powerful vibratory force. Everything, myself included, seemed to respond to this vibratory force. (That's the best way I can describe it). One such thought was that with the aid of this force, gravity meant nothing. Most of the rest of my ideas, then, were even more asinine. I don't know how long I lay there, wet from the spilled bucket, but peculiarly not at all afraid. Just as inexplicably, the thing took off with amazing speed to the north, and the vibratory feelings seemed to slacken and disappear. It took its lead position in the triangle, and all three zoomed off at the same rate of terrific speed. In regard to the light—after the thing left I was aware that I had a reddish glow before my eyes, as though I had been staring at a light bulb. Had the light been as in welding, I feel that the length of time I looked would have ruined my eyes.

It left me with an overpowering feeling of humility and insignificance. I sincerely hope this above will be of use to you.

S.E.

(This report was followed by a second letter six weeks later):

I received your acknowledgment to my earlier letter and was reminded of a plea which I heard when I sent the first letter off to you. I had taken the draft of my letter to G, a close personal friend, for his criticism of my attempt to recount a very personal experience to strangers. My friend insisted that I take the draft to Dr. B in that city. Dr. B is an advisor to the Atomic Energy Commission in Biophysics and biochemistry and served with the U.S. government as a scientific consultant. He is also a representative for the People's Division of the United Nations. He read the draft through carefully, and when I asked him whether people would think it asinine to mention the impact of thought I was subjected to he smiled and said no, that it had long been recognized that sudden and great exposure to gamma rays had an effect such as I described. He urged me to tell all that I could.

First of all, the thing represented energy-powerful and elemental, but still controlled. There was nothing haphazard about it, whatever. The perfect proportion of the equilateral triangle in which the three moved, the regular spacing of the windows, the graceful and beautiful proportions of the thing itself, as well as the undulating, vibrational pattern I felt all pointed to wonderful thought, coupled with careful planning and execution.

The length of time which I spent on the ground could not have been long, but I honestly do not know how long I was there. I felt a desire growing to join myself to the thing. It was somewhat like hypnosis from what I have observed, although I have never been a successful subject for hypnosis. It seemed to have a much greater power than gravity. I had an impression that gravity was a cold magnetic action and that it was inferior in power to the hot magnetic action of the thing.

When I went to the barn, which has its opening on the east, I was startled to see my cow. An Angus, like the rest, she had two marked characteristics. First, she was definitely antisocial as far as humans were concerned, and second, she had never had a calf without aid. When I got to the barn I was dreading, after the experience I had been through, roping her and helping her calve. She was standing facing the entryway, with her hide shaking all over like a horse trying to shake off a swarm of flies. But she was not afraid. Her eyes showed no white whatsoever. She would let me touch her anywhere, and when I examined her I knew I did not need to go back for more water. She was back, in appearance, to a point weeks from calving. I turned her out and, as I recall, she had her calf unaided the next day.

Many of the mental impressions which I received were new to me. At least I don't recall ever having come across them before. However, they charged my mental battery, so to speak, so that I got into encyclopedias and other books, and found that all had been expressed before. In every case, which I can recall, the seemingly simple truths had been called to peoples' attention long ago. One result—after many years away from it—I returned to church when the full impact of realization finally struck me. It took two years and has changed a cocky guy into a very humble person.

I do not feel in any way that I deserve any credit for this experience. I stumbled into it both figuratively and literally. I again renew my request for anonymity.

S.E.

THE ASTOUNDING UFO SECRETS OF JAMES W. MOSELEY

A key turning in the door of the cheaply furnished office awakened me from my perusal of the relatively dull magazines. In walked a handsome man in his 30's with circles under his eyes and a worried look on his face.

"I'm Frank Miller," he said, offering his hand. His assistant filled him in on my mission.

"There's very little to it, except the Air Force ruined me," Miller told me ruefully. He flopped down in a chair and offered me a cigarette from the battered pack.

I began to like this man immediately, and I am extremely glad he has done well since our meeting. I recently ran into him on a plane and found he had lost none of his wit and down-to-earth manner. It is difficult to believe that he was giving me a leg-pull back in 1953.

"It all began when I engaged a friend of mine to make some sixteen millimeter film for me in Alaska. This chap bums it all over the world, picking up jobs here and there, including film assignments when he can. I was doing pre-production work on a science fiction film about a prehistoric monster which comes alive due to atomic bomb experiments. It is first seen in Alaska, then heads south for L.A.— and the whole bit. There is no good film clip library on Alaska and I needed some shots of the coastal region which we could use as background. If you shoot sixteen millimeter color film you can blow it up to theatre-size film pretty easily, without much distortion.

"Well, Skippy shot a couple hundred feet of film and was ready to send me the batch when he decided to make part of it over due to better weather. While getting a shot of the surf, this character notices a bright flash in the viewfinder and looks up.

"There, hovering a few hundred feet above him is a real weird flying saucer. Jerry, dig that original letter out of the files, and I'll even let him copy it if he wants to."

"I think you may have the most sensational sequence of film ever released by a Hollywood studio," the letter to Miller read, "and that you won't have to use any special effects after all. Now, I'm no scriptwriter or producer, but I think I have something for you and if you change the plot of your picture you can announce that you have actual photographs of a flying saucer in your picture.

"I'm air mailing the film directly to the lab you specified and you should get it from them without delay.

"Here's essentially what I saw and it should come out good on the film. When I looked up I saw an object like two dinner plates stuck together. On top of this was a dome with round windows or portholes. The object was a bright silver in color, with a greenish glow coming from underneath. As I watched and shot my film, I became aware of a high-pitched tone which made me rather uncomfortable. Then this flying saucer, if that's what it was, began to move in a strange kind of gyration. It seemed to sway back and forth, describing a wide arc, just as if it were on an object suspended on some giant cable from the sky. As this swaying motion became faster, it suddenly shot upward at about a 75-degree angle to the southwest, the greenish glow changing to a bright yellow, then a deep red. There was a kind of 'shooshing' sound as it did this, but both the sound and the machine vanished within an incredible second or so."

As soon as he received the letter Miller immediately had a quick rewrite done on most of the script. He changed it from the atomic monster theme to that of a flying saucer appearing and warning the public to stop nuclear testing, following somewhat the successful major studio film, *The Day the Earth Stood Still.*

He made the mistake, however, of sending out blurbs to all the columnists and to the trade press, announcing that his film would be the first to contain actual close-up movies of a genuine flying saucer.

This led to his undoing.

"An Air Force major in a natty uniform showed up," he told me, "and said he would like to know more about the film. Get me right, he didn't at any time discourage me from finishing studio shooting of the film, releasing it, or anything.

"At the time, in fact, he seemed to be quite a decent chap. We had both been in the Pacific, and had seen action on the same island. But I had been an enlisted man and he had served as an officer throughout the war, so we had never talked to each other before. We went out to a bar and had a few drinks while he discussed the general flying saucer situation. "He told me that many saucer sightings were dreamed up by crackpots and that many of the cases involved misinterpretation of various natural phenomena. The Air Force was greatly concerned about the reports, however, and actually had a special division set up to investigate many of the sightings.

" 'That, of course is the official Air Force policy line on the situation,' the major said.

"I asked him what he personally thought of them, and he said that although he was probably too much of a science fiction buff to be objective, he personally believed there was something to it and that it could be boiled down very simply- we were being observed by an advanced civilization from Mars!

"The Air Force, he told me, wanted to examine our film for authenticity. I told him I wanted no part of it, since frankly, if it were a fake or some sort of natural phenomena, I certainly didn't want this to get out and ruin our publicity. I had already made costly alterations to our shooting schedule.

"He assured me that the results would be kept in strict confidence, and noted that his superiors had anticipated just such a reaction from me. If the film we released caused a great deal of controversy they would wait a respectable length of time until it got through the key money play dates before announcing they had analyzed it. Regardless of how good the film was, it was the policy of the Air Force to attempt to explain all photos and sightings, the major added.

" 'Gee thanks!' I told him, 'but I still don't buy that. Are you demanding the film or just asking a favor?' I asked him.

" 'I wish I had the authority to do so, but I don't,' the major told me.

"Then he began to fill me in."

Miller said the major had described the Air Force's role in flying saucer investigation as a great dilemma. They had gotten into it because their job was to keep the nation secure from enemy aircraft attack. Any unidentified flying object suggested the possibility of enemy aircraft penetration. Suddenly the whole impact of the possibility of superior interplanetary civilizations had hit them, and they found themselves holding a much bigger bag than they anticipated.

The year 1952 had brought a big UFO scare. Flying saucers were seen everywhere across the Nation. Many were reported as landing. A monster scare gripped West Virginia.

"Whether it was just hallucinations or something real, there was the possibility of real panic if the Air Force had another *1952*. They were trying to dig into all the cases and explain the ones they could honestly solve and to gather evidence which might provide the key to the solution of the mystery."

Miller hadn't believed in saucers from space, feeling they were some sort of secret military craft, but the major's appeal partly changed his mind. If it were one of our own craft his photographer had filmed, why would the Air Force be so anxious to examine the footage? So he put in a call to the lab, releasing the three rolls of film for a local Air Force officer to pick up, with the promise that they would immediately return the two rolls of background film, make a quick duplicate of the saucer footage on the third roll and forward the original to the studio where he was renting space and equipment for the movie.

"Three weeks passed and no film," Miller continued, so I called the major. He expressed surprise and promised quick action."

"He got quick action all right and I got a screwing. Skippy vows he sent about 25 feet of exposed film of the 100 on the saucer roll to the lab. I got back the two background footage rolls intact, but only about 15 feet of the other film, by registered mail within a week.

"I brought my two writers down to the apartment and ran the film off for them. It was the first time I had seen it, since the bulb in my projector had burned out and I had to look around the stores for the special kind it took. When I turned up the lights I must have looked like a fool; at least I certainly felt like one. " 'How do you write anything around that?' Bill, one of the two, observed, and he was correct.

The movie showed a small speck in the sky which moved around slowly for about 30 seconds. What's more it wasn't even over the water, it clearly was a desert scene, though there wasn't a horizon reference. If you've caught the picture you'll know what I mean."

Miller trusted the free-lance photographer implicitly and was certain he had told the truth. He was a cinematographer of at least 25 years of experience. A telephone conversation with him, when he finally could be located, further confirmed Miller's suspicion that a substitute film had been foisted upon him.

Miller was in a real bind, for the "saucer film" really showed nothing that would convince anybody. The picture, already oriented around the sequence, had been completed, using the substitute saucer, but caused no stir and little patronage at the boxoffice. In fact it had received only a couple of hundred bookings, and these in second feature slot at minimum rentals. The corporation formed for the movie had taken bankruptcy and Miller was now desperately trying to get back on his feet.

I am happy to observe that Miller has since risen above this sort of producing, has garnered a couple of minor Academy Awards, and is no longer on the lookout for process servers.

1:00

KIDNAPPED BY SPACEMEN

The advent of something which is pleasant, or something which is sad or, more often, with Ufologists, something tremendously exciting, usually starts with the ringing of a telephone. So it was on the Long John Show, and so it was in L.A.

Only John's phone doesn't ring. It either lights up or somebody motions from the control room to pick it up. As we continued the discussion John entered into his own private, but visibly heated, discussion with some unknown party on the other end.

Listening to the tape of this particular show and remembering what I could reconstruct from the audio reminders, I really think that whatever troubles beset the Long John Show that night started with John picking up the telephone. If John ever retires, which I sincerely hope he will never do, though he live to be a hundred, I'll probably ask him what happened, if I'm around to do so. Meanwhile I'm sure he doesn't want to discuss it. But something strange was afoot that night, something that might help us all explain a lot that we don't know about official suppression of saucer information.

In L.A., the telephone had also rung, and I had it in my hand before I realized I had been awakened at 2:00 in the morning. It was Manon Darlaine, and her voice was shaking.

'Jim!" she said, "I should have let you in on this when I gave you the lead on the confiscated film. I promised to keep this quiet, but I think you should know about this. Anyhow, the papers are swarming all over the story. It's no longer a secret."

I fumbled first for the light and then for my cigarettes.

"What! Manon! What's up?"

Although myriads of still pictures of UFOs have been taken, a relatively few motion pictures have been reported. Perhaps one of the most authenticated movies is represented above in the single-frame blowup inset. Major Colman VonKeviczky, of the American Institute of Aeronautics and Astronautics, and currently at the United Nations, New York, doing photographic technology, is seen here holding a series of blowups from the film. The movie was taken by Ellis E. Matthews, of Alberton, South Australia.

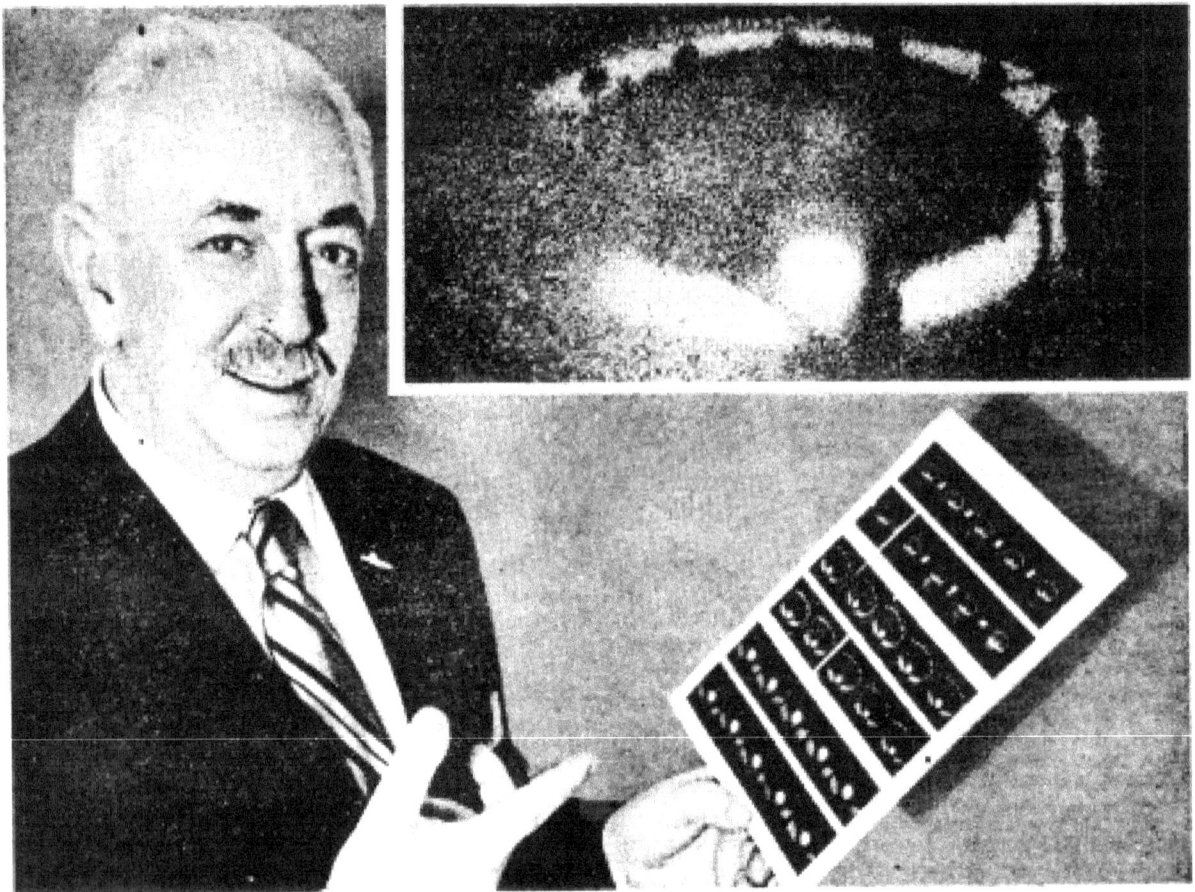

THE ASTOUNDING UFO SECRETS OF JAMES W. MOSELEY

"A couple of men have been kidnaped by a flying saucer!" Then she gave me some details.

Two nights previous Karl Hunrath had telephoned her at about midnight. He and Jack Wilkinson were ready to keep an unusual rendezvous, and invited her to come along. They were on their way to meet a flying saucer crew and take a ride in their craft!

Although I gathered that since she was still evidently a part of the terrestrial scene, she had declined the invitation, I could detect a note of real excitement, fear and belief in her voice.

"I've just had a call from Mrs. Wilkinson," she continued. "Yesterday Hunrath and Wilkinson just walked off their jobs and rented a plane at the Gardena County Airport—that's near L.A. They didn't file any flight plans and they have completely disappeared!"

Maybe Manon was being overly dramatic as she first started to fix my breakfast in her studio apartment, went into an adjoining room and brought out a strongbox which she opened with a key tied around her neck. Inside were several file folders. She withdrew one and told me to digest it as thoroughly as possible, for she couldn't let the material out of her sight.

I have just dug the elaborate notes I made that morning from my research files, in order to put together the strange background of this duo of Hunrath and Wilkinson.

Karl Hunrath and His Associates was the title of the file folder, written on the tab with the elaborate calligraphy which she evidently reserved for important cases.

She apparently sensed some importance about the activities of the two men, for she had typed up an elaborate report. It introduced a third party, Jerrold Baker, a saucer researcher, who had been personally acquainted with the missing men for many months prior to their disappearance. Manon Darlaine first met Hunrath at George Adamski's house in Palomar Gardens, California, in November of 1952.

(The late George Adamski is the author of several books in which he claims to have contacted space people from Venus and other planets. What I hope is a sensible review of Adamski's claims appears later in this book-JWM).

At that time Baker, Hunrath and a George Williamson were forming the Adamski Foundation, a kind of Grand Authority or clearing house for flying saucer information. Each of these three was to contribute his own special knowledge of UFOs to the Foundation's fund of information. Hunrath qualified, in that he was an electrical engineer; before coming to California he had performed experiments in electromagnetism and had constructed a machine which not only would demonstrate the effects of that phenomena but accomplish remarkably demonstrable results as well.

This machine, contained in a black box, and to which he had given the strange name Bosco was designed in an effort to duplicate the magnetic power by which the saucers were assumed to operate. (One of its more sinister purposes was to create a magnetic fault, which would cause any saucer operation in its proximity to crash in the vicinity of the machine!)

Bosco's contribution to saucer research was soon to run into some snags, however, as The Adamski Foundation became sidetracked into metaphysical rather than mechanical research. And thus began a series of fantastic episodes at Palomar Gardens where Adamski held court and conducted his researches.

Williamson would go into medium-like trances, and receive space messages, which he would repeat to his listeners in a voice different from his own, as if the space intelligences had taken possession of both his will power and his vocal chords. At times he even spoke in unknown languages.

The group would take elaborate notes, make tape recordings of the messages and later try to decipher the information given by Williamson in trance. Later, Williamson would assign pictograph symbols to the languages in the messages, based (he said) on his knowledge of anthropology and ancient symbology.

"Can you give me some details on this?" I asked Manon Darlain, pointing to her simple note, *"Personal falling out."*

"I had been sworn to secrecy on this point, and anyhow I don't believe in 'personalities,' but now that Hunrath and Wilkinson have disappeared, maybe I had better clear this up.

"Adamski is peculiar among the crackpots—and don't mean this in a disparaging way; I'm just using this term as it is used on the West Coast—in that he doesn't go in for any psychic or occult explanations for flying saucers. Although Adamski believes in telepathy, this to him is a purely physical matter, the ability of a superior brain to transmit messages to another brain, electronically. Adamski did not approve of Ric's (Williamson's) trance-mediumship method of obtaining information, and some of the other activities of the threesome, who in my personal opinion, were in part simple freeloaders of Adamski's bed and board, did not meet with his personal approval. The relationships apparently became more strained and the final breakup was precipitated by Hunrath's announcement that he was going to use the Bosco machine to interrupt the magnetic fields of saucers, which appeared regularly over Mt. Palomar, and bring them down.

THE ASTOUNDING UFO SECRETS OF JAMES W. MOSELEY

"Adamski, if insincere, would probably not have believed this; instead he became enraged with the idea. He ordered Hunrath to remove the black box from Palomar Gardens, and when the latter refused, an argument ensued and all three guests were ordered to leave the premises."

(Madame Darlain's information once more proves to be valid. A recent book, Gray Barker's book of Adamski (Saucerian Books, 1966), presents a lengthy personal letter to the publisher from Adamski in which he elaborates at length on his relationships with Hunrath, the black box, and the argument which ensued-JWM.)

After the schism in The Adamski Foundation, Hunrath, Baker and Williamson went to Los Angeles to seek employment. Since Williamson through his study of anthropology and extensive living among the American Indians, had knowledge of Indian dances, for a while he and Baker considered the idea of performing these dances publicly, with Baker doing the narration. While these two pondered this unique self-employment, Hunrath with his technical background, obtained a job with an aircraft company. A few months later, Williamson returned to his wife, Betty, in Prescott, Arizona.

Baker and Hunrath moved into an apartment in Los Angeles.

The tale hereby began to hang, I gathered from Manon, from the introduction of another character into the bizarre Ufological plot.

"In August, Wilkinson, who had worked with Hunrath in some of his earlier experiments with Bosco, joined him. He had quit a job as foreman at an electrical plant in Racine, Wisconsin, before coming back to L.A. to look up his former buddy.

"Hunrath and Baker introduced the newcomer to Williamson, and Wilkinson also appeared soon to fall under Williamson's spell. The three made several trips to Prescott to confer with Williamson and to listen as he received his mediumistic messages."

I began to suspect that the seed of this weird idea had been planted by Adamski, with his talks of meeting space people. According to Manon, all four of the persons assumed space names: Baker was Markon, Williamson was Mark III, while Hunrath and Wilkinson were content with Firkon and Ramu. The symbols which Williamson had previously begun to assign to his apparent gibberish now started coming to Hunrath and Wilkinson as visions, at any time of the day or night. They began to write down and interpret them.

"At this point Baker's mother became seriously ill," Manon Darlaine continued, emerging from the kitchen with my breakfast. "Baker left the association; and this probably is the reason he is safe today. I learn from my sources, however, that he received a letter stating that the writer, which was Wilkinson, had found out definitely when and where a saucer was going to land. The letter asked Baker to hurry back as soon as possible and participate with them in a meeting with the occupants of the craft."

The three were not only invited to meet the saucer occupants, but to fly away to Mars in the saucer!

A knock at the door interrupted her remarks. A young man entered and handed her an ink-stained roll of paper. She unrolled a proof of a widely-circulated afternoon newspaper.

KIDNAPED BY SPACE MEN, the headline declared.

Then I realized partly why Manon Darlaine had been free with this somewhat exclusive information: the papers were now on to it and it was no longer the hidden property of her Seven Safes.

During my survey of the West Coast Saucer scene I had begun to learn to take no information too seriously, particularly when it involved the so called lunatic fringe. But subsequent investigation has indicated that the Hunrath-Wilkinson disappearance is one of the most puzzling items in that vast lexicon of saucerology and still remains one of the major unsolved mysteries of the field.

Although many conflicting rumors continue to circulate about the disappearance, there is no definite evidence that Hunrath, Wilkinson, or their plane were ever seen again. One rumor had it that the plane, partly dismantled, was spotted from the air by a search party, but no ground expedition has succeeded in locating it, although a thorough search was made.

Several other facts serve to heighten the baffling mystery. A few weeks after the disappearance, the airport from which Hunrath and Wilkinson rented their plane was destroyed by fire.

The day after the disappearance a peculiar man in a white uniform visited Mrs. Wilkinson and told her that her husband was alive and safe. He gave no details, but did leave his name and address. Baker contacted him, and became convinced that the man did not know anything. Later, other stories circulated, contributing to the idea that the men might still be alive. One such story involved a newspaper ad in the personals column of a Los Angeles newspaper, in which the writer of the ad stated in a cryptic manner that he was interested in saucers and would like to contact like-minded people. Some of the people who had known the missing pair though that Hunrath or Wilkinson had placed the ad in order to contact their friends. Baker also followed up this lead and found the writer to be unconnected with the case. Another story had it that the missing men skipped for Mexico, in an effort to get away from personal problems in California.

THE ASTOUNDING UFO SECRETS OF JAMES W. MOSELEY

Today, looking at the case objectively, the balance of evidence favors the opinion that the men are dead. It is known that Hunrath, who flew the plane, was not an experienced pilot. He had taken a refresher course in flying just the week previous to his disappearance. It is believed that the pair were flying in the direction of Prescott, Arizona, for a saucer rendezvous in that area. This would have taken them over a long stretch of desolate, unexplored country in which there are mountain regions where a plane could crash and not be located for years.

Recently, I came in late to my office and found my secretary, without the usual cheery look on her face. I could sense that she had bad news which she would probably get around to giving me in the afternoon.

Surely enough, in time she handed me a large manila envelope which contained the latest issue of *Saucer News*, my UFO publication. I recognized the envelope as belonging to the usual bundle returned daily by the post office as undeliverable.

Across the face of the envelope was marked the simple word, *Deceased*.

I knew Manon was getting up in years, but I always looked forward to the letter I would always receive commenting on every issue.

No comments, no criticisms, no kudos from this issue .It had been addressed: Manon Darlaine P.O. Box 2048-North Wilcox Station Hollywood 28, Calif. I knew Pam had not removed this mailing plate from the file, for she had a kind of sixth sense about friends of mine whose mail had become permanently undeliverable.

Two or three days later, late in the evening, I personally would get around to the task.

PLANE VANISHES IN MYSTERY

Wife Fears Hubby in Flying Saucer Kidnap

Rare clipping from THE LOS ANGELES MIRROR tells of mysterious disappearance.

BY CHARLES RIDGWAY, Mirror Staff Reporter

Two missing electricians may have been kidnaped by interplanetary invaders in a flying saucer, fears Mrs. Wilbur J. Wilkinson of 1933½ LeMoyne Ave., wife of one of the missing men.

The two flying saucer fans, Wilkinson and Karl Hunrath of 2315 S Flower St., took off in a rented airplane from Gardena Airport last Wednesday with a three-hour gas supply.

Despite a widespread search, no trace of the plane or its occupants has been seen.

Wilkinson's wife told The Mirror today that Hunrath was an avid believer in flying saucers. He and Wilkinson believed the end of the earth was nearing, and that strange little men from the planet "Maser" were ready to invade.

Hunt Saucer

Hunrath claimed to know the whereabouts of a flying saucer recently landed. Wilkinson's den, in their rented hillside home, is lined with flying saucer pictures, weird signs and formulas, which his wife says were supposed to be the new interplanetary language.

"Of course, I don't quite go for all the flying saucer talk, but Karl had convinced Wilbur they actually existed," Mrs. Wilkinson related.

"He had tape recordings of conversations with men from other planets who landed here in saucers."

She also pointed to messages tacked on Wilkinson's walls, supposedly received by radio from the interplanetary visitors. One was from a "Prince Reggs of the planet Maser."

The Wilkinsons, who have three children, Patricia, 12, Judith, 5, and John, 2, moved here from Racine, Wis., June 28. Wilbur is employed by Hoffman Radio Corp., where he was recently promoted to be in charge of the inspection department, Mrs. Wilkinson said.

The 38-year-old electrician has a den full of electronic equipment, radios and tape recorders.

"He was planning to go into the recording business," his tearful wife told The Mirror.

"He really didn't seem too interested in flying saucers except when Karl Hunrath came around. Karl was the one who talked us into coming to California because he said he could actually show a flying saucer to Wilbur."

Deputy sheriffs took a dim view of the "saucer kidnaping."

They warned Mrs. Wilkinson the two missing men might be in for a prison term if it is shown they "stole" the plane.

Mrs. Wilkinson admitted having an argument with her husband the night before he disappeared, but insisted it had nothing to do with him leaving. "I just can't help but think flying saucers had something to do with it," she concluded.

WILBUR J. WILKINSON
One of missing men.

FROM OUTER SPACE?
These weird symbols and words were found on wall of Wilkinson's home. Some have English words penciled lightly beneath. In upper photo, "Losh-tai," next to last line, is translated "Create Life." Lower, second line, "Xenph-mau" has scribbled under it: "Poseid Returning." Third from bottom, "Josh-tau-marin," is translated: "Births give cataclysms."

1:45

SCOUT SHIP FROM VENUS

Long John's microphones stand on a long table, above garish, noisy Times Square; yet, high on the 24th floor, with no windows, and sound proofed, the panel member or guest is transported far from the reality of everyday things.

After an hour or so talking on the show you forget you are before microphones. You get the feeling that there is nobody listening and the broadcast becomes almost an unreal thing.

Of course, Long John periodically jokes about his original Society of Eight, the legendary eight listeners who he avers were, at one time the only people tuned in. The truth is that immediately after John went on the air he gathered about a million listeners. In New York, the late movies may drown him out in a few homes, but across the eastern part of the nation truck drivers, travelers and others of a large and avid section of the radio audience regularly lose their sleep listening to Long John's fantastic interviews. It is this wide and enthusiastic audience which gives him his fantastic ratings.

This evening when Yonah opened a large strange book of more than a thousand pages I knew he was ready to make some interesting comments. I leaned over and glanced at the opened pages of the two-column format with text which read like the Bible. "This is *Oahspe*, or New Bible," Yonah told me off-mike, during a recorded commercial. I would later know why Gray Barker was obviously trying to avoid the subject of *Oahspe*. As a commercial bookseller, he had offered the book to his customers and sold a number of copies. Although he made a good profit on the high-priced books, the customers; he later told me, often read *Oahspe*, accepted it as the Whole Truth, and would not buy any other books for months, as if they already had all the answers!

The book, however, as I would learn later, certainly was mysterious enough in its conception and writing, let alone its contents. Its authorship is remarkable in that a human agent transcribed the words, while in trance, at the direction of heavenly beings. John B. Newbrough was an Ohio boy who came East to enter the dental profession, and soon became one of the leading dentists of New York City.

Newbrough happened one evening to be visiting a circle of friends of social note when the host suggested that one of the guests, who had some fame as a medium, conduct a seance for the group.

Newbrough reluctantly assented to join, and then was astounded. Once the seance had begun he found that he could not control his hands, which could not lie on the table without flying into "tantrums", as he put it.

"Often they would write messages, left or right, forward or backward," one of his letters declared.

Newbrough became interested in seances and attended many. He found his strange power growing and his hands continued to move in these tantrums, much to his annoyance at times. When he would control his hands by withdrawing them from the table, the baffling power would attack his tongue, his eyes, or ears, at which times he claimed to hear "differently from my normal state."

Newbrough spent more than twelve years traveling hundreds of miles, investigating various mediums, trying to disprove them. Finally, entirely convinced, he decided he wanted to know more about the spirit world.

The dentist began a series of fasts, frequent bathing, and rising before daybreak for meditation, in an effort to develop his powers.

According to a letter Newbrough wrote to *The Banner of Light*, Boston, Mass., on Jan. 21, 1883:

"A new condition of control then came upon my hands. Instead of the angels holding my hands as formerly, they held their hands over my head and they were clothed with sufficient material for me to see them. And a light fell upon my hands as they lay on the table. In the meantime I was directed to get a typewriter. This I did.

"One morning the light struck both my hands on the back and they went for the typewriter for some fifteen minutes, very vigorously. I was told not to read what was printed, and I had worked myself into such a religious fear of losing this new power that I obeyed reverently. The next morning, also before sunrise, the same power came and wrote again. One morning I accidentally looked out the window and beheld the line of light that rested on my hands extending like a telegraph wire toward the sky. Over my head were three pairs of hands, fully materialized.

THE ASTOUNDING UFO SECRETS OF JAMES W. MOSELEY

Behind me stood another angel with her hands on my shoulders. My looking did not disturb the scene.

"For fifty weeks this continued every morning and then it ceased and I was told to read and publish the book *Oahspe*.

Although this was the twentieth century and we were broadcasting from a New York far removed from the days of Newbrough, I remember, as we talked about contactees, thinking that the case of the dentist's visions and contacts were not much different from those of George Adamski, Howard Menger, and the others of the present. Instead of seeing angels, the modern contactees saw spacemen, *and space women*. Maybe it was because of the age involved, a mechanistic one, when man himself was on the threshold of space.

Now it was not so remarkable that Newbrough should see angels, I thought, but that he could come up with such a monumental volume—for sheer size alone! Even though the contents might not be generally accepted, and even though they may have come from his subconscious, as some claimed, his subconscious must have been remarkable.

According to the angels of *Oahspe* (the celestial authors) one of their numbers, Sethantes, was appointed by their government about 79,000 years ago to take charge of the earth and to people it with beings like themselves, capable of immortality. With Sethantes came millions of other space-dwelling entities and they accomplished that mission. They caused a new race of primates to appear here called man-flesh of the earth with an imperishable spirit.

Since that day (all of this according to *Oahspe* enthusiasts) "the etherean hosts of the Most High," aided by their heirs and successors, have maintained a vigilant jurisdiction over the earth and its inhabitants. Since then, they have never ceased trying to make mankind aware of his dual heritage, trying to make obedient "to the spirit within" and appreciative of its great possibilities. By psychic means and strategems they have tried to keep us making progress toward a higher world civilization, and then toward a higher spiritual development.

Flying saucers were not new to the thousands of *Oahspe* students who have studied the book for almost a century. The vehicles that *Oahspe* ethereans used for travel correspond quite closely with what people are seeing today. Whatever flying saucers are, they certainly are nothing new.

Yonah had brought up the subject of *Oahspe* in order to make a point. George Hunt Williamson (whom we met in the previous chapter through his associations with Hunrath and Wilkinson) was, according to Yonah, a very serious student of the huge book, and believed practically everything it expounded. Williamson interpreted certain sections as a prophecy for a contact to be made with a spaceman on a certain date—a date which he predicted for George Adamski, who went out onto the desert to help fulfill the prediction. Yonah held that the entire Adamski affair was a made-up-thing, concocted to make the *Oahspe* prediction come true.

Gray Barker had defended the contactees in some of his publications and books. Yonah's inference was that he also may have had something to do with the Adamski story. This I doubted very much. Probably no reporter or investigator in the field had spent any more effort and time than had I in trying to expose Adamski, the author of three popular books claiming that he had met and talked to men from Venus.

I had been before the Long John microphones on one previous occasion with Adamski, and thoroughly enjoyed interrogating him. In fact I suppose you could say that we had become friends—of sorts—though our beliefs differed.

As I thought of Adamski, I thought of the pleasant evening I had with him back in 1953. I had driven my car up the winding road to the very top of Mt. Palomar in search of him. As I ascended the mountain I mused over the many strange situations I had run into as a result of Manon Darlaine's leads. While I had come to California with the idea of writing an "expose-type" book about the UFO "fringe" crowd, I had run across a lot of exciting material. Maybe it was the heat, maybe it was the emotional climate: but I had to prevent myself from beginning to believe a part of what I'd heard and investigated.

Manon Darlaine had never discussed Adamski at any length. It was not until I was preparing to leave California did I hear the rumor that, if it checked out, could be mighty important—a rumor that there was proof that flying saucers and visiting space people were real!

A Mt. Palomar astronomer, the story went, had come out with a book, published in England, which declared that he had met a Venusian pilot of a saucer on a California desert and talked to the creature with the aid of sign language. The astronomer's name was Professor Adamski.

Not having telephoned ahead, I had some doubts about being able to see the professor, but I had previously found that the best way to see a relatively inaccessible public figure was to show up in his outer office and to talk my way in.

I had met such a figure on my way to California. Stopping off in Independence, Mo., I had been able to walk into former president Harry S. Truman's office and interview him about flying saucers. This interview, however, was less successful than my entrance. In answer to my first question about UFO, Mr. Truman succinctly replied:

"I've never seen a purple cow . . . . .But I'd rather see than be one'" And with that, my interview came to an end!

Instead of a hard time at the Palomar reception office, I got a horse laugh from a passing staff member when I asked about Professor Adamski'

"The Professor," and he emphasized the title in a mocking manner' "lives half way down the mountain. You'll find him running a hot dog stand down there."

The receptionist gave me a more thorough and restrained explanation: No there was no Professor George Adamski at the Observatory: the man I was looking for could be found at Palomar Gardens, a restaurant on the slopes of the mountain which catered to the tourists who came to see the 200-inch telescope at the crest. Yes, Adamski had written a book about flying saucers and had claimed to take photographs of them.

"You'll have to pardon Dr. I'm afraid he can be very blunt at times," she added.

Adamski didn't really own the restaurant, but lived nearby. He spent a great deal of time in the restaurant, however, telling his story to the people who were beginning to flock there to see him. The receptionist herself had stopped by on one occasion, and had found his story most interesting, though she was skeptical about his claims.

I drove back down the mountain to Palomar Gardens and parked in the lot almost filled with cars. Inside I quickly spotted a gray-haired man who appeared to be in his sixties, seated at one of the tables. A crowd of thirty to forty people sat open-mouthed as he related his story.

Adamski did not claim to have any connection with Palomar Observatory. "I am a philosopher, teacher, student, and saucer researcher," he told us. "For several years I have been an amateur astronomer, and have two small telescopes, one of them a 15-inch reflector, and the other a six-inch refractor."

Long interested in the possibility of life on the other planets, Adamski had written a fictional book wherein interplanetary visitations took place. He had also conducted a school of Tibetan philosophy, known as The Royal Order of Tibet.

His real interest in flying saucers began, Adamski said when two men from the Point Loma Navy Electronics Laboratory, near San Diego, visited him. These men, J. P. Masfield and G. L. Bloom, assured him that the flying saucers were probably interplanetary and that an Earth government was also developing such machines.

The purpose for their visit was to secure his cooperation in photographing the strange craft, on the assumption that his small telescopes could maneuver more easily than the large one at the Observatory. They planned to make a similar request to the Observatory Staff.

Thus, having been asked by the military, as Adamski put it, to cooperate with them, he purchased additional photographic equipment and began to watch the sky for the spacecraft.

"Night after night I stayed outdoors with my telescope aimed, camera attached. Some nights I thought I might freeze because of the cold winds.

"Alice K. Wells, owner of Palomar Gardens, brought hot steaming coffee by the dozens of cups but this was very little comfort. Once I caught an extremely bad cold and was away from my task for weeks while recovering, but still I persisted."

Even though Adamski's liaison with the Point Loma technicians soon terminated (for some unexplained reason), he continued his efforts at saucer photography and was rewarded with some sightings and some reasonably good photos, though most of the pictures did not turn out well. Not being a photographer, Adamski had to master the art as he went along. Absolutely convinced of the saucers' reality after the sightings, he began to hope that the time would come when he could make a personal contact with some person from another world. Many times he wandered out onto the desert, feeling he had received telepathic messages from the saucers.

But it was not until November 20,1952, that Adamski's wish became a reality.

In August, 1952, he had met two Prescott, Arizona, couples, Mr. and Mrs. Bailey, and Dr. and Mrs. George Hunt Williamson. Since the couples were also interested in possible contacts with space people, they asked to be invited to come along the next time he made one of his desert trips. Accordingly, Adamski phoned Williamson on November 18 and arranged to meet the two couples near Desert Center, California, two days later. Adamski's secretary Lucy McGinnis, and Alice K. Wells, were invited to go along.

The seven people met on schedule and proceeded to a point on the highway about eleven miles from Desert Center. The Baileys brought a movie camera, the Williamsons a still camera; Adamski took along his 6-inch telescope, binoculars, and a case containing his still camera and gadgets for attaching it to the telescope. He also had seven cut film holders and an inexpensive camera.

Williamson, who still claimed to be an anthropologist, had even brought along plaster of Paris in case any ground markings needed to be preserved. Thus, the party was quite well prepared in case a meeting with a saucer or a space man should come about.

"The first unusual occurrence," Adamski told us, "was the sighting of a huge mother ship type of saucer, that's the dirigible-looking type, which appeared at a very high altitude and was seen by all our party. We had camped right next to the highway, and I'm sure this mother ship could have been seen by any passing motorist.

"But I had the feeling that this would not be the spot where we might make contact. I had Lucy drive me to a spot a half mile or so from the highway. I then asked her to return and rejoin the others for the period of an hour, after which I would return if nothing had happened. I had a very strong feeling that this would be the day for a contact and that I should be alone."

He set up his telescope and related equipment, and within five minutes was rewarded by the sight of "a small scout ship type of saucer some distance from me. I took seven photos of this ship, though these did not turn out well for some reason.

"Right after this, I saw motion out of the corner of my eye, looked and saw a man approaching me. Although this person looked very much like an ordinary man, he was dressed in a peculiar type of ski suit clothing and had long flowing hair."

To quote from Adamski's book, "The beauty of his form surpassed anything I had ever seen. . . I felt like a little child in the presence of one with great wisdom and much love, and I became very humble within myself, for from him was radiating a feeling of infinite understanding and kindness, with supreme humility."

Although the story Adamski was telling was fantastic, I was impressed by the many photos, tacked up on the wall, of disc-shaped objects with portholes, dome-type superstructures and spherical landing gear. I also realized almost immediately that I personally liked this man, for he seemed to radiate a humble attitude and good will. Although other members of the restaurant audience became vituperative, including a skeptical heckler who tended to disrupt Adamski's colorful narrative, the "Professor" displayed remarkable patience and interrupted his story to answer his objections and to go into irrelevant details.

Later, when I published many articles critical to Adamski in *Saucer News*, and when I appeared with Long John as a skeptical panelist, Adamski never displayed any personal animosity toward me. Instead he treated me kindly and spoke well of me to others.

Although I have, in later years, become known as one of Adamski's chief critics, I must confess that during this restaurant audience he held me enthralled, as he continued his story:

"The meeting lasted about three quarters of an hour. During this time, by using gestures, I learned that the man was from the planet Venus and that his visit here on Earth was due in part to concern over our use of atomic weapons. To express the idea of atomic explosions, the Visitor said Boom! Boom! Unfortunately, he would not allow me to photograph him. I got the mental impression that perhaps many of these Venusians were already on Earth, mixing with Earth people, and that possibly some distinguishing feature in such a photograph might enable people to identify them more easily."

Toward the end of the interview, the Venusian made a point of calling Adamski's attention to his footprints in the sand. It developed that the soles of his shoes were inscribed with symbolic markings. After he returned to his scout ship and departed, Adamski rejoined the others and excitedly led them to the Scene. Williamson, fully prepared for such an eventuality, made plaster casts of the footprints. Subsequently, many people had tried to interpret the strange symbols impressed by the shoes, but had failed to come up with anything definite.

In the course of his talk with Adamski, the Venusian asked permission to borrow one of Adamski's film packs, with the promise to return it to him shortly. About three weeks later a similar—or the same—scout ship flew over the vicinity of Palomar Gardens, and the pilot dropped the film pack out one of the portholes.

The film, upon development, revealed more strange symbols, similar to those in the footprints. Adamski had a number of language experts at work on the "writing," yet without results, though one of them pointed out that the symbols appeared similar to a language called Urdu, which had been reproduced in a strange book titled **From India to The Planet Mars**, in which a French woman claimed to have obtained messages from Mars while in trance state.

The next month, December 13, however, Adamski succeeded in getting several good pictures of the scout ships—these were the ones displayed on the wall. Another photo of one of the ships, though blurred, had been made by Jerrold E. Baker, who said he snapped it with a Kodak Brownie camera as the saucer flew away and passed rapidly over the low hill on which he was standing.

Adamski further strengthened his account with a sworn statement made by the witnesses, a photostat of which he took from a brief case and passed around through our group. I copied it after it had finished its full circuit:

I/we the undersigned, do solemnly state that I/we have read the account herein of the personal contact between George Adamski and a man from another world, brought here in his Flying Saucer "Scout Ship," and that I/we was/were a party to and witness to the event as herein recounted.

I was determined to have a private audience with Adamski, so I remained in the restaurant until he had gone through the account at least five times. I must say, however, that this repetition was not particularly boring, for the Professor, though his handling of official Earth Language was unique indeed, delightful—his apparent sincerity and sense of the dramatic made it all worth while.

Each recounting was somewhat different, in that Adamski added details he had not mentioned as the groups who came and went constantly, like the audience at some fantastic grand movie house.

The foregoing is a composite of his various tellings of the story.

When the last of the diehards left the restaurant, including (finally) the lady who imagined that her husband was really a man from outer space and wanted means of positively proving the case. I told Adamski that I was a prospective author of a saucer book. Surprisingly, Adamski took great interest in me and graciously gave all the time I wanted to ask questions. Mostly, however, his end of the conversation was a rehash of what he had already related.

As a very brash, unprofessional and quite naive young man, I'm afraid I asked Adamski:

'Would you tell me honestly, and just between the two of us is all of this the truth-or were you merely writing an exciting book?"

I suppose I wanted him to answer "Yes. It's the truth." Adamski showed no anger or discomfort at the question. Instead, he put a fatherly arm on my shoulder, led me over to the counter where, finally' after the tedious hours of the lectures, he could relax. He drew a half-filled bottle of vodka from behind the counter, and somebody brought some orange juice. He mixed a screwdriver for both of us, and although I never did like this drink, I enjoyed that one.

Adamski, relaxing still further, departed from the subject of flying saucers altogether, as if, filing away my unanswered question for further reference, he wanted to get away from the general matter. He asked me where I was from, and in a number of other friendly questions, made me feel he was genuinely interested in me.

Warmed by the drink, he raised his eyes to a calendar on the wall, which displayed a well-rounded female, and his eyes twinkled. Then he ripped off a couple of jokes that really shocked me, not because I was unused to such stories or did not thoroughly enjoy them, but because they seemed so much out of context.

"When you are older," he then told me, and a grave look came over his face, "you may learn the truth about the mission of the space brothers. It may be, but I hope that this is not the case, that you will be too old a man, as, alas, I am, to do much about this.

"What I have told you and the others tonight is absolutely true. But who is it that asked in the poem, 'What is truth?' I don't remember, I am not a literary man. You must not only take my truth, but you must discover the truth for yourself. In that manner, you will truly believe, as I do."

All of this, despite Adamski's charming hospitality, sounded like double talk to me; and I have as yet not discovered just what he was getting at, if anything, even though I am much older. And I am still waiting, of course, to see if there was any meaning to a very odd prediction he next made:

"If you don't believe in the space ships," Adamski went on, "and the space brothers, as I don't think you do, young man, wait until 1968 and you will find more understanding—or at the most until 1969."

As I drove down the winding slopes of Mt. Palomar I wondered if he had been predicting something or engaging in occult mumbo jumbo.

The rock 'n roll on the car radio suddenly halted and a voice blurted in, announcing that Soviet scientists had just predicted that artificial satellites would be orbiting the earth by 1957. I laughed. The Soviets were even crazier than anybody I had met on the West Coast.

2:10

THE SAUCER BUG

I had planned to remain in the Los Angeles area for only a week, to gain a general overview of the UFO situation there. Already I had been there fifteen days, yet I decided to check out some of the claims I had heard, particularly those of Adamski, who seemed to be the most important, or at least the most controversial figure I had met.

A good lead might be G. L. Bloom, one of the two men from the Point Loma Navy Electronics Laboratory who, Adamski said, visited him and created his interest in photographing the saucers. In the course of their conversation with him they had also, Adamski alleged, confirmed the landing of a flying saucer in Mexico City.

A telephone call to Bloom brought a very quick denial about part of Adamski's story. He claimed to have no knowledge whatsoever of a Mexico City landing incident. Strangely enough, he would not be specific in confirming or denying that he and the other man had encouraged Adamski. His only positive statement was that "I have been grossly misquoted in *Flying Saucers Have Landed*." Apparently he had seen an advance copy.

Although Bloom's brief testimony certainly did not deny the meeting, the fact that Adamski might embellish the conversation with the Mexico City incident certainly did not put him in favorable light in terms of his total veracity.

I was unable to reach the other man, who Adamski said was J. P. Maxwell.

Another point that troubled my mind was Adamski's remark that if his pictures of saucers were really photos of U. S. secret military aircraft, the Air Force would not have allowed him to distribute them. He said he had sent a complete set to Wright-Patterson Air Force Base, in Dayton, Ohio, scene of the Project Bluebook

George Adamski claimed that he met a Venusian space pilot in the desert. He is shown standing beside a painting of the spacemen. The painting was executed by Gay Betts.

saucer investigation, and that no interest was taken in them. Had the photos been genuine space ships, I reflected, surely the Air Force would have been even more interested, and would have requested the negatives for evaluation.

The fact that Adamski had witnesses to his desert contact had been a point which almost clinched my total belief; however this began to slowly fall apart as my visit ran into its third week.

Although at least two of the witnesses were close personal friends and might not be completely impartial (one was the owner of the property where he lived, and the other his secretary); at first glance the other four seemed to be free from prejudices toward spaceship reality.

Dr. George H. Williamson, who had been accompanied by his wife, was impressive, until I remembered that he had been the person involved with Karl Hunrath and had lived at Adamski's place during the incident of the "black box." He had also engaged in telepathic reception of space messages while there, and possibly connected with the Hunrath-Wilkinson disappearance. An anonymous Los Angeles source told me that Dr. Williamson had no doctor's degree; that indeed he had never received a diploma from an undergraduate college, and had in fact been expelled because of poor scholarship. (this evidence was later formally confirmed in a letter from The University of Arizona, formally signed by a responsible official of the University.)

A personal visit to Al Bailey, who with Mrs. Bailey, comprised the other two witnesses, convinced me that he had been an ardent believer long before the desert incident. Further, he did not see the spaceman with whom Adamski allegedly talked, nor did he see the scout ship which Adamski said landed. He did, however, see a dirigible-shaped mother ship, and some flashes of light in the direction where Adamski was supposed to be during the contact.

To the best of his knowledge, no one else present saw any more than he did! Furthermore, a drawing, supposedly made by Alice K. Wells while watching Adamski and his visitor through binoculars, could not in his opinion have been made from that distance—about a mile away.

Nevertheless, despite this negative evidence, Bailey believed that the contact may actually have taken place, though he personally could not vouch for it.

According to another West Coast informant, it would have been almost impossible for the space man (unless of tremendous weight) to have made such sharp imprints in the sand. There had been no rain for several months and the loose sand would not have received such a definite impression.

I wondered that if the space man were indeed from Venus, how he had been able to defy all scientific evidence by existing so easily and comfortably in Earth's atmosphere, since it is an established fact (confirmed, later, by the Mariner space probes) that the Venusian atmosphere is much different from ours. How, also, did the spaceman defy the laws of probability by looking so much like an Earth man?

Why had no one succeeded in taking any movies or decent still pictures of the mother ship seen during the November 20 contact?

Not only did Adamski's story need a great deal of further reappraisal; in fact, almost everything I had seen on the Coast did also.

Probably Gray Barker could fill me in on many of these things, I thought, if I were able to see him on my way back home. Barker had put me off when I had called him earlier, with the excuse that he was departing on a three-week trip to the southern part of West Virginia to act as a consultant for a school system which was making a film. I suspected that he simply did not want to see me. On the phone he seemed somewhat nervous speaking to me.

I remembered, however, that Dominick Lucchesi and August C. Roberts had been suspicious of me when I visited them, until they talked with me for a while and became convinced I was not one of the Three Men in Black!

By now, or more likely five minutes after my visit to Augie and Dom had ended, they had probably been on the phone to Barker giving him a report on me. Since there must have been some contact since then, Barker probably now knew that I was not somebody coming to shush him up, seize his files, or do any of the other half-feared, half-hoped-for misfortunes which I found so many saucer enthusiasts expected would soon happen to them.

This time, my phone call to Barker drew a much more favorable response. He invited me to stop at his apartment and invited me to stay overnight. I declined, but made an appointment to see him for an hour or so.

I was reminded of the story of the missing film when I saw how the drive-in theatre industry had apparently made Barker most affluent.

In his letters he had just moved from a rooming house to a beautiful apartment which he had just furnished, and now had his own private office.

At his apartment Barker spent an hour subjecting me to demonstrations of his high-fidelity record player and color television sets, two items which, at that date, were quite novel.

Whenever our talk finally settled down to UFOs, Barker became noticeably nervous and fidgety. He pulled out a large file of letters, reports and correspondence—from and regarding the International Flying Saucer Bureau—most of which were letters to and from the director, Albert K. Bender.

"I'm trying to put all this together, but somehow it just doesn't make sense," he stated.

Barker finally revealed that he had been visited by the FBI before Bender's hush-up, and he believed that the visit had something to do with the Bender mystery.

A man from out of town, being treated in a local hospital, had in his possession a business card issued by the IFSB, and having heard of Barker's interest in saucers had come to get information from him.

Barker did not know how the man could have got hold of the card, since he had just received his package of cards a few days before. "Did the FBI investigators discourage your investigation?" I asked.

"No, and that's peculiar, if it has anything to do with Bender. They just asked a few questions about the organization, and if I knew this chap, and that's all. I guess I must have got overly frightened for I should have asked them some questions. But I had never before been visited by the FBI and was very nervous."

Barker had pulled out all of his files on the IFSB and was trying to search out the possible "answer" that Bender had come up with before being visited by the men who had confirmed the information and offered even more. Also he was beset with some devils of doubt, and was wondering whether or not Bender was telling the truth.

Worst of all, Barker feared he would be interfered with in some way and wondered if he should stop his investigations and the publication of a small magazine, *The Saucerian* which he had just begun.

"I'm truly fascinated by the study of UFOs and I don't want to stop. Yet if it's something the government doesn't want me to do, as a loyal citizen I would give it up."

Barker had just received a review copy of Adamski's *Flying Saucers Have Landed*. A skim reading disclosed that it followed essentially the same story I had heard from the author. Most of the pictures I had already seen at Palomar Gardens.

"I don't know quite what to think of Adamski's part of the book," Barker told me, "but Desmond Leslie's part is tremendous."

He was referring to the fact that the book was really written by two different authors, the part by Adamski comprising approximately half the volume, after a long introduction by Desmond Leslie.

THE ASTOUNDING UFO SECRETS OF JAMES W. MOSELEY

Leslie's contribution consisted mainly of a history of flying saucers, from which he drew largely on the works of Charles Fort, the books Dom and Augie had acquainted me with. Going into old manuscripts, however, Leslie came up with what seemed to me very wild interpretations of some of the ancient Indian poetry, which, according to Leslie, was filled with flying saucers, the "magic carpets" of those ancient days.

"I think that the subject of flying saucers has great occult significance," Barker interjected during my comments on the book. "From my contacts in the field it seems that people who are interested in occult matters such as Yoga, ESP, ceremonial magic and the like are also tremendously interested in UFOs. With me, it's the other way around. I'm now trying to find out all I can about the occult."

Although Barker had been very helpful, had given me much material, and cleared up some of my questions about the field, I remember that I could not help being disappointed by his preoccupation with the Three Men In Black story, and by his interest in occult subjects which I felt had no part in an objective investigation.

This was my last stop driving back to New York, so as I maneuvered my Ford around the twisting West Virginia roads, I began to think back and review my trip.

Barker's account of the closing of the saucer organization and Bender's strange visitors in black, (the same story told by Dom and Augie) was most dramatic, and even entertaining. And Barker's sincerity was, like Adamski's, convincing.

But what facts had I really learned about the case? The information was mainly second hand, and Bender had not disclosed the identity of the men who discouraged him.

What facts had I really obtained in any of my investigations?

The story that Mortimer Bane had told me included, as proof, a piece of engraver's metal with deep scratches on it. True, the lab report looked authentic, but the mark need not have been made by a Venusian's fingernail, but by a hoaxer's machine tool.

Since the film which the air force had allegedly confiscated was still confiscated it could not be proven that the movie had ever been taken at all. I had only the producer's word for it.

The only proof existing in the strange Hunrath-Wilkinson case was the fact that they were still missing. They could have been whisked away to Mars, could have crashed in the mountains, or maybe they took a powder to Mexico.

THE ASTOUNDING UFO SECRETS OF JAMES W. MOSELEY

My strange interview with Dom and Augie, prior to my West Coast trip, had contained little more than wild claims about a possible earth tilt, saucers coming from inside the earth, and other assorted information of similar value.

The writing of a book, such as Krippine had suggested, however, which made fun of the crackpots of California, was repugnant to me. Whether they were crackpots, seers, or frauds, I found that I had liked most of these people I had interviewed and investigated.

Most of them, especially Adamski, expressed philosophies of peace and the brotherhood of man, ideals of some value, even if they had been received from space people from the mouth of the Big Dipper itself. The majority of the "contactees" were kind, friendly people.

The "saucer bug" had bitten me. Although my California visit had left me skeptical and disillusioned, I was slowly reaching the conclusion that there must indeed be something behind all of the reports, particularly some claims by airline pilots which Barker had shown me. If, out of a thousand crackpots, only one of them had actually seen a machine from outer space, here was a man who should be heard. In any case, my research had led me into many interesting situations and created dozens of valuable friendships.

I had just read a book by Major Donald E. Keyhoe who claimed that the United States Air Force knew what the flying saucers really were, but had classified the information and was withholding it from the American public. Was Keyhoe the true prophet of the space age, as many believed? Or was he, like the others, a prophet without substance? Though I frankly expected to learn nothing, I decided to take a short cut and seek my information direct from the horse's mouth—a winged horse, the USAF itself!

The Air Force would open its files to me, then snap them shut, right on my figurative fingers! I would run into more mysterious people with even more mysterious ploys.

Most everybody engaged in civilian saucer research would think that I was secretly on the payroll of the Air Force. This rumor has persisted so widely that at times I have been half-ready to believe it myself, but I'm still waiting for my first check!

2:35

THE AIR FORCE FILES

"Jim, I'd like to ask you a question. This has been on my mind for some time because this had been kicked around and kicked around. We've heard so many rumors about James Moseley.

"Is there any truth to the story that you are employed by the United States Government; that you are a member of the Air Force, or that you have been a member of the Air Force, and that it has been your job to kill the contactee stories in any way that you can, by appearing on radio programs, television programs, and printing brochures?"

Long John Nebel had suddenly turned the interrogation from Gray Barker to me. I was surprised at this. In the past John had helped me field such questions. I had assumed he thought I just might be a secret Air Force representative and was giving me a chance to cover it up.

I knew what Barker was ready to bring up at the drop of a hat from the Three Men In Black incident. While he didn't believe that I was employed by the government to kill the saucer mystery, he wasn't quite sure whether or not I had ever been in the Air Force. One of his investigators had written the AF and received a very confusing letter about a James Mosley (the name spelled slightly differently) who had indeed once served with that branch.

John might be serious in his questioning, or he might be giving me a chance to throw in a note of mystery. Anyhow I decided to play it safe and field the question by saying it wasn't relevant to the evening's discussion whether or not I had ever served in the Air Force. (By avoiding the question about employment by the government, I left this open to even more doubt. I was beginning to enjoy the many rumors going around.)

THE ASTOUNDING UFO SECRETS OF JAMES W. MOSELEY

Gordon H. Evans, a New York executive and expert on far eastern politics, had, on more than one occasion, insisted to my face that I was employed by the CIA, and I couldn't convince him otherwise! This is understandable; I have come to believe that Evans, himself, is a CIA member, and so the suspicions run in the flying saucer field.

But then there are the strange little things, like the letter Barker had just published, at the time of this broadcast. It was on official stationery and no doubt authentic.

Now, though I may never be able to convince some of my readers that I have never served in the Air Force, I, myself, know that I haven't.

Several months before the broadcast an anonymous correspondent had written Roger Pierce and Howard Neuberger, editors of the UFO magazine *Cosmic News*, including a strange and ridiculous detail about my hiding behind a counter in a department store! It also claimed that I had been in the Air Force.

I could detect that Barker, not too serious at the moment, was getting a kick out of belaboring the Air Force rumor, and that he was going to ask permission to read the latest letter. John assented and Barker read it.

DEPARTMENT OF THE AIR FORCE WASHINGTON

OFFICE OF THE SECRETARY 6 July 1959

Dear Mr. Ogden: Reference a letter from this office to you dated 23 June 1959. We have obtained more information concerning a James W. Moseley from the Air Reserve Records Center which follows:

The Air Reserve Records Center does not have a record of 1st Lt. James W. Moseley, New Jersey, but a check shows Captain James W. Moseley's name changed to Captain James W. Mosley, A0-2089932, last address Florida. Officer discharged effective 18 December 1957, per Reserve Order 173, dated 1 December 1957.

We do not know if this is the same person you were inquiring about.

If we can be of assistance, please let us know.

Sincerely,

(Signed) James M. Dyer

Lt. Colonel, USAF

Chief, Reserve Forces Liaison

Office of Information Services

THE ASTOUNDING UFO SECRETS OF JAMES W. MOSELEY

As Barker read the letter I thought about the average person's reaction to it. The coincidence was too great! And there was the business about the spelling of my last name, always a sensitive point to anyone whose name is constantly misspelled.

Was somebody consciously and deliberately trying to perpetuate this rumor? If so, the Air Force would have to be in on it. I would think of this again when, in 1959, the infamous Straith letter to George Adamski, allegedly written on official U.S. State Department stationery—but obviously spurious—was the main subject for discussion in UFO circles. Both Barker and myself were accused of having been behind the letter, much to our discomfort and embarrassment.

(For a complete report on this and other letters which were apparent hoaxes, but as yet unexplained, see **The Book of George Adamski**, *SaucerianBooks, 1966.)*

Although I have subsequently visited the Air Force Information Desk at the Pentagon a number of times, and have even, later, visited the sacrosanct confines of Project Bluebook at Wright Patterson Air Force Base, my first contact with the AF proved to be the most fruitful, so far as saucer data was concerned.

I often suspect that the chief gripe of spies, when they get together to talk shop, is not the quality of U.S. Government security in Washington. Their beef probably is that simply finding the locations of the departments or offices in the Pentagon is more difficult than the actual heisting or microfilming of military secrets!

In my own experience, obtaining secret saucer information from the Air Force was much, much easier than simply finding the Public Information Office. Maybe that is why the Public is not informed about the reality of flying saucers! I had gone to the Pentagon in the late fall of 1953 expecting to be rebuffed, for Major Donald E. Keyhoe (U.S.M.C. Ret.), in his book, *Flying Saucers From Outer Space*, had told how, in the beginning of his research, the AF had given him data on reported sightings but had later clammed up and classified all of the UFO information. In fact, when I was admitted to the office of Lieutenant (later Major) R. C. White, the information officer at that time, I was surprised to receive a very friendly reception.

"I'm writing a book about flying saucers," I explained (although I had given up on the book, I still found this excuse a wonderful door opener). I know your files are secret, but. . ."

"Now who told you that, old buddy?" the lieutenant interrupted with a big smile, rising and walking to some filing cases. He pulled out several bulging file folders and bound material and handed it over.

"How's this for a starter?" and he gave me a slap on the shoulder. As I slowly opened the folder and peered inside, out of the comer of my eye I could see him pause to light his pipe while he observed my reaction with a quizzical look on his face.

I was so nonplussed that my grip on the bulky folder slipped, and its contents spilled, with a dozen or so Air Force flying saucer sightings falling all over my lap and onto the floor.

"Aren't these classified?" I blurted.

"I was sort of pulling your leg. I'll explain the situation," White replied. "You came in at the right time. You're in for a bit of luck. We've decided to make all of these Status Reports available to interested members of the press and public. In fact it was just last week that this policy was decided upon. We didn't make any federal case out of it with the press, so few people know about it. In fact you're the first person from the saucer press to drop in since this policy went into effect."

I asked him about Major Keyhoe's assertion that the files had earlier been open to him. White explained that although the major had access to most of the information, he had never seen the actual files, the reports either having been transcribed for him, or read to him orally.

"Some people make too big a thing out of their claims about Air Force secrecy. True, these reports haven't been available in the past. Frankly this saved us a lot of trouble with kids and crackpots running in here asking us to see little green men they said we had captured."

Both of us had a laugh. "Can I use this information?" I asked, still incredulous.

"If you wish you can borrow one of these broken down G.I. typewriters and copy anything you please. Spend as much time as you want. We can't let the reports leave the Pentagon, but they're public information now and you're welcome to copy and use as much as you want."

There was but one restriction:

"I must ask you that in the interest of privacy of witnesses involved that you not use their names, unless, of course, the case and the names are previously known to you. You'll be sort of on your honor there, I suppose."

To have copied everything made available to me would have taken several days. I settled for transcribing only the most dramatic material, and this now occupies more than twenty single-spaced typewritten pages in a private notebook of mine. This is a story I have never revealed during more than ten years of saucer research.

As I copied the reports on the old Underwood, I thought how different they were from the wild stories, supported mainly by rumor, which I had collected in California. In fact a quick look at these Air Force files began to revive my respect for the possible reality of the UFOs.

Here, for example, was a report of a saucer which left contrails! It was observed by military pilots. This and the other reports presented here are printed, with a few minor deletions as we will explain later, exactly as given me by Lieutenant White:

Luke AFB, Arizona-March 3, 1953. In this instance, the object was never observed, but a high altitude condensation pattern was observed. When first sighted, the contrail was approximately 300 to 500 feet in diameter. The pattern began with a smooth knife-like leading edge, very thin in depth and with an irregular trailing edge. As the source gave chase, the contrail made a slight dip to the NW and began climbing at 20 degrees. During this maneuver, source and object were at right angles, and he observed the pattern to appear as a sharp-nosed, very thin object about 300 to 500 feet long with an irregular, wispy trailing edge. Immediately, a heavy condensation trail began to form and extended for approximately 1000 feet back, at which point it separated into a double trail which again was approximately 1000 feet long, ending abruptly. At this time, the object was traveling at an estimated 400 mph true air speed. The most unusual feature was that the contrail stayed with the unsighted object, and did not extend across the sky as in the case of conventional aircraft contrails. . .

The contrail was observed by the pilots of three F-84 aircraft, with only one giving chase. This pilot chased the contrail for fifty to sixty miles before breaking off. . .

During the chase, this pilot took approximately thirty feet of gun-camera film. This film was received in very good condition, and had been analyzed, by the photographic laboratory at Wright Patterson Air Force Base. Their conclusions are:

(a) The white streak photographed is probably a vapor trail from a rapidly moving object of unknown velocity. The object itself is invisible in the photographs.

(b) The exhaust vapor trail, apparently from a twin propulsion unit, is more pronounced at the end of the film. The configurations in the trail appear to be due to maneuvers performed by the object.

(c) An additional vapor trail, thought to be due to lifting surfaces, is also in evidence, but it dissipates rapidly. This additional vapor trail appears to be centered about the exhaust trail.

(d) Within the period of the time represented by the film, the photographic plane may have reduced the distance between the object and itself. However, the flight paths are not parallel by a considerable angle, so that the object's distance and velocity with respect to the plane cannot be determined with useful precision. Since there was nothing gained by the photo-analysis, that would actually aid in identifying the object involved, this report is being sent to the Aircraft Laboratory of WADC for further analysis. Until the report is returned from WADC, this incident will be carried by Project Blue Book as unknown.

Conclusion: Unknown

Another report which deeply impressed me involved sightings by visual and radar means:

Continental Divide, New Mexico-January 26, 1953. On January 26, 1953 at 2115 MST Air Force personnel stationed at an AC&W station in this area observed an aerial phenomenon simultaneously by electronic and visual means. To the naked eye the object appeared to be a very bright reddish-white object estimated to be ten miles west of the radar site. The object passed behind a hill and then reappeared apparently heading in a northerly direction at a slow speed. The airmen making this visual observation reported it to personnel manning the radar equipment. They stated that they had an unidentified blip on the radar scope, appearing west of the station approximately nine miles away. The scope showed the object to be on a 270 degree azimuth at an altitude of 10,000 to 15,000 feet, moving away from the site at 12 to 15 mph. It was eventually lost on radar at the eighteen-mile range. The object was under visual and radar observation intermittently for forty-five minutes. The elevation of the station is 7,500 feet above sea level. Weather at the time was characterized by a high thin overcast and low scattered clouds. Winds aloft were from 270 degrees at 30 knots at 10,000 to 30,000 feet. An atmospheric inversion layer existed at 18,000 feet with the top at 21,000 feet.

[This is the most complete report ever received by ATIC (Air Technical Intelligence Command) on the sighting of an unidentified object. . . . . . The combination visual-electronic sighting is the best type to work with because it affords the most information.]

Conclusion: Unknown

Or consider this dramatic close-up sighting, reported by civilians:

Craig, Montana-at 4 A.M-, January 3, 1953. Three sources observed an aerial object 25 to 40 feet long and 18 to 25 feet thick with the appearance of two soup bowls put together. There were several lighted windows with what appeared to be a porthole on the side. The object moved slowly at first, then began to climb rapidly. The manner of disappearance was unspecified. The object first appeared at 200 to 300 yards from the observers at an altitude of 10 to 15 feet. An investigation of the sources revealed that they are mature, reliable, and in at least one case, a relatively experienced person.

Conclusions: Unknown

Sightings by Airline Pilots came in for many good reports, as the following:

Minneapolis, Minnesota-The only information available on this incident is this letter. "Time: 6:30 A.M., October 11, 1951. Dick and I were flying at 10,000 feet when I saw a brightly glowing object to the southeast of the University of Minnesota Airport. At that time we were a few miles north of Minneapolis and heading east. I pointed it out to Dick, and we both made the following observations. The object was moving from east to west at a high rate of speed and a very high altitude. We tried keeping our ship on a constant course and using the reinforcing member of the windshield as a point. The object moved past this member at about 50 degrees per second. This object was peculiar in that it had what can be described as a halo around it with a dark under surface. It crossed rapidly and then slowed down and started to climb slowly in lazy circles. The pattern it made was like a falling oak leaf, inverted. It went through these gyrations for a couple of minutes and then with a very rapid acceleration disappeared in the east. Dick and I watched this object for approximately five minutes. I can't describe its size. Shortly after this we saw another one, but this one didn't hang around. It approached from the west and disappeared to the east. Neither object left any trace of vapor trail."

Status of Investigation: Observers were positive of the following facts: (A) The object, though vaguely defined and blurred, retained a definite shape. (B) No vapor trails, exhaust flashes, or jet propulsion were observed. (C) The object definitely seemed to be controlled. The sources are experienced engineers with General Mills balloon projects and have been observing all types of balloons for several years.

Conclusions: No conclusions can be made. It is significant, however, that the sources can be graded as very reliable and that they observed an object with which they were entirely unfamiliar.

Another combination visual-radar sighting, involved an aircraft scramble to intercept a saucer, was typical of the many similar exciting accounts:

Heneda Air Force Base, Japan. The object was first noticed by two airmen walking across the ramp at Heneda on the night of August 5, 1952 at 11:01 local time. The airmen were on their way to the tower to relieve the operators. On reporting to the tower, the object was called to the attention of the tower operators who were going off duty. The four operators agreed that the object, which they observed from 50 minutes to an hour through 7 x 50 binoculars, was circular in shape with a distinct brilliance. The light appeared to be a portion of a large, round dark shape which was about four times the diameter of the light. When the object was close enough for details to be seen, a smaller, less brilliant light could be seen along the lower edge of the dark shape. The object faded to the east twice but reappeared; it could have faded or actually gone away and come back. The size of the light, when closest to the tower, was approximately the same as the ceiling balloons that are released near the tower. A comparison was made of these 24 foot diameter balloons at 2000 feet. This would make the object fifty feet in diameter at 10 miles. During the observation, a lighted balloon was released but this light was extremely dim and yellow compared to the object. An airborne C54 was requested to check the object, which the pilot did, but he reported seeing only a star. The AC&W unit was notified soon after the original visual sighting and shortly after 11:51 picked up an unidentified return (on radar). The object was tracked at varying speeds from hovering to 300 knots. At 1:12 A.M. the return "broke into three pieces" and they maintained intervals of 1/4 mile. No visual observation was made from the AC&W unit although it was attempted and, at one time, the object was within 10 miles of the station. The radar was directed onto the target by visual observations from the tower, so it can safely be assumed that both visual and radar contacts involved the same object. At three minutes after midnight a fighter was airborne on a scramble and was requested to search the area northeast of Haneda Air Force Base. They could make no visual observations, but could see the north star and Venus. The fighter was vectored to the object by GCI (both the fighter and the object were in the scope), and held for 90 seconds. Shortly after this, both the object and the fighter disappeared into the ground clutter on the radar scope. At no time did the fighter make visual contact. Soon after the loss of the radar contact, the object was lost visually.

Conclusion: Unknown

That the Air Force is without a sense of humor is disproved by the following, which I toss in as an example of an AF conclusion that few can disagree with:

Friona, Texas-November, 1952. Source supposedly picked up pieces of an exploded "flying saucer" and sold half the pieces to the Soviet Embassy. He had previously notified the Pentagon, but hadn't heard from the Pentagon so he sold out to the Soviets.

Discussion of Incident: It is believed that this is a "crackpot" report. The original report was made to the F.B.I. and forwarded to the Air Technical Intelligence Command.

Conclusion: Hoax

The previous cases were taken from a file known as *Project Blue Book Status Report No. 7*. The information on the cover of *Report No. 9, which* I also saw, and which contained similar cases, read:

Confidential Security Information. Status Report. Project Blue Book-Report No. 9-Air Technical Intelligence Center, Wright-patterson Air Force Base, Ohio-Confidential.

Most people who are seriously interested in the UFO phenomena have actually read only one of these reports, known as **Project Blue Book Report No. 14.** This was made available to the public, and through the efforts of a private individual, an offset reprint, with some additional notes by the publisher, was produced and sold. Report No. 14 contains the famous *"Twelve Best Sightings"*, or, in other words, twelve saucer reports which were the most real, factual, and the most puzzling to the Air Force. *(The Twelve Best Sightings Appear in a succeeding chapter.)*

But the liberality with information did not last long at the Pentagon, mainly because of infighting by one of the best known saucer researchers in the nation.

After copying what I considered the most convincing sightings, I started going over my material and in the course of my research reread sections of Adamski's **Flying Saucers Have Landed**. Noting that the author had claimed to have had certain conversations with Al Chop, a former civilian member of the Air Force Press Desk at the Pentagon, then residing in Los Angeles, I decided to call him up and check Adamski's claims.

Since he had written a controversial letter to Major Keyhoe which he allowed him to use on the jacket of **Flying Saucers From Outer Space**, I also wanted to tell him the good news about the declassification of the Air Force reports.

As to Adamski, Chop claimed to have been grossly misquoted in the book. When I told him about seeing the Status Reports, however, I heard a little gasp, and for a few seconds there was complete silence at the other end.

"You mean they let you copy these?" he asked, somewhat incredulously; then he questioned me at length. Somehow he didn't seem too happy about the entire affair.

"You should be informed that you have seen classified information, and I would caution you not to use it," he told me.

Later, I learned, he wrote to the Air Force Press Desk and also to Major Keyhoe. I don't know what he told them, but Keyhoe immediately phoned the Pentagon, complaining that I had been allowed to see information which had been withheld from him.

On December 28, 1953, I received the following letter which is still in my files.

THE ASTOUNDING UFO SECRETS OF JAMES W. MOSELEY

The letterhead is the Department of Defense, Office of Public Information, Washington, 25, D.C.:

Dear Mr. Mosely:

We are in receipt of information indicating that you are in possession of classified information concerning radar sites and operating capabilities, and that you are citing this office as your source.

As we pointed out to you, while information concerning actual sightings is not classified, information concerning radar, electronics equipment, and aircraft operating capabilities is classified.

If any of this type of information has been available to you inadvertently or otherwise through this office, I respectfully request that you get in touch with me at the earliest possible moment so that we can determine if any security is involved.

Sincerely,

MONCEL A. MONTS

Lt. Col. USAF Chief, Air Force Press Desk

At the end of the Christmas and New Year holidays, I drove to Washington to find out what the letter was all about.

Lieutenant White, obviously embarrassed, but without any good reasons to give me as to why, informed me that the Status Reports had been "temporarily removed," supposedly just to have the SECRET and CONFIDENTIAL labels crossed off, since he still insisted that the sighting reports themselves were not classified.

I felt sorry for White, who had been so kind and cooperative. I felt that he might have inadvertently goofed in giving me the files to copy, so at his suggestion I wrote the following letter, dated January 22, 1954, which was filed at the Air Force Public Information Office:

TO WHOM IT MAY CONCERN:

There has apparently been some speculation as to the nature of certain material I received from the Air Force Press Desk in November 1953, concerning "flying saucers." The Status Reports made available to me had previously been shown to other interested persons, such as newsmen, etc. These Reports were at that time available to anyone sufficiently interested in "saucers," and they definitely were not classified. The only information I received from these Reports that could possibly be construed as classified was as follows: In a few cases the type of radar set was named, and in one or two cases the operating capabilities of radar was referred to. The value of these cases to my forthcoming book is in no way diminished by the omission of this radar information, and I will voluntarily withhold this information when I write up the cases for my book.

I have been very pleased with the help and cooperation given me by the Air Force Press Desk throughout my enquiry into the "flying saucer" phenomenon. However, I want to emphasize again that to the best of my knowledge I have not been granted any special favors, and specifically, I have been shown no documents not available to anyone ambitious enough to walk into the Public Information Office and ask for them.

James W. Moseley

Since the book I referred to was never written in its original form, that was one reason these files have not been printed until this time. As for Lieutenant White, many ardent anti-Air Force saucer fans might criticize me for going to such lengths to get him off the hook. All I can say is that I did not want to see a man penalized for having cooperated with me, and in the back of my mind was the thought that Major Keyhoe was a much more powerful man than I had realized and that he may have been responsible for the clampdown on public information from the Air Force.

In fact, this incident marked the beginning of the less-than-friendly nature of the relations between myself and Keyhoe, and later between myself and his organization, NICAP. (The National Investigations Committee on Aerial Phenomena, Washington, D.C.)

As for the classified information, it is now more than ten years old, and after elimination of information regarding capability of radar and speeds of aircraft, could be of no value to an enemy. I therefore have published these accounts without fear that I have violated security in any way.

3:10

THE PUZZLED PROFESSORS

I had made one exception to keeping the information from the Air Force files under wraps. In the November, 1954, issue of *Saucer News*, I would carry the brief announcement that I was unable to publish the "irrefutable documented evidence" I had promised in a previous issue.

That, of course, is another story, which I will attend to in a succeeding chapter.

As I was editing the issue in which I made the Announcement, I decided I should at least give my readers something which had been in my possession for some time, but never released: the official ATIC Project Bluebook Status Report on the Lubbock lights.

This report, along with the others reproduced in the preceding chapter, had been given to me to copy at the Pentagon.

Of the many cases I had in the Status Reports, this was among those which had impressed me the most. It concerned one of the best publicized sightings in the history of flying saucers. The story and associated photographs had appeared in *Life Magazine*, the bestselling Adamski book, *Flying Saucers Have Landed*, and many other media.

Here, with only minor editing for the sake of clarity, is the text of the Air Force report:

Lubbock, Texas, August 30, 1951: The first of a series of sightings related to this incident occurred on the evening of August 25, 1951, at approximately 9:10 P.M., Central Standard Time. Four Texas Technical College professors were sitting in the back yard of one of the professor's homes, observing meteors in conjunction with a study of micrometeorites being carried out by the college.

THE ASTOUNDING UFO SECRETS OF JAMES W. MOSELEY

At 9:20 P.M. they observed a group of lights pass directly overhead from north to south. The lights had about the same intensity as high cirrus clouds on a moonlight night. The altitude of the lights was not determined, but they traveled at a high rate of speed. The pattern of the lights was almost a perfect semicircle containing from 20 to 30 individual lights. Later in the evening a similar incident was observed, and during a period of about three weeks a total of approximately 12 such flights were observed by these men.

The observers included: Professor W. L. Ducker, PhD, Head of the Petroleum Engineering Department; Dr. W. I. Robinson, PhD, Professor of Geology: and Dr. A. G. Oberg, PhD, a Professor of Chemical Engineering. An unnamed Professor of Mathematics and a graduate student of Texas College were among the other witnesses on the campus, and in addition, over one hundred residents of the town observed the lights at one time or another.

These professors took a personal interest in the phenomena and undertook a study of the object. Attempts were made to obtain an altitude measurement by laying out a measured base line perpendicular to the usual flight path of the object, and placing angle measuring devices at the end of the base line. All these attempts failed because the lights did not appear on the nights the professors were waiting for them with this equipment.

However, from the series of visual observations, they obtained the following facts: (a) The angular velocity of the object was very nearly *30 degrees of arc per second* (italics mine), i.e., from horizon to horizon in about six seconds. (b) The flight path of the object was from north to south in the majority of flights although some were from northeast to southwest. (c) There was no sound that could be attributed to the object. (d) The color of the lights was blue-green. (f) There were 15 to 30 separate lights in each formation. (g) The first two flights observed were a semicircle of lights but in subsequent flights there was no orderly arrangement. (h) The object always appeared at an angle of about 45 degrees from the horizon in the north, and disappeared at about 45 degrees in the south, i.e., the object did not come gradually into view as would an aircraft approaching from a distance, nor did it disappear gradually. (i) There was no apparent change of size as the object passed overhead.

Attempts were made by the professors to obtain the relative height of the object in respect to the clouds, but were unsuccessful because the object passed between widely scattered clouds. Attempts were made to determine whether or not there was any form between the lights by trying to see stars between the lights. These attempts were also unsuccessful due to the short time the object was in view.

(Note: A clue to the solid nature of this phenomenon may have been revealed by

112

THE ASTOUNDING UFO SECRETS OF JAMES W. MOSELEY

the Air Force chronicler's unconscious use of the word "object" rather than "objects" in describing this series of lights. Also, this same Status Report describes a sighting which occurred a few miles from Lubbock, on August 25, 1951, in which a low-flying unidentified flying wing type aircraft was sighted in daylight by two people. The shape and lighting of this flying wing was sufficiently similar to the Lubbock affair to cause the Air Force writer to state that a tie-in between the two incidents is considered likely.-JWM)

On the evening of August 31, 1951, at about 11:30 Central Standard Time, a Texas College freshman named Carl Hart Jr. observed a flight of the unidentified objects fly over his home in Lubbock. The flight was observed through an open window. Upon observing the first flight of these lights, Hart obtained his camera and went into the back yard of his home in an attempt to get photographs of additional flights. Two more flights allegedly did occur and were photographed by him; two photos of one flight and three of another were obtained. The Air Technical Intelligence Center has four of the negatives but the other one was lost or misplaced by the photographer. (Note: Since this report was written, the Air Force has returned the negatives to Hart). The photographs show a V-shaped formation of lights. In one photo a single V of lights appear, while on three other photos there is a double-V. The separate lights, which appear to be pinpoint light sources, vary in intensity.

One or more members of the O.S.I. made a trip to Lubbock to investigate the incident firsthand, and the photographer was interrogated at length. His account of the incident seemed logical, and there was no obvious indication of a hoax. The photographer had previously been interrogated by the Lubbock newspapers and the photos inspected by the Associated Press and by representatives of *Life Magazine*. It was their opinion that the photos were not obviously a hoax. However, the college professors were doubtful as to whether or not the photographs were of the same objects they had observed, because: (1) They had never observed a V-shaped formation of lights. This is not too significant, however, because the arrangement of the lights that they had observed varied, and since there were several flights, the college professors possibly did not see the flights that were photographed. (2) The lights that the professors observed were, in their opinion, not bright enough to be photographed. This is, however, an estimate, and could be an error.

The Air Technical Intelligence Center at Dayton, Ohio analyzed the photos, and their conclusions were: (1) The images on the negatives were caused by light striking unexposed film, i.e., the negatives were not retouched. (2) The individual lights in the formation varied in intensity. (3) The intensity was greater than any surrounding stars, as the stars did not register. (4) The individual lights changed position in the formation.

The O.S.I. was requested to reinterrogate the photographer in another attempt to determine the authenticity of the photographs. A preliminary report concerning this reinterrogation stated that there was no indication that the photographs were not authentic.

As I retyped the report for my magazine, there seemed to be little doubt that the Lubbock light photos represented the same phenomena that the Texas College professors saw.

But as I carefully proofread the article, twice in fact, as I cogitated, a great deal of doubt began to creep into my mind, and I began to notice a very odd attitude in the Report:

We usually think of the Air Force as subtly or directly trying to discredit genuine sightings and photos, but in this instance we had a most peculiar situation in which the AF was for some strange reason apparently trying to uphold the authenticity of pictures which they knew or strongly suspected to be clever fakes.

An unofficial AF admission to this effect, plus my own findings during an on the spot investigation, substantiated my belief that the sighting was genuine but that Hart's photographs were not.

Some of the objections have come directly from one of the professors who had witnessed the sightings.

"You can identify me as one of the professors mentioned in the Bluebook report, but please not specifically by name," he told me at his office.

"The things we saw were never in view more than six seconds. For the photographer to have taken the pictures under the conditions we observed would have been impossible."

I had to agree with the professor. In a personal interview with me, Hart had told me that the camera exposure he used was very slow-only 1/10 of a second-and other people I saw who had talked to Hart said he had given them the same shutter speed. Yet, even with my inexperience in the field of photography I knew that any fast moving object would produce a blur at that setting.

Yet in only one of the four pictures is there any evidence of blurring and only slightly in that one.

"Suppose that Hart panned the camera," I asked the professor, "moving with the object, to avoid blurring; would that have resulted in a sharp picture?"

"I doubt that 100 per cent," he replied. "I believe I can safely say that no amount of panning could have given him clear photographs of the phenomena we witnessed.

"Further, O.S.I. officers, who investigated our sightings and Hart's photos, told me that his pictures were of lights whose total brilliance would be of several times that of the full moon. Yet the lights we saw were of no such brilliance; in fact these lights were not even bright enough to be photographed at all."

After interviewing two of the other professors, who gave me essentially the same story printed above in the Status report, I talked to many other people in the town, and was further convinced that the photographs were fakes.

In another incident, not involving photographs and a much more serious matter, I was told that Hart stuck to a false, preconceived story in spite of definite evidence against him. Furthermore, another informant told me that Hart, an ardent amateur photographer, once told him that he would do "anything" to get a picture of his own in a newspaper.

To me it seemed quite evident that the famous Lubbock lights photographs were nothing more than clever fakes that had "taken in" dozens of editors and authors. Taking advantage of the genuine phenomena being seen almost nightly over his home town, Hart apparently found the opportunity he was looking for to achieve a small degree of fame.

But of the phenomena itself, the lights positively could not have been the results of reflections or temperature inversions, nor any of the other popular explanations then in vogue. According to the opinion of the Lubbock professors, they were either a totally unknown unnatural phenomenon, or else one or more solid craft of some sort.

3:15

THE WRIGHT FIELD STORY...OR "WHO'S LYING?"

Now, technically, by the Ground Rules, Yonah was supposed to be on my side on the Long John Show, and to help me castigate Barker, by means of the article by Lonzo Dove in *Saucer News*. But you can't knock Yonah's sense of humor, and I could tell from his quizzical expression that the note he was passing to Long John contained some awful retribution directed to me.

"Let me ask you this. . . ."

John was reading the note. "In the apartment house where you live," John continued—and I knew what was coming.

John was going to give me a hard time on this, and his face betrayed not one trace of the smile I knew was building deep within him. That, I suppose, is the reason why Long John is the best radio man I know. When you are on the Long John show, he subtly leads the guest—or panelist—into a magic world of belief; in which every word of the Master (L. J.) is imbued with an authority or seriousness.

"How is your name spelled on the building directory?" John continued—and I could see Yonah trying to repress hysterics.

Of course, as Yonah and Long John were forcing me to admit, the name on my apartment house directory was spelled incorrectly, without the "e" in Moseley!

"M-O-S-L-E-Y," John spelled out the name.

Of course, this was supposed to have something to do with the letter Barker had read, which involved the changing of name of "Moseley" to Mosley." I should have appreciated the gag, but somehow when you are on radio, you don't want somebody to be one-up on you, especially Barker that night, since he was supposed to be the person I was "exposing."

THE ASTOUNDING UFO SECRETS OF JAMES W. MOSELEY

"If you aren't in the Air Force," Yonah, still the turncoat, insisted to me, "isn't it strange you can't get a letter from them saying that?"

I launched into the usual complaints of the Average American who writes to the Government and of the *Strange Replies* he usually receives.

While I was talking I was thinking seriously about the Air Force. About the files I had seen which had been suddenly withdrawn. About the crackpots who claimed the Air Force had little men from flying saucers pickled in formaldehyde. Then there were, of course, the tales of crashed saucers, and reported scientific examination of them.

When I reviewed such stories of disabled saucers, I always think of my involvement with the Air Force which led me to the most fantastic report I have ever investigated.

And somebody was lying—either the AF or "Miss Y."

The scene had been perfectly set for a weird bit of business. An odd weather condition had added a note of unreality and spectral quality to the Ohio city. It was sunset, and the sky had taken on a frightening red color. Somehow it seemed appropriate, for I had gone to this city to visit an Air Force base where a flying saucer had reportedly crashed. I was locating the base so that I could find it easily the next day.

I planned to find a nearby motel and look for "Miss Y" tomorrow. If my lead had been reliable, she would have a fantastic story to tell.

In looking through the Air Force files I hadn't expected to find, nor found, any reports of captured saucers or little men. Despite official AF denials, however, such rumors still persisted.

The late Frank Scully, well known and highly respected Hollywood writer, had caused a sensation with his book, **Behind the Flying Saucers**, in which he related how a government scientist had been called in to examine a saucer which had allegedly crashed in New Mexico. Few people now believe Scully's story, which he had obtained from two acquaintances, Silas Newton and Leo Gebauer, for a **True** magazine article had pretty well exposed it as a hoax. It probably wasn't Scully's fault. The article, and other reports suggested that the author had simply been taken in.

But at that time the basic rumor, with many variations, vividly haunted the saucer scene. Every month or so a new crashed saucer report, complete with little men, would appear. Most of these reports came from the southwestern U.S., but there was one from Scandinavia and another from Europe.

THE ASTOUNDING UFO SECRETS OF JAMES W. MOSELEY

I had little faith in the accounts until I bumped into a bizarre investigation of a saucer said to be in the possession of the AF at Wright-Patterson Air Force Base!

Since my perusal of the AF files late in 1953 I had begun corresponding with people all over the U.S. and was becoming fairly well known as a civilian UFO researcher. In April, 1954, one of these correspondents floored me with a letter, from which I quote: My opinion is that the Air Force is holding a saucer or parts thereof at Wright-Patterson Field. I base this opinion on a great number of collective items-and one solid item, the testimony of a woman who was a WAC at Wright in the fall of 1952 when there was a Red and White aircraft attack alert for two weeks. She learned that a saucer had been brought to Wright Field, and she saw a picture of it!

According to the correspondent, the Air Force had found an operative radio transmitting device inside the machine which regularly gave off "beeps." They were afraid the saucer had signalled for help and might attract other craft and a possible attack. The correspondent believed the saucer had crashed near Columbus, Ohio, but wasn't certain. He also said that bodies of six little men had been found and hauled to the base, along with the machine.

I put down the letter and pulled out my special file on crash rumors. I had dozens of them: A professor of anthropology at Columbia had supposedly been called out to Wright-Patterson to examine these creatures; a scientist in Massachusetts had made X-rays of the bodies; a man in Los Angeles knew of a saucer that landed in Mexico; a man in Florida had talked to a man who knew of, in turn, a man who had driven a truck for the Army, in which a captured saucer had been carried from the place it had "crashed" to a nearby military base; a doctor in New York had examined bodies of little men in a funeral parlor there . . .

And so it went. The reports had a great deal in common besides crashed saucers: the people involved were not named, so most of them were uncheckable.

The ones I had been able to check turned out to be hoaxes, or else they had no discoverable factual evidence to back them up. I finally decided that all of the accounts had been appropriated right out of the pages of Scully's book.

So I stuck the letter into the "crash file" to lie with the many unsubstantiated yarns. I would have forgotten it had I not found myself routed through the correspondent's home town about a month later. I decided to stay overnight, got myself a hotel room and rang him up. The man, whom I will call Bill, greeted me enthusiastically on the phone and invited me to his house. From his conversation I gathered he might be the first informant who could provide any real, concrete lead on a captured saucer, for he claimed to have a tape recording of a key informant. For the first time I became really enthusiastic about such a matter. I wished

THE ASTOUNDING UFO SECRETS OF JAMES W. MOSELEY

I had not waited so long to follow it up.

When I arrived at Bill's house he already had his recorder set up, and after a preliminary cup of coffee, I began to hear a tape made by a woman who sounded very much as if she really knew what she was talking about!

Immediately impressed by her apparent sincerity, I quickly decided that here at last was something concrete; a first-hand account of what a woman working for the government had seen and heard in the course of her duties. Although uncertain about many details (just as many people would be in relating an event which had transpired months before), she in general told her story in such a manner that I could not help feeling that she was probably telling the truth.

There was only one fly in the Ufological ointment. Although the woman's first name (I will refer to her as Miss Y) was on the tape, Bill would not give me her full name, nor tell me how to get in touch with her.

"The fellow who made the recording promised her she would receive absolutely no personal publicity, and made me pledge likewise when he entrusted the tape to my safe keeping. When I wrote you I had no idea that you would take the trouble to come out here and follow it up."

"But Bill," I pressed, "you may be sitting on the hottest news story of all time. Don't you think the public should know about this if it's true?"

"I agree with you, Jim, but a pledge is a pledge. Miss Y is already sorry she made the tape for she fears repercussions should her story leak out."

Miss Y's apparent sincerity on the tape made me determined to smoke her out and talk to her personally for I was convinced that this was one "crash" report really worth following up.

How I finally located Miss Y, three months later, is certainly worth telling, for it is almost like a detective story. But to tell the story I would have to give out many details which most likely would violate the secrecy of the identities of not only her, but others involved: and this I will not do, even at the expense of reader disbelief that these people do really exist. I know this is not good reporting, but if the reader will go along with me in this respect, I will relate what is to me the most fascinating part of this book.

Miss Y turned out to be a rather fragile-looking woman, probably in her late thirties, bespectacled, with her hair neatly done up in a bun. Her entire demeanor was that of meekness, and I think she finally decided to talk with me because she felt sorry for me after my expressions of disappointment.

Now I know that some fragile little old ladies, and middle-aged ones as well, embezzle banks and other employers by the dozens, but I must say that Miss Y seemed to me to be almost the last person in the world who would make up a real whopper—and if Miss Y were lying, she had manufactured a colossal one!

First she straightened me out on some points which Bill had either assumed or got confused. She did not work at Wright-Patterson, but at another large military base in that area which I will not name; she was not a WAC, but rather a civilian employee of the Signal Corps, working under the Army and the FBI (she has since retired and moved away). Her duties, those of a night girl on teletype, included decoding messages and handling classified material of many different sorts. If this were true, I thought, this alone would vouch for her trustworthiness, for such work would require a security clearance granted only after a very thorough check of her background.

* * * * *

"In August—or was it September—of 1952, I walked into the photographic lab to get an aspirin from —, who was in charge of this section (The Army photographer in charge of the lab will be referred to as Mr. Z.). This lab was in the same section of the communication building on the base which I worked in. When I walked in he was developing a number of prints, and I couldn't help noticing that about a dozen of them looked like the newspaper drawings I had seen of flying saucers.

"At first he expressed some concern that I had seen the photos; he thought he had the door locked but had gone to the rest room and forgotten to relock it. Knowing that I had a clearance and being a good friend of mine, he apparently decided to relieve my curiosity."

"Mr. Z had personally taken the photos during a recent special assignment at a location Miss Y described simply as "north of the Base." There, according to the technician, a flying saucer had crashed. That in essence was all the information he would give her, as he warned her that the pictures were classified and carried top security designation.

"At the time," Miss Y told me, "I thought this was more or less a routine photographic record of experimental military aircraft which frequently were tested at the base, and thought little more of it until I handled some startling messages.

"The first communications involved information that the aircraft, which was thought to be of interplanetary nature, was being brought first to our Base, under very heavy guard, where it would receive a preliminary examination and then be trucked to Wright Field.

Further messages ordered a Red and White Alert for the base, since it was

120

feared that the crashed saucer had communicated with other similar craft still flying. This made me very nervous, for it sounded to me as if the base commander believed that other machines might attack in an effort to recover the disabled craft."

Security had been clamped down very tightly. Officers and one scientist were brought in from other bases to complement the staff, and no enlisted men except Mr. Z had anything to do with the matter. No less than a major, Miss Y told me, drove the truck that hauled the craft to the base. Enlisted men were told that the alert was for practice only and that the officers had been flown in to observe how well it was carried out.

"How large do you think the saucer was, from seeing the photographs?" I asked.

"I'm not good at this, but I would say thirty feet in diameter. In a couple or three of the pictures there was a jeep parked by it and this gave a good frame of reference. It would be forty feet at the most, I would say.

"It had no protrusions, other than a rim where the upper and lower halves of the machine met.

"It appeared to be made of pieces of metal riveted together, though I couldn't see any rivets, only the different sections. It didn't have any windows that I could see. Some of the messages, however, mentioned that it had windows or portholes of one-way glass which you couldn't see through from the outside."

Miss Y also said she had heard from Mr. Z that scientists employed by the government had trouble getting inside the saucer, and that it was composed of one or more alloys not found on Earth.

And here her description departed from the classic tale: this saucer contained no dead little men. It was a remotely controlled device, evidently equipped with devices to collect and transmit information. Also, the saucer hadn't really crashed, having floated gently to the ground due to a "lack of magnetic power on which they run."

Miss Y had heard vague information about other saucers which had previously been captured, these actually containing bodies of humanoid creatures. I discounted this part of her story, however, feeling that she had perhaps overheard conversations about the Scully book (she had never read it). I was still greatly convinced with her sincerity, but I felt I still didn't have quite enough to warrant the conclusion that the Government did actually have a captured saucer and possibly little men.

So I begged Miss Y for the name of Mr. Z, the photographer, which she finally gave me after much hesitation.

THE ASTOUNDING UFO SECRETS OF JAMES W. MOSELEY

"He won't talk, though. I can tell you that right now. He's still on active duty with the Army. He's getting almost ready for retirement and fears anything that might get him discharged'"

Whether for the reason that Miss Y gave, or whether she had for some almost unbelievable reason, concocted the story and was indeed lying, she was certainly correct about one thing:

Although Mr. Z did talk, it wasn't in confirmation of her account. He began with a summary denial of having any knowledge of flying saucers, what's more photographing one. During the two-hour conversation, the latter part of which was in the presence of his superior, a Signal Corps officer, he completely refuted her claims.

Miss Y did work as a night girl on teletype during the period she claimed to have been there, but she had never read any highly secret messages. She most likely had handled coded messages, but she had no way of decoding them. If any highly classified messages had indeed come through she would not have known what they contained.

"Sure we know about flying saucers," Mr. Z told me, "but only what we read in the papers. If you run around and investigate these sightings, you know a lot more than we do."

Certainly no saucer had ever passed through their base, and they certainly had no knowledge of saucers captured anywhere by the government, or so they said.

They described Miss Y as a very efficient worker and "an upstanding woman." They couldn't guess why she would be telling such a story.

Walking out of the officer's club, where I interviewed the two, the seemingly almost organized confusion of the saucer mystery began to trouble me. If the two men were telling the truth, Miss Y was lying. One thing was obvious: Somebody was lying!

As I drove by the rows of barracks to the base exit, I tried to analyze the situation.

First I assumed that Miss Y was telling the truth. She had said that the facts she gave me were "public knowledge" and that she was not breaking security to tell them to me, though on that point I tended to disagree. It was quite understandable that she didn't want her name connected, even though it may have been public knowledge. She also had said that the government was holding back the facts from the public because of fear of panic, and also because they didn't have all the answers yet themselves; these observations probably were only her own personal opinion.

If indeed Miss Y had been telling the truth, it certainly would fit in with Mr. Z's statements. He would be required to say she was lying and deny having made the photographs or having knowledge of them.

If the government did indeed have captured saucers, it probably would be known to only a few people, which would include a few with the necessary skills, such as photography, for investigative purposes. Probably none such people would know the full story, only his or her tiny part in the drama. Only a handful of brass at the very top would have all the details, anyhow.

The whole thing would be guarded as well, if not better, than the atomic bomb. If all that Miss Y had told me were true, I doubted if even the people at the Pentagon, whom I had talked with and who had let me see the files, knew it. It was then that I got a fantastic idea. Suppose that the Project Blue Book was merely a cover-up, which analyzed routine saucer sightings; while somewhere else, within a highly guarded section of Wright Field, or some other base, a super-secret group was prying open saucers and desperately trying, in an attempt to get ahead of the Russians, to find out what made them and their extraterrestrial operators tick!

In keeping these secrets, the government had many advantages, and the main one probably was that the saucers themselves carried a ridiculous connotation in the minds of most of the public. Quite possibly; of course, there were very effective ways of dealing with individuals, in or out of the service, who knew too much or and talked too much.

In Scully's case (if his story had some truth to it) it was fairly simple: he was not dealt with in any dire cloak-and-dagger manner, but by the simple technique of ridicule. At first his book caused a sensation; now very few people believe it, for every possible effort has apparently been made to discredit and make him look ridiculous. Two principal characters of the book had been arrested on fraud charges, and they, their cases then undisposed of, were claiming that they were being persecuted for their saucer revelations. Could they be right and could Miss Y be right? There probably was a fifty-fifty choice either way.

I thought of the flying saucer the Canadian Government had first started building and later sold to the U.S. Department of Defense. Were we desperately trying to build such a machine, basing our design on what we had learned from the possible inspection of genuine interplanetary craft? True, the news releases said the AVRO Saucer would employ conventional jet power. (Later the government put the AVRO saucer on public display and indicated its design was unsuccessful. But its design would be strangely changed from that of the much publicized jet craft and turn out to be a ducted-fan hovercraft much like the model the British experimented with about the same time. Was the AVRO saucer a red herring or a possible preparation of the public to accept some startling announcements and increased congressional appropriations?

If saucers were real, they certainly didn't run on jet power. Many technicians had suggested that they must employ control of gravity and likely involve an electromagnetic drive. If the government had indeed captured a saucer or saucers it certainly appeared likely that they could unravel the power secrets involved.

When would the public be informed about the entire matter? Probably only when the government was good and ready, and only after they had mastered the secrets of the captured discs and learned from their operators the purpose of the visits. We would probably be told only after years of being gradually prepared and indoctrinated. This could be done in many ways, with more red herrings, such as George Adamski; with carefully conceived reports such as the AVRO saucer.

I wondered if the public should know sooner. After all, I was part of the public, and I didn't think I would panic if I suddenly knew the saucers were real. And I was becoming convinced, more and more each day, that they certainly weren't temperature inversions and all the other things the government said they were.

Yes, somebody was lying. If Miss Y were lying, there wasn't anything to the captured saucer. Yet if Miss Y were not lying, somebody should be able to prove it and somebody should tell the public.

If Miss Y were not lying, Mr. Z would have to lie !

What could I do about it? Not much for I probably exaggerated my own effectiveness.

But there was one way I could raise a lot of hell in the field, and probably get a lot of public awareness going. Albert Bender had done it and lately Gray Barker was arousing a lot of public interest with his Saucerian.

Knowing very little about how to do it, and with a bravado effected, it seems, only by brash people who have been hooked on saucers, I headed my Ford back toward Fort Lee, New Jersey.

If I drove hard I could make it back home sometime in the early hours of the next morning. I doubted if I would even go to bed. For the next day I would start my own flying saucer magazine.

3:25

DR. D'S STRANGE THEORY

As I referred again to my expose article in *Saucer News*, and Gray Barker further defended himself on the Long John Show, I noted the difference between the neatly-printed offset publication as it was now, and the old *Nexus* I began publishing after returning from Ohio.

The first issues of *Nexus* were cranked out on an old mimeograph machine. Physically, its publication was as simple as typing the material out on a stencil and then helping August C. Roberts, whom I named associate editor, turn the crank.

I wondered which version I really liked the best—the old crudely-printed issues or the slick new ones I had passed out to the Long John panel.

It was in the *Nexus* days when I first ran into the *Earth Theory*. I sometime regret that I ever got started on the "Theory" at all, for it alienated popular support for my magazine and made me disliked among many segments of saucerdom.

But I had a lead and I wanted to check it out. And the best way to check out a theory is to publish information about it and seek public reaction.

It all began when I picked up the phone and rang up Leonard Stringfield, a prominent UFO civilian researcher of Cincinnati. I thought I'd pass the time of day, compare notes, and ask him for some ideas.

"I have just received a letter from a fellow you ought to meet," Len told me. "A scientist who lives in New York State. I'll give you his name but I warn you, agree to refer to him only by his pseudonym, Dr. D., or you'll get very little information out of him."

"What gives with him?" I queried.

"His theories on saucers are ridiculous, but you know I'm an interplanetary buff from A to Z. He thinks the saucers come from Earth, are built by the U.S. Government. It may not be too popular with your readers, but it would be interesting if you interviewed him or had him do an article for you. He seems to be very cooperative with the UFO press. Personally I think his theories can't hold up—you know, saucers are nothing new and have been flying around since the dawn of recorded history. What really interests me about "Dr. D.' is . . ."

There were some noises on the line and Len paused.

"Well, make up your own mind on him. The most I can say over the phone is that I think you'll find it interesting if you read between the lines of everything he tells you."

Then he gave me Dr. D.'s name and address and I promised to drop by Cincinnati as soon as possible and see Len personally. Although I frequently heard the usual noises on the telephone, I really hoped the Silence Group, if indeed there was one, was actually listening. In phone conversations I had the habit of kidding whoever might be listening. While Len and some of the other saucerers seemed to fear being wire tapped, I would usually throw them some whoppers, especially while talking with close friends who were "in" on my own little bit of paranoia. I usually announced that I was planning to assassinate the president of Brazil, or that I had a secret informant in the Pentagon who had given me classified Bomb secrets. This, I figured, would provide anybody really listening in something to check on for a few weeks. Then I always gave names of my imaginary accomplices, specific dates and so on.

After I had hung up with Len I put a long distance call through to this man, whom I will dutifully refer to as Dr. D.

"Oh yes, Jim," he said. "I've been thinking of calling you but haven't got around to it. Say, I've enjoyed your magazine very much." (I wondered how he had read the magazine since I had the small mailing list almost memorized and he wasn't on it—nor was it on the newsstands.)

Dr. D. said he would be very happy to grant me an interview, and that he had many things to discuss which he would rather not go into over the phone. Yes, if I drove up that very night, he would be glad to see me.

"My wife and I were thinking of going out tonight, then I caught this cold. If you aren't afraid of catching it, drive on out. We'll probably have something to eat about 7:00; why not start early enough and join us at dinner? Nothing fancy, but you're welcome."

Dr. D. turned out to be a very affable man in his late thirties with a very fine sense of humor. Although he began by calling many of the civilian researchers "big nuts" (much to his wife's censure), I could tell he was deeply interested in the subject.

"Now there's some of this stuff (the saucers) that I can't figure out. But my background and certain information at my disposal should qualify me to explain at least some of it. The Adamski bit and some of the other contactees is a bit more difficult, but I think I have a line on them too. Still there are a few sightings that just don't fit into the information I have."

Dr. D. then gave me a persuasive argument that saucers are made on Earth.

"First let me assure you that if it were permissible I could show you some photographs and documents which would be very convincing. You can publish anything I say and later I may write an article or so for you if you wish. What I have to say is in no way classified because I do not have this particular information in documented form and speak only as a private citizen."

I was all ears.

"As you know, the Army and the Army Air Force were made two separate entities in 1947 . This still didn't help the interservice rivalries, for the old feud between the Navy and the Army was merely carried over into the Air Force itself. This the general public may not be aware of, except for occasional outbursts such as the Navy fight against the B-35, the Air Force fight against the Forrestal-class supercarriers and so on.

"Those who read the aviation and military journals and follow the Washington news reports closely, accept the continuing Navy-Air Force fight as one of the facts of American political life.

"I claim that no one can understand the flying saucer situation without a good knowledge of this grudge."

Dr. D. paused, and rather impishly asked me if I knew that the AF had secretly changed the name of its saucer investigation to Project Grudge early in 1949. I had heard about it, though had ascribed no particular significance to it.

"Prior to 1952 the Air Force denied, not only that the saucers were interplanetary, but U. S. made as well. If you'll think back however, Jim, I don't think you can come up with any official Navy statements to the effect that they were not made on earth."

I tried to recall any such statements, but couldn't. Come to think of it, the Navy had been very quiet on the subject. "The year 1947, when the sightings first commenced on any big scale, has another significance as being just prior to the 'unification' of the U.S. Armed Forces. The interservice rivalry between the Army and

Navy, and between each of these and the Air Force, is well known, and still exists.

This rivalry would have assured that the Air Force would have been kept uninformed of secret aviation developments by the Navy in 1947. It is documented in the Project Grudge report that it was in early 1949 (after unification had got well started) that an Air Force general instructed the flying saucer investigators to change the project code name from Sign to Grudge, to stop spending money on special investigations and to wind up the project during 1949. To me, this indicates that the general had at last been informed of the Navy's developments, and was stopping the ridiculous investigation of our own devices. Prior to unification, the Navy had felt that it was perfectly fair to let the Air Force try to find out for itself what the saucers really were.

"To be brief, the Air Force found out that the Navy had saucer-shaped craft in 1952, and that was the year that General Samford came out with his somewhat befuddling but widely publicized statements that saucers were not extraterrestrial."

I checked some newspaper clippings and transcripts Dr. D. handed me describing and quoting the conference. One reporter had asked General Samford if the saucers were "some very highly secret new weapon that we're working on." Samford evaded the question the first time, but the second time he gave as his answer a very definite but misleading statement: "We have nothing that has no mass and unlimited power!"

"That statement," said Dr. D., pointing to the clipping," as anybody with a high school education knows, is a definite evasion of the question, not an answer, not a denial, since every real object must have some mass.

"To sum up, the Air Force has a 98 per cent assurance that the saucers are Navy made. They will not say this because of the security involved and the fear of giving credit to their arch rival. Then Project Bluebook, understaffed and a sort of Siberia, it often seems, for Air Force officers, may not really know what is going on. They still have to run out, chasing the saucer stories, probably in the dark as to what those at the top really know."

"You mentioned Adamski," I reminded Dr. D.

"There may be nothing to his story, but the UFO field is flooded with contactees these days. I frankly don't believe these yarns but I haven't discounted them entirely. I sort of think that where there's fiery-eyed saucer zealots, there just may be some saucers to be smoked out."

"I haven't made a study of the other contactees, for the information wasn't readily available to me," Dr. D. continued, lighting his pipe in which he had put some aromatic tobacco.

"I'm a poor man, but if I weren't I'd lay money on Adamski. But I'm still not laying money that he contacted a long-haired Venusian. "

"Whom did he contact then?"

"Probably the CIA, though there are other agencies. There was an elaborate setup. George was taken inside a mock-up flying saucer which didn't actually fly. You've seen Cinerama and how it looks so real. Take a gooked-up saucer and a little hypnotism to a man who wants to believe in it anyhow and even a 16 mm. projector on a screen through some portholes, and you have a real tour to Mars, Venus, or even Perth Amboy, depending upon where they want you to think you went!"

"But the CIA isn't interested in collecting the royalties from Adamski's books—he's in for all the dough," I protested. "Now I don't believe Adamski, but what you're telling me is more fantastic than his story."

Then Dr. D. launched into an elaborate framework which he thought explained the role and motives of the CIA. Though not very convincing to me, I don't think I should publish the material, just in case the theory is valid. Suffice it to say that the theory involved the cold war and U.S. relationships with the Soviet Union.

I drove back to New Jersey not a little dazed by Dr. D's theories. I had asked him to write some articles for *Nexus* outlining his strange views, and for several years these would appear. I remember thinking that his theories, while they sounded logical at the moment, were just a little too pat. Also, they could not account for the historical sightings. But there seemed too much of a possibility of truth in what he had told me to completely discount his statements.

3:30

THE TWELVE BEST SAUCERS

Later I was even more puzzled about Dr. D.'s role in the flying saucer drama.

On May 5, 1955, the Air Force released a controversial document to the public. With the excuse that the reproduction costs of the document for any wide public distribution was prohibitive, the AF made the report available only to people who took the trouble to visit the Information Offices in the Pentagon, New York and Los Angeles.

But the lengthy document, running more than 75 pages, did not prove too expensive for Dr. D., a private individual without apparent wealth, to reproduce and distribute widely! The print job that the AF. with millions at its command, could not allegedly afford, Dr. D. managed to finance!

He promoted and distributed it widely, its modest price tag obviously only a part of its actual per copy cost.

To the average individual with only a surface interest in the UFO enigma, *Project Blue Book Special Report No. 14* was a time-consuming bore, which, by the employment of elaborate graphs and statistical gobbledegook, purported to prove that only a small percentage of reported sightings (3 per cent or less) remained unexplained.

When I heard that Dr. D. had reproduced the document, I dutifully sent my check for $1.50 and in due course had a copy in my hands. Paper-wise, it certainly was worth the money, but the graphs and statistics I found quite taxing.

The civilian publisher had seen fit to follow both the then current AF line and provide a dramatic cover illustration. The stiff paper cover (appropriately, blue) carried the current artist's conception of the flying saucer the Department of Defense was building—the famous AVRO saucer discussed above.

THE ASTOUNDING UFO SECRETS OF JAMES W. MOSELEY

The illustration, widely carried by the press, suggested that the flying saucers Joe Doakes was seeing probably involved an already-developed device comfortably in the possession of the United States Government.

Later the AF would admit that the AVRO saucer, though it cost a lot of dough, actually failed to fly. Rumor had it that the test pilot who tried to get it off the ground almost got killed in the process, when the U.S. saucer, unlike the alleged interplanetary ones, took a nose dive like *Darius Green's Wonderful Machine.*

Report No. 14, however, displayed a characteristic ambivalence the AF often let sneak into their official pronouncements. If it figuratively swore on a stack of statistics that flying saucers were the bunk, it nevertheless always left itself a loophole by admitting that a small percentage of sightings submitted were unexplained, or involved "unknowns," as the apparently honest-to-goodness saucers are termed by the AF.

So the literary saving grace of *Report No. 14* consisted of what the AF termed the *"Twelve Best Sightings"*-terrestrials' encounters with saucers which were the most difficult—or impossible—to explain. The twelve sightings were accompanied by some dramatic drawings which would tend to put some of the wildest UFO books to shame. We reproduce both the text and the drawings in the following pages:

Case I (Serial 0573.00)

Two men employed by a rug-cleaning firm were driving across a bridge at 0955 hours on July 29, 1948, when they saw an object glide across the road a few hundred feet in front of them. It was shiny and metallic in construction, about 6 to 8 feet long and 2 feet wide. It was in a flat glide path at an altitude of about 30 feet and in a moderate turn to the left. It was seen for only a few seconds and apparently went down in a wooded area, although no trace of it was found.

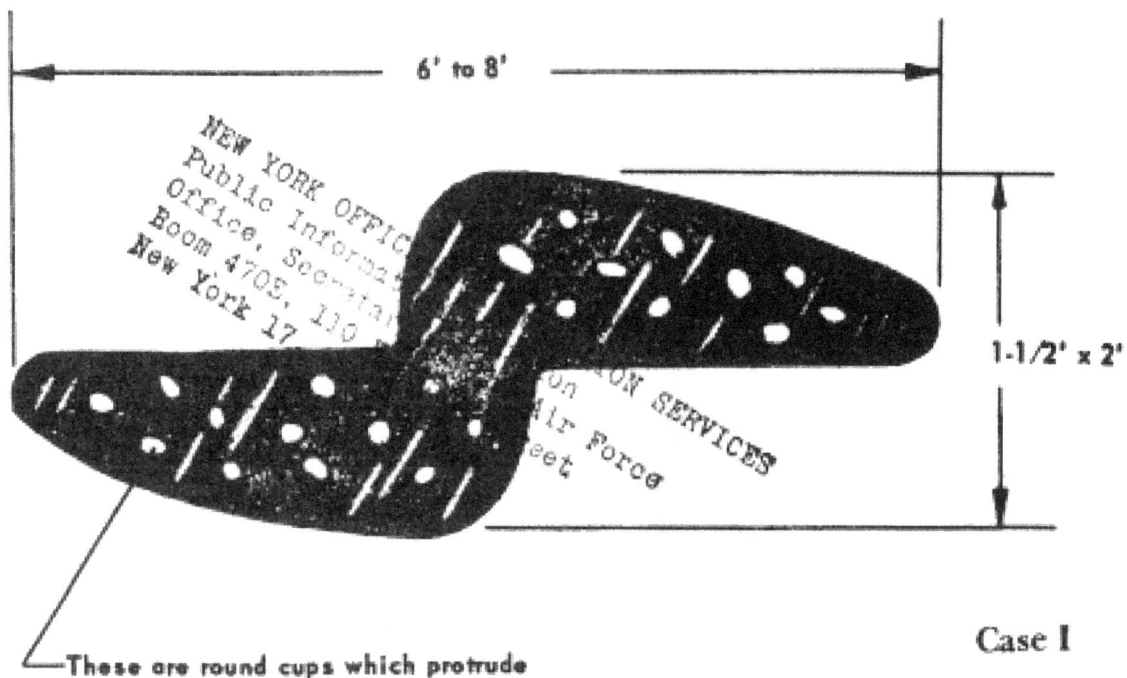

6' to 8'

1-1/2' x 2'

These are round cups which protrude

Case I

Case II (Serial 4508.00)

A naval aviation student, his wife, and several others were at a drive-in movie from 2115 to 2240 hours on April 20, 1952, during which time they saw several groups of objects fly over. There were from two to nine objects in a group and there were about 20 groups. The groups of objects flew in a straight line except for some changes in direction accomplished in a manner like any standard aircraft turn. The objects were shaped like conventional aircraft. Their unaccountable feature of the objects was that each had a red glow surrounding it and was glowing itself, although it was a cloudless night.

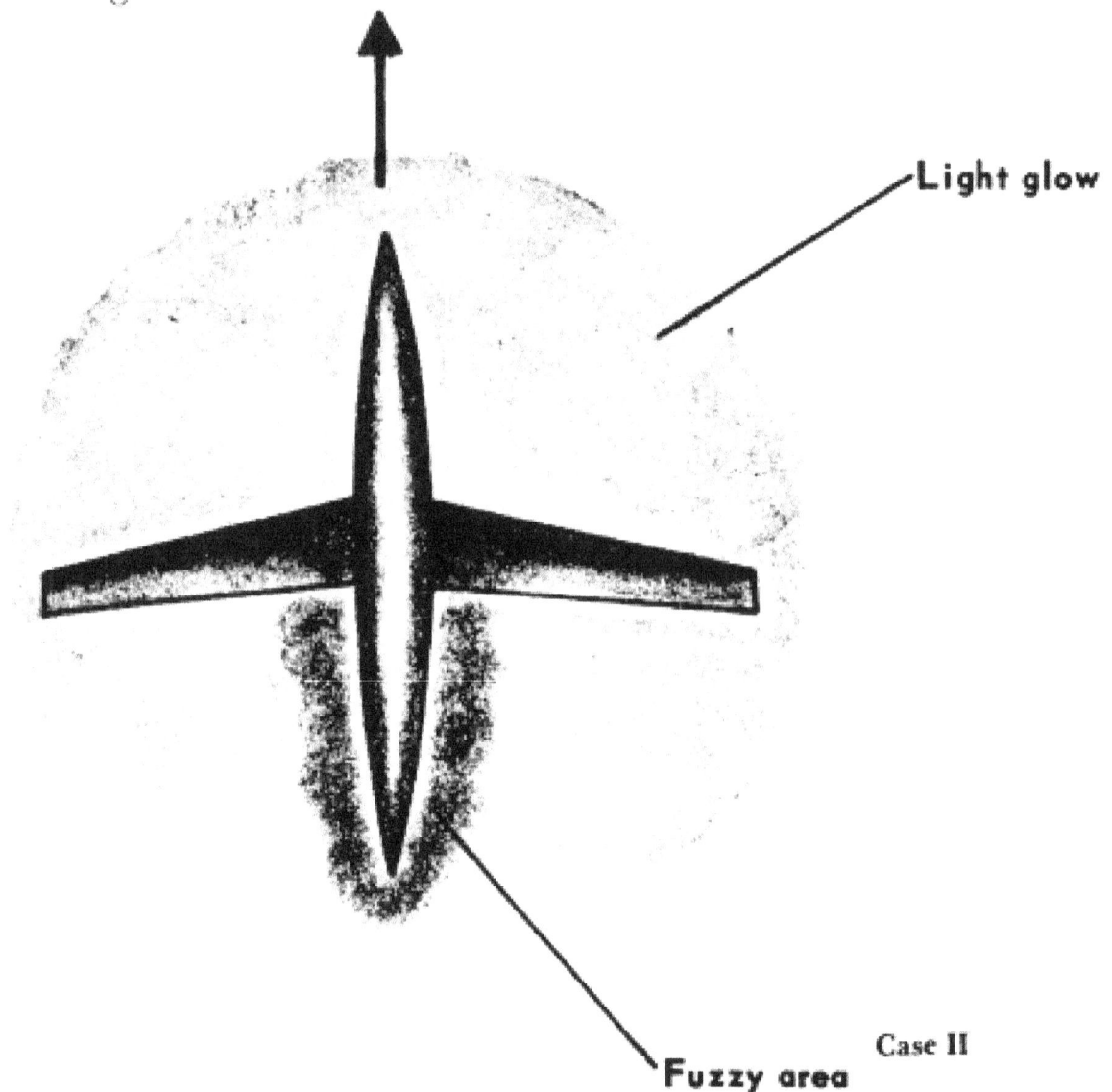

Light glow

Fuzzy area

Case II

THE ASTOUNDING UFO SECRETS OF JAMES W. MOSELEY

Case III (Serial 2013.00, 2014.00, and 2014.01)

Two tower operators sighted a light over a city airport at 2020 hours on January 20, 1951. Since a commercial plane was taking off at this time, the pilots were asked to investigate this light. They observed it at 2026 hours. According to them, it flew abreast of them at a greater radius as they made their climbing turn, during which time it blinked some lights which looked like running lights. While the observing plane was still in its climbing turn, the object made a turn toward the plane and flew across its nose. As the two men turned their heads to watch it, it instantly appeared on their other side flying in the same direction as they were flying, and then in 2 or 3 seconds it slipped under them, and they did not see it again. Total time of the observation was not stated. In appearance, it was like an airplane with a cigar-shaped body and straight wings, somewhat larger than a B-29. No engine nacelles were observed on the wings.

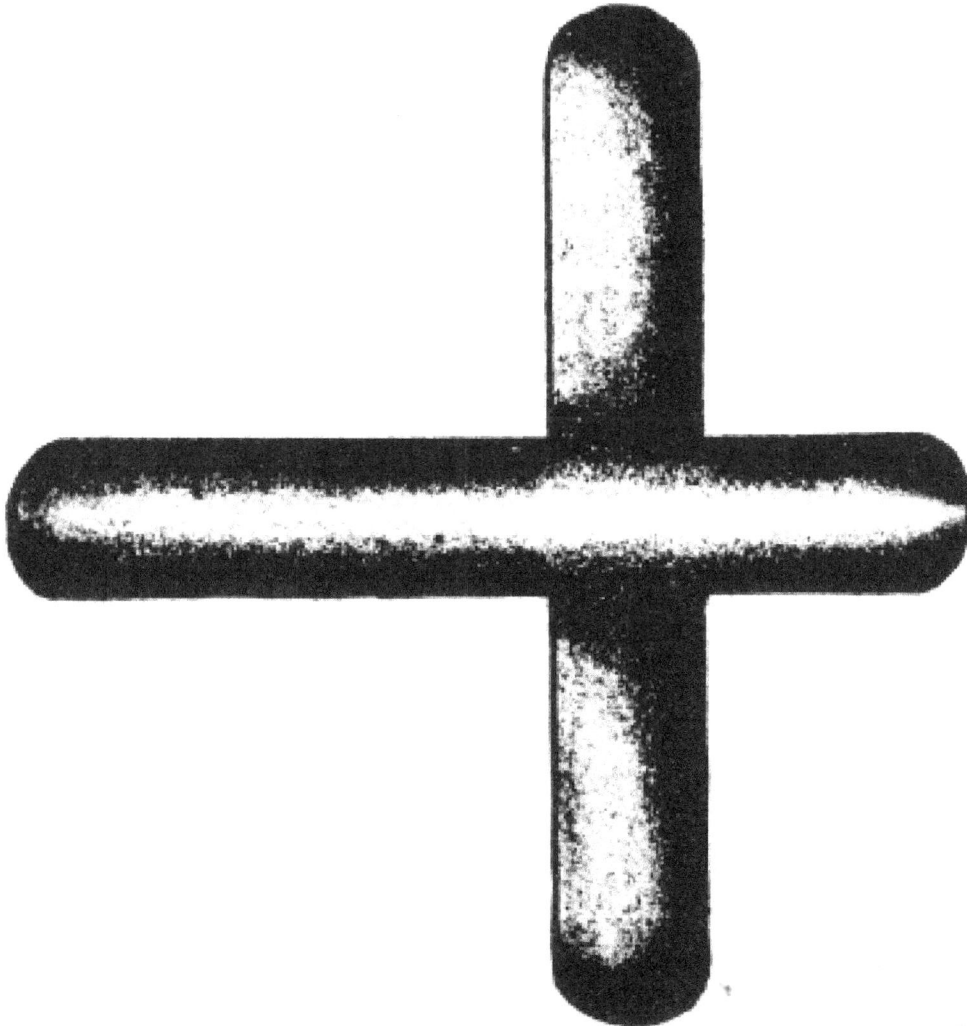

Case III

135

Case IV (Serial 4599.00) A part-time farmer and a hired hand were curing to-bacco at midnight on July 19, 1952, when they looked up and saw two cigar-shaped objects. One hovered while the other moved to the east and came back, at which time both ascended until out of sight. Duration of observation was 3 to 4 minutes. Both had an exhaust at one end, and neither had projections of any kind. It was stated that they appeared to be transparent and illuminated from the inside.

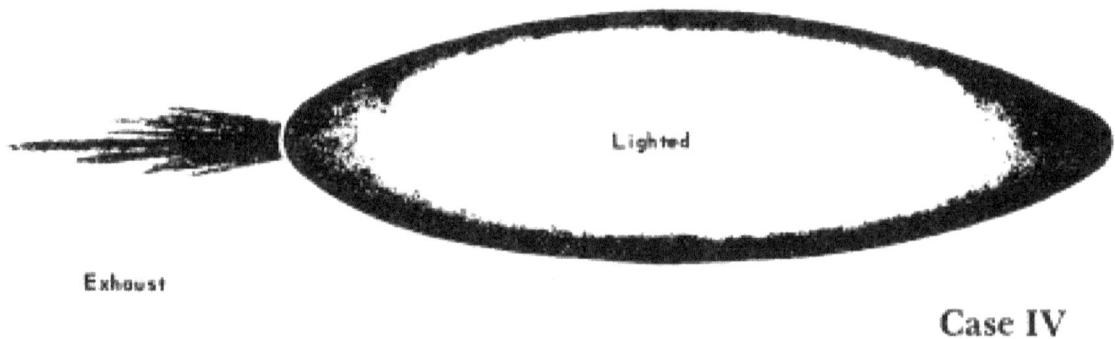

Lighted

Exhaust

Case IV

Case V (Serial 0565.00 to 0565.03)

A pilot and copilot were flying a DC-3 at 0340 hours on July 24, 1948, when they saw an object coming toward them. It passed to the right and slightly above them, at which time it went into a steep climb and was lost from sight in some clouds. Duration of the observation was about 10 seconds. One passenger was able to catch a flash of light as the object passed. The object seemed powered by rocket or jet motors shooting a trail of fire some 50 feet to the rear of the object. The object had no wings or other protrusion and had two rows of lighted windows.

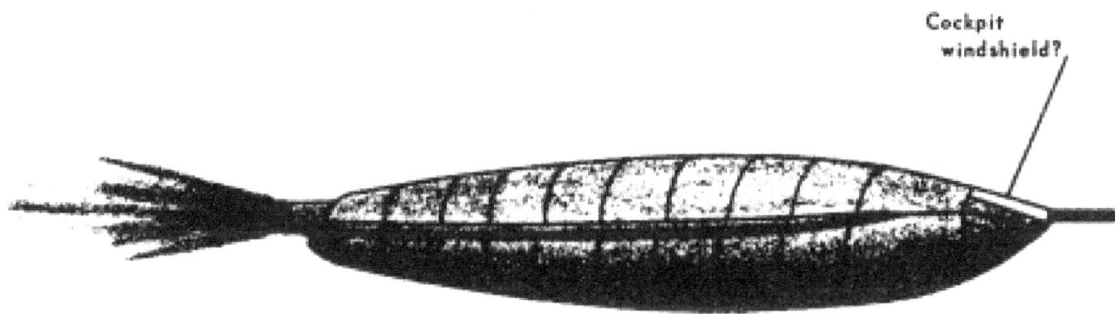

Pilot

Case V

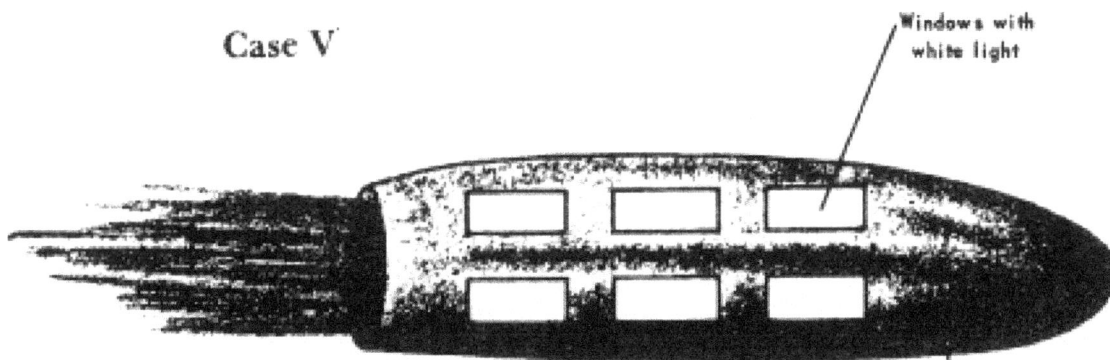

Copilot

THE ASTOUNDING UFO SECRETS OF JAMES W. MOSELEY

Case VI (Serial 4822.00)

An instrument technician, while driving from a large city toward an Air Force base on December 22, 1952, saw an object from his car at 1930 hours. He stopped his car to watch it. It suddenly moved up toward the zenith in spurts from right to left at an angle of about 45 degrees. It then moved off in level flight at a high rate of speed, during which maneuver it appeared white most of the time, but apparently rolled three times showing a red side. About halfway through its roll it showed no light at all. It finally assumed a position to the south of the planet Jupiter at a high altitude, at which position it darted back and forth, left and right alternately. Total time of the observation was 15 minutes. Apparently, the observer just stopped watching the object.

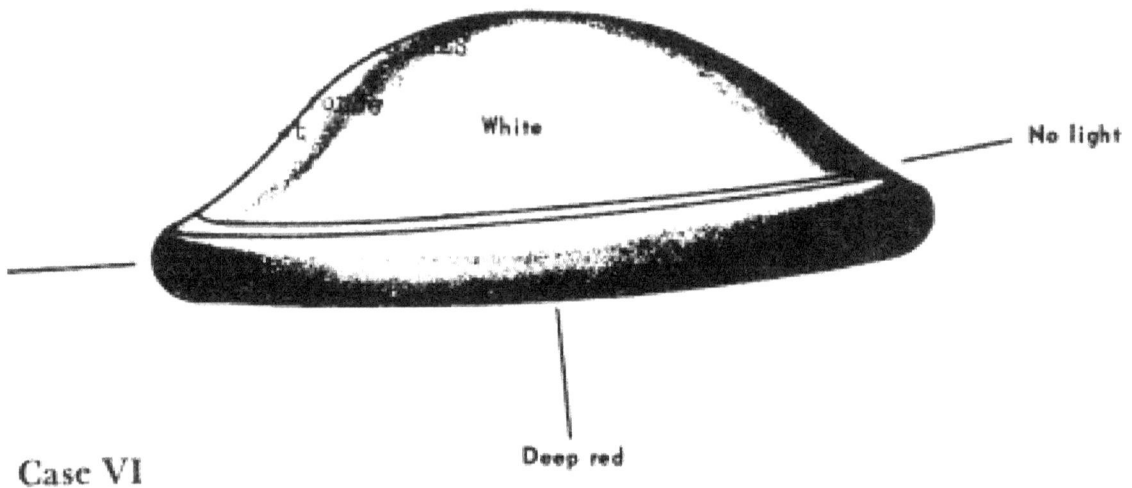

Case VI

Case VII (Serial 2728.00)

A Flight Sergeant saw an object over an Air Force base in Korea at 0842 hours on June 6, 1952. The object flew in a series of spinning and tumbling actions. It was on an erratic course, first flying level, then stopping momentarily, shooting straight up, flying level and again tumbling, then changing course and disappearing into the sun. It reappeared and was seen flying back and forth across the sun. At one time an F-86 passed between the observer and the object. He pointed it out to another man who saw it as it maneuvered near the sun.

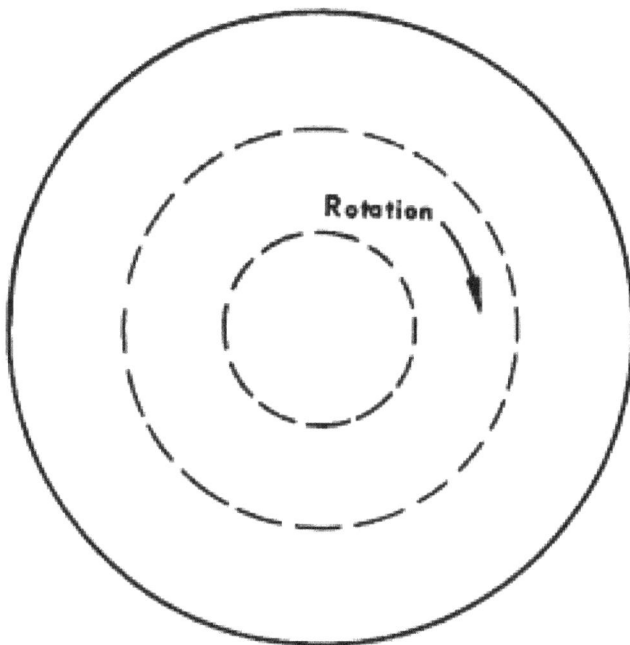

Rotation

Black lines evenly spaced

Case VII

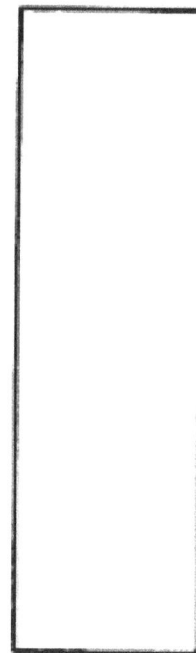

Proportion 7 to 1

(Dimensions are as shown in observer's original drawing)

Case VIII (Serial 0576.00)

An electrician was standing by the bathroom window of his home, facing west, at 0825 hours on July 31, 1948, when he first sighted an object. He ran to his kitchen where he pointed out the object to his wife. Total time in sight was approximately 10 seconds, during which the object flew on a straight and level course from horizon to horizon, west to east.

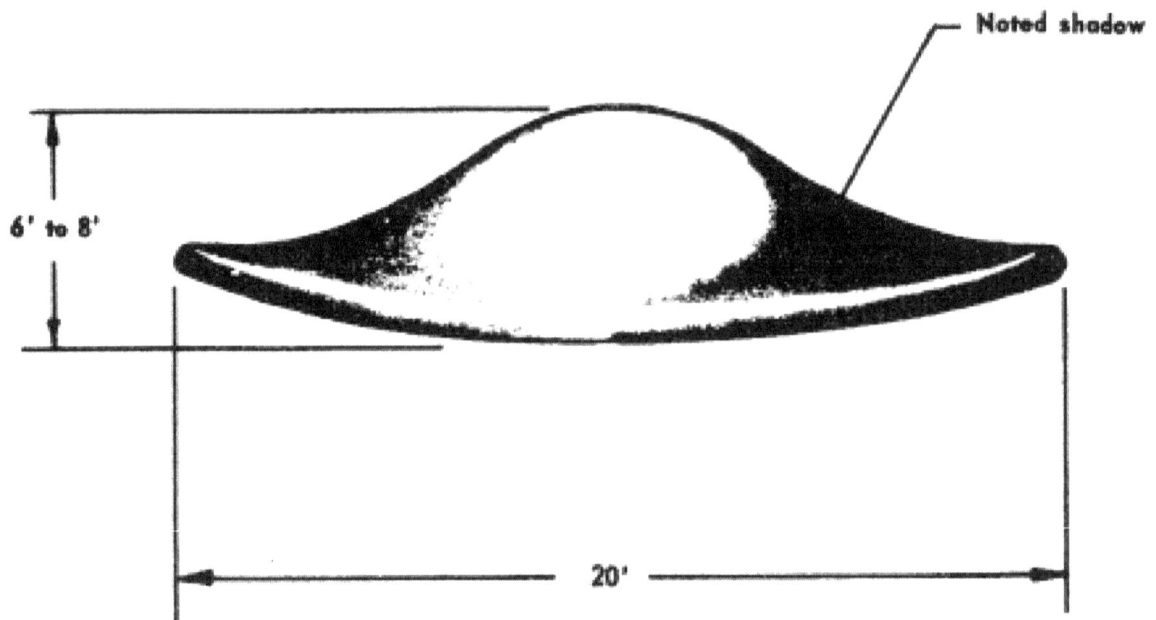

Case VIII

(Ratio approx. 3:1)

Case IX (Serial 0066.00)

A farmer and his two sons, aged 8 and 10, were at his fishing camp on August 13, 1947. At about 1300 hours, he went to look for the boys, having sent them to the river for some tape from his boat. He noticed an object some 300 feet away, 75 feet above the ground. He saw it against the background of the canyon wall which was 400 feet high at this point. It was hedgehopping, following the contour of the ground, was sky blue, about 20 feet in diameter and 10 feet thick, and had pods on the side from which flames were shooting out. It made a swishing sound. The observer stated that the trees were highly agitated by the craft as it passed over. His two sons also observed the object. No one saw the object for more than a few seconds.

Side view

Case IX

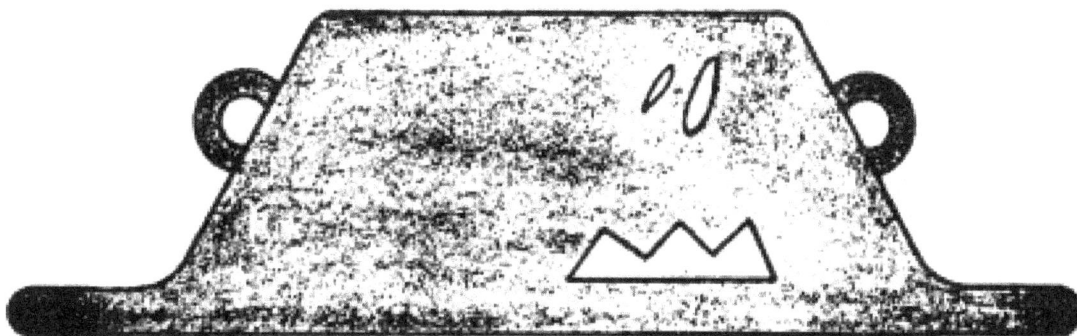

End view

Case X (Serial 1119.00)

An employee in the supersonic laboratory of an aeronautical laboratory and some other employees of this lab, were by a river, 2-1/2 miles from its mouth, when they saw an object. The time was about 1700 hours on May 24, 1949. The object was reflecting sunlight when observed by naked eye. However, he then looked at it with 8-power binoculars, at which time there was no glare. (Did glasses have filter?) It was of metallic construction and was seen with good enough resolution to show that the skin was dirty. It moved off in horizontal flight at a gradually increasing rate of speed, until it seemed to approach the speed of a jet before it disappeared. No propulsion was apparent. Time of observation was 2-1/2 to 3 minutes.

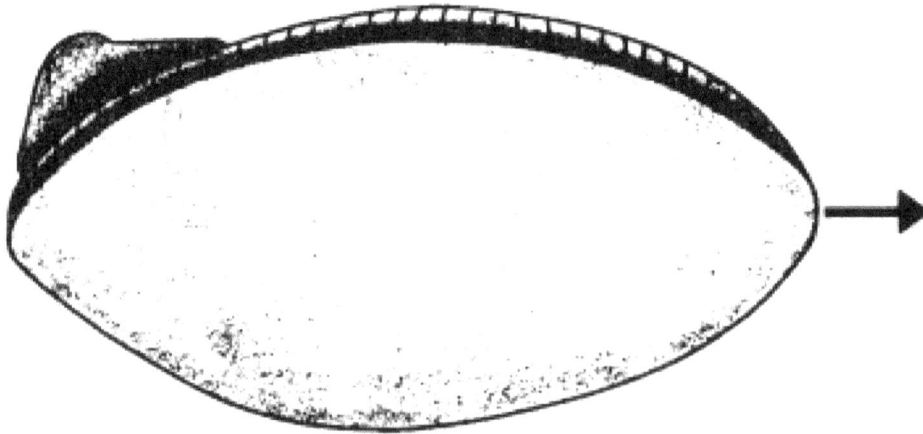

Case X

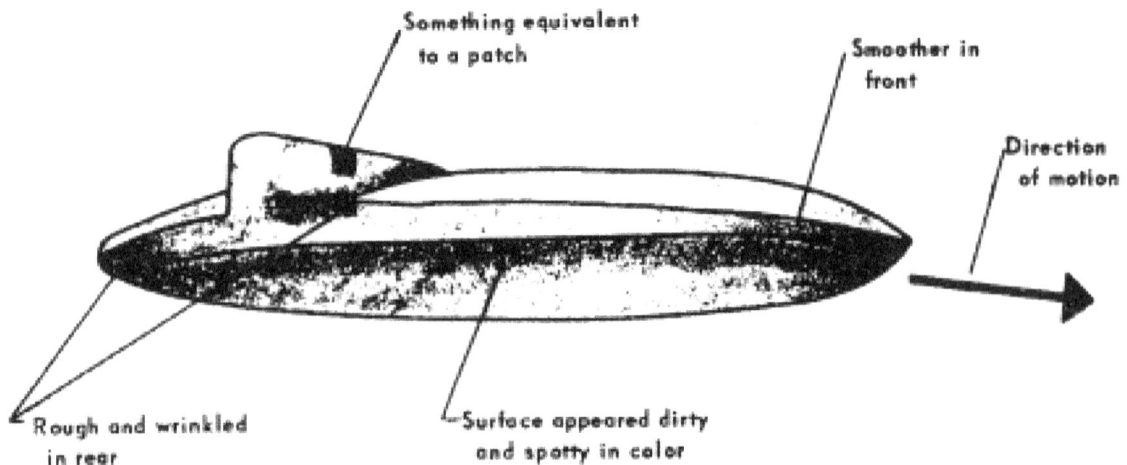

Something equivalent to a patch

Smoother in front

Direction of motion

Rough and wrinkled in rear

Surface appeared dirty and spotty in color

THE ASTOUNDING UFO SECRETS OF JAMES W. MOSELEY

Case XI (Serial 1550.00)

On March 20, 1950, a Reserve Air Force Captain and an airlines Captain were flying a commercial airlines flight. At 21:26, the airline Captain directed the attention of the Reserve Air Force Captain to an object which apparently was flying at high speed, approaching the airliner from the south on a north heading. The Reserve Air Force Captain focused his attention on the object. Both crew members watched it as it passed in front of them and went out of sight to the right. The observation, which lasted about 25 to 35 seconds, occurred about 15 miles north of a medium-sized city. When the object passed in front of the airliner, it was not more than 1/2 mile distant and at an altitude of about 1000 feet higher than the airliner.

The object appeared to be circular, with a diameter of approximately 100 feet and with a vertical height considerably less than the diameter, giving the object a disc like shape. In the top center was a light which was blinking at an estimated 3 flashes per second. This light was so brilliant that it would have been impossible to look at it continuously had it not been blinking. This light could be seen only when the object was approaching and after it had passed the airliner. When the object passed in front of the observers, the bottom side was visible. The bottom side appeared to have 9 to 12 symmetrical oval or circular portholes located in a circle approximately 3/4 of the distance from the center to the outer edge. Through these portholes came a soft purple light about the shade of aircraft fluorescent lights. The object was traveling in a straight line without spinning. Considering the visibility, the length of time the object was in sight, and the distance from the object, the Reserve Air Force Captain estimates the speed to be in excess of 1000 mph.

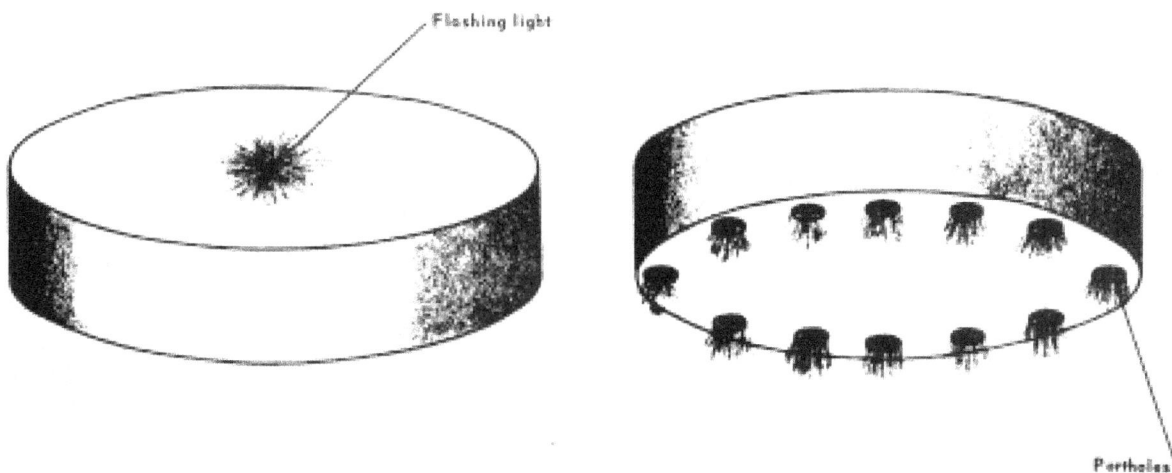

Case XI

143

Case XII (Serial 3601.00)

At 0535 on the morning of August 25, 1952, a musician for a radio station was driving to work from his home when he noticed an object hovering about 10 feet above a field near the road along which he was driving. As he came abreast of the object, he stopped his car and got out to watch; having an artificial leg, he could not leave the road, since the surrounding terrain was rough. However, he was within about 100 yards of it at the point he was standing on the road. The object was not absolutely still, but seemed to rock slightly as it hovered. When he turned off the motor of his car, he could hear a deep throbbing sound coming from the object. As he got out of the car, the object began a vertical ascent with a sound similar to "a large covey of quail starting to fly at one time". The object ascended vertically through broken clouds until out of sight. His view was not obscured by clouds. The observer states that the vegetation was blown about by the object when it was near the ground.

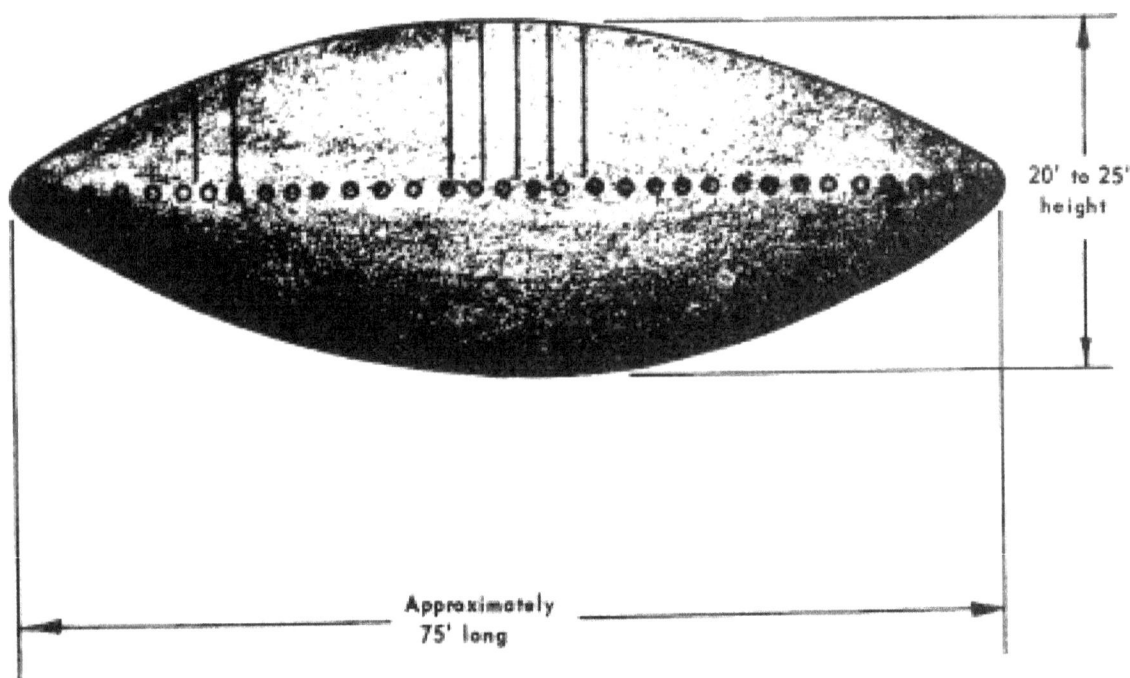

Case XII

THE ASTOUNDING UFO SECRETS OF JAMES W. MOSELEY

Description of the object is as follows:

It was about 75 feet long, 45 feet wide, and 15 feet thick, shaped like two oval meat platters placed together. It was a dull aluminum color, and had a smooth surface. A medium-blue continuous light shone through the one window in the front section. The head and shoulders of one man, sitting motionless, facing the forward edge of the object, were visible. In the midsection of the object were several windows extending from the top to the rear edge of the object; the midsection of the ship had a blue light which gradually changed to different shades. There was a large amount of activity and movement in the midsection that could not be identified as either human or mechanical, although it did not have a regular pattern of movement. There were no windows, doors or portholes, vents, seams, etc., visible to the observer in the rear section of the object or under the object (viewed at time of ascent). Another identifiable feature was a series of propellers 6 to 12 inches in diameter spaced closely together along the outer edge of the object. These propellers were mounted on a bracket so that they revolved in a horizontal plane along the edge of the object. The propellers were revolving at a high rate of speed.

Investigation of the area soon afterward showed some evidence of vegetation being blown around. An examination of grass and soil samples taken indicated nothing unusual. Reliability of the observer was considered good.

* * * * *

Dr. D. would continue to be a puzzling personality in the UFO investigation field.

For a while he dropped out of active research, only to show up again at a party given in New York in the honor of Al K. Bender, finally coaxed from his Bridgeport, Conn., home to make a short appearance on the Long John Show.

"Dr. D. did a real peculiar thing," Al told me after drawing me aside.

"So you think he's mysterious, too," I half kidded Al.

"He asked permission to take my picture with his Polaroid, and of course that was all right," Al said. "But then he asked me to get up and stand aside while he took a picture of the empty chair. Then he sat me down again and snapped the picture. The picture of the empty chair and then me in it turned out fine. He even made an extra print for me."

"Did he explain the empty chair bit?" I asked.

"Only that it was what he termed 'a control shot,'" Al replied.

I doubt very much if Dr. D. was or is a member of the Silence Group, and I doubt very much that I will ever completely believe he isn't.

A couple of years later Dr. D. ran out of copies of *Project Blue Book Special Report No. 14.* Whatever the merits of this special Air Force report, it must have a special place in the heart of Dr. D. (Through special permission of Dr. D., a new expanded edition of *Project Blue Book Special Report No. 14* is now available from *Saucerian Books*, Box 2228, Clarksburg W. Va. at $5.95. This limited edition contains much additional documentation by Dr. D., and consists of more than 100 large 8 x 11" pages.

3:47

UFOS FROM ANTARCTICA

"I think I know what Ray Palmer's fact is," Yonah averred.

All of us on the Long John Show turned and looked at him, mouths wide open. For we'd all read Palmer's many statements and had often kicked this around in bull sessions.

Tonight it had come up again and we were wondering if Palmer really knew some fact which enabled him, as he claimed, to know whether a given account about flying saucers' contactees, and so on was true or false.

Where Palmer had got the fact, nobody knew—if indeed he had one. For Palmer always stopped there. If he revealed the "fact," it would invalidate his use of it, for people might deliberately fabricate yarns to conform with it.

"Ray Palmer invented flying saucers!" Yonah continued. "He knows there is nothing to them since he made them up in the first place!"

True, Palmer had publicized Kenneth Arnold's famous 1947 sighting, the first one to gain any publicity, in *Fate* magazine and in a book co-authored by Arnold titled *The Coming of the Saucers*.

I wish Ed had Ray's "fact"—if indeed there were any such thing. It might help me evaluate one of the strangest experiences I have encountered while involved with saucer research.

As each year goes by, my suspicions grow. And those suspicions are that I was hoaxed. As time goes by, and I reflect on it, the whole thing just doesn't make sense. If I were hoaxed, the hoaxter must have had sick and complex motives.

I wonder if Bender, the subject of most of the discussion that evening, might have had some similar experience. I didn't really think that Gray Barker had hired the three men in black to visit and frighten Bender, but the subject we were discussing did, come to think of it, contain some similar content.

About a week after I had talked with Dr. D., a knock came at my door.

"Are you the James Moseley who publishes the flying saucer magazine?" a young man, probably in his thirties, asked. The man, about five feet nine and just beginning to bald, was dressed in a gray, Madison Avenue suit, and employed some of the mannerisms and vocabulary of that establishment.

I decided to invite him in, for he did not seem to be the usual type of saucer fan who came to my place to ask me questions (which I always enjoyed answering) but who usually harangued me for an inordinate period of time about the flying saucer he had seen, and his own private theories.

It developed, however, that the man was, after all, like such fans in one respect. He didn't want to find out anything, but he did want to tell me many things.

"Look," I told him, "I'm very busy. I have these stencils almost typed for my next issue and have to put in three or four more paragraphs and proof read the thing in order to 'get it to bed.' "

While I was thus remonstrating the man was unzipping a neat leather portfolio, and he then withdrew about seven photographs from it and tossed them on the coffee table between us.

I must have sounded like a phonograph running down. "Are...you...submitting...these...for...publication?"

"You might say that. All seven of these can be published in your. . .what is it, **Nexus, all** for the sum of. . .well, let's be reasonable and settle for a couple of beers."

This guy had the most tremendous saucer photographs I have ever seen. Real close up stuff.

Saucers, yes, but unlike the ones I had seen. Portholes, doors, antenna, and even markings in unfamiliar symbols. I can't remember the details now, but I do recall that one of them was very much like a photo Gray Barker had published in his **Saucerian**. It had a large "tail rudder," or "handle," and I had kidded him that it looked like a flying cup. Barker claimed it had been found in the reject bin of a color lab that did secret work for the Air Force.

The man's photos were not black and white, but had a reddish, sepia-like quality. In fact they reminded me of the proofs I had received of my high school graduation pictures.

"They're all yours, Jim—that is, if you can publish them in the next hour before they fade. Soon you'll have seven nice big eight by ten pieces of black photographic paper. I'm going to talk to you about five minutes longer than that," the man, still friendly, but now with an almost cynical touch, announced. Then I remembered how the photographer had made several graduation photos of me and gave these to my mother. The prints, however, had not been "fixed" with hypo and soon faded out after we had selected the particular pose we wanted the prints and enlargements made from.

"Just who are you, pal?" I asked him.

"I represent the F.P.S.—that's the Free Photo Service. To you at least, Jim. That is with just one condition. You have just seen seven samples. I could have brought you six or eight or nine, or any reasonable quantity; but somehow seven seems to be a mystical number you fanatics go for."

"Are these photos fakes?"

"Take them to any photo expert in the country," was his evasive reply. "Only get them there quick before they fade."

I wondered what the man's game was. I didn't think he was a nut, for he approached me in such a cynical non-nut fashion which was completely disarming. But suddenly he became more serious.

"Jim" he said, "I have a real story for you to publish—just the way I tell it to you and no other way. And do you know what my safeguards on this are?"

"I think I do," I replied, "and I'll bite." I thumbed once more through the photos, even then having turned indictably darker.

"O.K. You get the photos and I give you something to go with them."

I asked him to explain the conditions. "I'll deliver these photos in time for your November issue. Only they will be real photo prints and won't fade out when the light strikes them.

"Write the article based on the material I'm about to give you and put it under a pseudonym, such as Fred Broman, or Richard Cohen, or other names you have used for your own articles.

"By the way, what is your name?"

"I'd 'like for you to call me Bob," was the way he evaded that question.

"All right, when can I have the real photos?"

"I will contact you again in two weeks. Show me the finished article and if it's accurate you may have the photos to back you up."

"What if it isn't accurate?"

"I'll ask you to rewrite or not to publish the article. "

"What could you do if I misquoted you and insisted on publishing it," I asked, subtly suggesting that he might be a government agent.

"You don't look like the type who would go back on his word," again came the evasive answer. I wondered if there could be any pitfalls in listening to what he had to say.

"You aren't going to tell me something about UFOs and place me under security are you?"

"Don't be ridiculous. How could I do that?" Bob indicated he was ready to give me his information.

"Now if you'll get out lots of notepaper, I'll talk to you exactly one hour. If I go too fast, tell me and I'll slow down."

I got the notepaper, an extra pack of cigarettes and noticed that I had a half-filled bottle of Scotch. I asked from the kitchen if he'd like a drink, and he accepted. I brought him some ice and a mixer, deciding not to have any myself, for I very seldom drink.

"First," he began, "let me qualify somewhat the information I am about to give you. Some flying saucers may come here from some far galaxy, but then once, say, in a thousand years or longer. The only planet in our solar system where saucers might originate is Mars, but that's extremely unlikely. The flying saucers, the ones you're currently hearing the reports about and possibly have seen yourself, are coming from right here on this planet, known to us Earthmen as Earth."

I put down my pad, and was ready to remonstrate when Bob interjected with "Uh !-Uh!-Uh ! —just a minute ,Jim. "

He told me I was going to say this wouldn't explain the historical sightings.

"Did I say they are made by our government? Or some other known government? Of course not."

This guy was a real wild one. Next, he'll probably tell me that they came from the South Pole!

'Jim, the flying saucers are manufactured and based in the vicinity of Antarctica!"

I had heard from Roberts and Lucchesi that Al Bender had been exploring an Antarctica theory before he had been hushed up by the alleged three men in black. He had been working with Harold H. Fulton, of Australia, on this, though neither had reached any conclusions.

"Let's start with a little background," Bob said, and drew a folder from his portfolio. He did not offer to show me the document.

"It seems that in many investigations of UFOs by teams of qualified scientists, it has been established that the background radiation content of the atmosphere increased sharply on several occasions at the same time a flying saucer was observed visually in the vicinity of the radiation measuring equipment.

"The report I have here continues and says that this proof was not sufficient to reach any conclusions because no photographs were ever taken of any of the saucers seen visually when the radiation count on the instruments increased."

"I don't see why a photo would be needed for proof," I interjected.

"I don't either," he replied, "unless these scientists didn't trust peoples' eyesight.

"Anyhow," he continued, "the radiation clue mentioned here is correct. Some people in the government know this, but not necessarily the air force. Sure the people at the very top all know this, but they don't deal directly with it in the investigations which are still being carried out. I'm not talking of a government agency you would know about—nor the air force, nor the other services.

"For convenience, I'll just refer to it from here on as The Organization.

"Interplanetary saucers, if there be such and our group has nothing to do with them, does not concern The Organization. The type The Organization does not want us to know about operation atomic energy. They employ a means of converting atomic radiation into electrical energy, and they operate by means of this combination, which, of course, represents an entirely new and previously unknown type of propulsion. These machines vary in size from about two to thirty feet in diameter. And there aren't any little green men in them; they are remotely controlled. That's why they can perform the so-called impossible maneuvers which would kill a pilot with the G-forces involved.

"What I'm going to tell you next is not the big secret, but it has to be dealt with carefully because it is a part of the big secret."

"Why," I interjected, "is it a big secret—fear of panic as is often claimed?"

"Yes and no. And politics. A test was recently run in a small town wherein the residents were led to believe that flying saucers were real and were, as I recall, from some mythical unknown planet hidden behind the moon. The citizens were fearful, all right, but not overly-alarmed. A poll taken by evaluators proved, for one thing, that their politics had become more conservatively oriented, and surveys showed more ordering of flying saucer literature from the occult book distributors. The people did some minor hoarding. You won't believe this but many people set up souvenir stands, whether to sell stuff to the space people or to possible tourists, we don't know. Otherwise, the town remained pretty normal. In other words, the old panic argument is not a good one."

Bob added a little more mixer to the half-consumed drink and asked me if I had heard of the scare which citizens of a large midwestern town (not a city) experienced as a result of rumors about an atomic pile running out of control. I hadn't.

"Stories were taken out of the paper after an early edition. Actually the pile hadn't run away at all. But there were rumors that radiation had raised in the vicinity and as a precaution CD leaders urged citizens to go to their basements. There was widespread panic, looting, all that bit. I could show you this private study our group made, but I don't have it along."

"But what of this Antarctica business? Who is responsible for these saucers anyhow?" I asked, impatiently. His story was beginning to make a little sense and he began to sound less and less like a crackpot.

"Bob" then pulled a small book from his briefcase. It was titled "Agartha" by a Buddhist lama named Robert Dickhoff. Then he looked at my library shelf and exclaimed, "Oh I see you don't have this. . .work."

I took it from his manner that he was being facetious.

"There is an occult tradition that the inside of the earth is inhabited. This finds expression in tales of Rainbow City, the Dero Hell, giants in the earth, and all of that. Of course occult tradition always contains some truth, but greatly distorted from reality.

"Do you remember the Admiral Byrd story?" he continued.

"Oh yes, something. About his flying over an uncharted territory and finding warm climate. Is there really something to this?"

(Later Ray Palmer would publish the Admiral Byrd legend in his magazine, *Flying Saucers*, and it would arouse much controversy)

"A bit, yes, but this was greatly distorted. First of all, to my knowledge it didn't appear in any of the news media, but facts have a way of leaking out as scuttlebutt. The fact is that on a certain flight Byrd did find all his charts confused. The temperature suddenly rose and he found himself flying in darkness. It was probably miraculous that he got out of this alive ."

"You mean he flew into the center of the earth?"

"Of course not. What actually occurred is not fully understood. We don't really know too much about magnetism and the why of magnetic fields. It seems that the same phenomena which make our compasses work create a magnetic field distortion somewhere near the geographic south pole. It seems that somebody entering this field would first find himself in total darkness. Then, if he knew how to navigate the field, he would find himself in recognizable form of reality that would not be like our own. It is at the other side of this distortion field that the saucers originate."

My credulity momentarily decreased. This man was getting on the "4-D" kick, and that in my book was madness.

"You mean this mat and demat business?"

"You've been reading too much nut literature," the man replied.

"But suffice it to say there is a barrier there, which can be controlled or passed through with the correct technical know-how. Just what is on the other side nobody can be quite sure of. But the saucers originate there.

"Behind this field is a race of people civilized beyond all of our dreams. It is a very old race, about which there are many theories, which are not important to go into here, for if you published it, you would really sound way out."

The man suddenly rose. I looked at my watch. Although I have greatly condensed the conversation in the foregoing pages, I noted that he had talked exactly one hour.

"Hey," I remonstrated, "Why some silly rule about an hour when you're just started !"

He smiled. "I've given you all the keys. Let's see what you come up with."

"But you left out the real key. Sure, you say the saucers are from Antarctica, maybe a few from Mars and what not, but you haven't told me why they don't contact Earth people, what they are doing here. . ."

"You're trying to say that I didn't tell you the WHY of saucers. You see, the origin of saucers bothers nobody. People only set up concessions stands to sell the space people rebel flags. You have a great point there, Jim, and I want to see if you can come up with the rest of it. Call this a psychological experiment. Call it a hoax, call me a Commie, anything. But I think you're convinced that it is the WHY of saucers that is important."

He finished off the drink, visited the bathroom and walked out with the renewed promise he'd contact me within two weeks.

As soon as he was out of the room, I ran to the window for I was suddenly consumed with a curiosity about the man who had visited me.

A large black Cadillac had pulled up near the entrance to the apartment building and a man, presumably a chauffeur, waited inside. Soon my friend Bob, appeared, the chauffeur got out, opened the door for him, and took a large brown suitcase from him and placed it in the trunk. They soon drove off. I'm sure this has no significance, but the man had no suitcase with him when he visited me. It probably contained some data he had thought about bringing in and had probably left outside the door. I'm sure the man didn't live in our apartment building for I have checked this out.

"Bob" left me in a really puzzled position. The import of it all, in fact, wouldn't hit me until a few days later, after I had published the following announcement in the October, 1954, issue of **Nexus**.

The information I have discussed so far is a matter of public record. However, just before this issue of **Nexus** went to press, I received irrefutable documented evidence which fully confirms these ideas.

". . .It is now too late to assemble this startling data for this present issue, but it will be presented in full in the November issue."

From my conversation with the visitor I had concluded, somewhat incorrectly, that if I wrote up the interview accurately, on his next visit he would reveal the rest of the mystery when he brought the photographs for me. Over the next two days, therefore, I did not concentrate on figuring out what the why of saucers might be, but on preparing an accurate report. I came up with fifteen pages, which I condensed to three, to fit into the limited format.

I had not expected another visit until two weeks later, the promised date for the delivery of the photographs. But just one week, to the day, the following Monday, my telephone rang at 11:00 A.M.

"Hi, buddy. Three guesses." The midwestern voice was unmistakable.

"Bob!"

"Right!"

"Did you bring the cup to go with the saucer?" I asked, as a disguised question about the expected photographs.

"Well. . .not exactly. Say, Jim. I called to see if you were there. I have to see you, buddy."

I told him to give me fifteen minutes to get dressed, for I had overslept. He said he was in Manhattan and that it would be a little longer than that.

When Bob arrived he appeared tense and morose. Since he carried nothing with him, I knew he had not brought the photos. I had entertained the suspicion that I would never see them again.

'Jim," he began. "I'm about to welch on the deal. I don't want you to print the article." I had started to hand it to him to inspect. He did not proffer his hand to take it.

"My conduct was inexcusable; you are under no obligation to kill your article. I can say that the article would get me into trouble. It probably would make you a laughing stock anyhow, if you did run it."

I did a real double take.

"Gee, thanks!" I exclaimed. I've already printed the issue in which I say I'll reveal the whole bit next issue. What will my readers think of me?"

"Jim, you do have a real problem. If I stuck my neck out again to help you solve it, I'd probably make the situation a whole lot worse."

"But why did you change your mind about the photos?"

"Believe me, Jim. The thing wouldn't be any good for you either."

I was getting hot under the collar, though I knew I would not use the material from my own volition, since he insisted on it. I still remembered the rules of ethics in journalism.

"You gave me this crackpot theory and got me half way to believing it. I published this notice in *Nexus*, and if I don't come up with something the readers will think I made up the whole thing trying to imitate Al Bender for publicity purposes."

"So you'll get publicity. But I'm sorry you'll have to get it this way."

"Let me get this straight now. You're not saying I can't print this but that it's simply off the record. Right?"

"Right," Bob said.

"O.K. It's killed. But I'll print anything I already knew before your first visit, and I'll have to find some way to get out from under the announcement I made. This is only a saucer magazine but somehow to me, it does represent the Fourth Estate and I'm serious about it."

4:00

"THE SOLUTION TO THE FLYING SAUCER MYSTERY"

Regardless of what I personally thought about Gray Barker's book, *They Knew Too Much About Flying Saucers*, and the hard time Yonah and I were giving the author on the Long John Show that night, it had been one of the two books which had affected greatly my direction in UFO research during the next few years after their publication.

The other book was *The Report On Unidentified Flying Objects*, by the late Edward J. Ruppelt, who had been head of Project Blue Book at Wright-Patterson. (Doubleday and Co., Inc., Garden City, N.Y., 1956. Now out of print but copies available from *Saucerian Books* at $5.95.)

As soon as I had read the Ruppelt book I had suspicion that it had been set up. A personal interview with Ruppelt and a hastily improvised sequel to his book brought out four years later would tend to strengthen those suspicions.

I looked across microphones to observe Barker as he defended his book and his position on the *Saucer News* article. He looked and sounded too sincere to be a conscious tool of any government pressure. I also had gotten to know him personally, and many conversations with him had also convinced me that, though a bit too credulous with the wild claims he published, here was a man tremendously enthusiastic about solving the flying saucer mystery, as it had grown to be called, though a man who sometimes let his enthusiasm get away with him.

His theory that flying saucer researchers had been silenced, combined with my own deliberate suppression of the promised article, convinced many people that I, also, had been hushed by the three men in black.

Long John's impish business about the spelling of my name on my apartment directory, Barker's digging out the letter "proving" my tenure in the air force, and the veiled suggestions that I was in the pay of the Silence Group (a term coined by Maj. Donald E. Keyhoe in his books), were all echoes of public reaction after Barker's book hit the stores.

The book had been tremendously popular, both in sales and reader acceptance. Some people claimed they had become terrified and couldn't sleep after reading it, but nevertheless went about buying copies for friends. People wrote me after reading it, accusing me of being a member of the air force, the Silence Group, and the CIA.

If I could at all believe in the part of the book outlining the visit to Bender by the Three Men, it was in the framework of a possible hoax. Lonzo Dove's *Saucer News* which we were discussing suggested this idea, though it went much too far. If a hoax, Barker had been drawn into it also and was an innocent victim.

When Bob had visited me with his fascinating photographs, and for a year or two afterward, I entertained seriously the idea that he had been a government agent, whether with the military or some civilian intelligence group. That was one of the reasons I had clammed up about the matter and had not even discussed it with colleagues in UFO research. Regardless of how much I wanted to print everything I knew, I was still patriotic, whether or not government policies were realistic or right.

Then came the realization, especially after the publication of Barker's Book, that I had been the victim of a hoax, as Bender might have been. I had often discussed possible hoaxes with Barker. Although he agreed there was some possibility, and that Bender could no doubt have been fooled, still he couldn't find the motivation for such actions, regardless of how he racked his brain.

The part of Ruppelt's book which had impressed me most was the chapter titled "*The Radiation Story*," pages 263-264. This was strangely similar to the ideas which Bob had expressed in our strange interview.

Bob had given me a really wild story, though with fairly good detail, about an Antarctic origin for saucers. The gist of his conversation also gave me the impression that he believed that the public would not panic if they heard that flying saucers were real, but that there was a great potential danger of panic which might result from a rumor or announcement about serious radiation threats (i.e. his example, whether fabricated or real, about the two towns and their reactions to rumors of both saucers and radiation). Ruppelt's narrative strangely tied in. In the chapter mentioned above, Ruppelt repeated 'Bob's' story, almost word for word, as to how several teams of highly qualified scientists proved that the background radiation content of the atmosphere increased sharply on several occasions at the same time a flying saucer was observed visually in the vicinity of the radiation measuring equipment.

Although I had promised Bob I would not reveal his information, I was severely tempted to break my word in the light of Ruppelt's printing some of the same information.

Even then, more than a year later, readers and friends were still pressuring me to tell what I had found out.

I had really found out nothing which was definite, though Bob had given me some ideas which nagged at the back of my mind. I might have come up with some clue to the saucer mystery, though a very small part of it.

I don't know if I made the right decision, but anyhow I decided to do something about it. If I created and published an article purporting to tell what I knew it probably would accomplish two purposes. It would get the public off my back and would serve as a trial balloon to determine whether I had something or not. If Bob had been a government representative, such an article likely would bring some reaction and I might have at least some indication of the validity of these theories.

Even today, I still believe that one vital clue to the origin and propulsion of saucers is the radiation that is associated with them, though certainly not necessarily within the framework of the article I published.

In preparing the article I took a far-out premise.

Many researchers and saucer enthusiasts who had been concerned about the radiation accompanying saucers, had been confusing cause and effect. Maybe saucers didn't cause radiation, but radiation, in some round about way, caused saucers!

What if saucers really did originate at the South Pole, either based there from an interplanetary or intergalactic source to escape detection, or built by some fantastic dero-ish or Rainbow City race there? What if their main concern was the dangerous radiation caused by our bomb tests? They might be measuring the ever-increasing radiation or trying to nullify it.

True, the theory was fantastic and possibly crackpot, but it also sounded as sensible as many of the others which had been advanced.

Dr. D. had told me that the scientific community, at the request of the government, was deliberately playing down the radiation dangers. The serious problem of the increasing radiation was confirmed by President John F. Kennedy, after he had successfully negotiated a nuclear test ban with the Soviet Union and other nations.

But what if Bob were correct, and that public knowledge of the seriousness of the radiation danger would cause panic? I should tread on this subject with caution. I therefore decided that it would be expedient to partially deceive my readers. Whether I did right or wrong will not be known until more progress is made toward a final solution of the saucer mystery.

Let me say that I still believe that the article, titled "*The Solution to the Flying Saucer Mystery*," which appeared in the June-July, 1956, issue of *Saucer News*, did contain a great deal of fact, though disguised.

In commenting on the chapter in Ruppelt's book, I told my readers, "I can tell you that this radiation clue is correct, and very important.

Ruppelt does not know it, but the type of saucers that the Government particularly does not want us to know about, run on atomic energy, and they operate by means of this combination, which, of course, represents an entirely new and previously unknown type of propulsion. They vary in size from about 6 to 30 feet in diameter, and they are remotely controlled, as a human being probably could not survive in these highly radioactive machines.

Research on this type of saucer was being done as early as 1946, and its startlingly advanced design and performance represents an improvement over earlier experimental saucer-shaped aircraft. These saucers are capable of speeds in excess of 4,000 miles per hour, and are also capable of hovering, changing course abruptly, and all the other performance characteristics that are usually attributed to saucers.

Then, switching what I had been told of Antarctica to a U.S. location, I stated, "This type of saucer operates from a supersecret underground base in one of our Southwestern states, and is being sent out over the country from there, and overseas, as well.

The whole project is so highly classified that ordinary military pilots and even the air force's saucer investigators on Project Blue Book could not possibly know about it. In fact, this type of saucer is not built by the American government as we ordinarily understand the word *government*. As fantastic as this may sound to you, these saucers are actually built, operated, and maintained by an organization which is entirely separate from the military and political branches of the Government that we know about. Although a handful of people at the very top of the Government know about the existence of this project, they have no direct connection with it. In the remainder of this article, I shall call this secret project "*The Organization*."

The main reason for the fantastic secrecy surrounding this project is not because of the new type of propulsion involved. The key to the saucer riddle is not what are the saucers, but the purpose for their operation. People naturally wonder why, if the saucers are American devices—why are they sent up over cities and other areas where people can see them, and where they would supposedly endanger civilian lives if they crashed or went out of control. The reason is that "The Organization" has no choice in the matter. These saucers were originally designed to test, in machines capable of very high speeds, the heat resistance of the metals that would later be used in the construction of larger rocket-shaped craft that would travel at lower speeds within our atmosphere, and which would use another, less dangerous system of power. But these cigar-shaped craft are another story, outside the scope of this article. The important fact is that the saucers, originally built primarily for the purpose stated above, were found to be far more vital for another purpose: that of absorbing excess radioactivity in our atmosphere.

This is the service they are now performing, and this is why the people of the United States have not been told about the very existence of the saucers, for "The Organization" could not tell us without revealing the fearful purpose that these machines are serving. The truth is that one or more of our secret tests involving atomic energy got decidedly out of hand. The atmosphere has been polluted to a dangerous and alarming degree. (In considering the above statement, please remember that not all atomic tests involve bombs; there are others which do not have anything to do with bombs.)

The saucers run on a small atomic plant. As they pass through or hover in a given area, they absorb radiation from the atmosphere. This they convert into what I will call, for lack of a better technical term, electrical energy. (I do not feel it necessary or advisable to go into technical details on this.) Thus, when a dangerously radioactive cloud is over a certain area, one or more saucers are sent to that area for the specific purpose of absorbing this excess. If the cloud happens to be over a populated area, there is all the more reason to proceed with the job of decontaminating it. If the cloud is over a foreign country, there is as much reason to absorb its excess radioactivity as if it were over the United States.

The saucers cannot absorb all the radioactivity in a given area, but they can reduce it to below the dangerous level. After a given flight, they return to their base for servicing; but at times it occurs that a saucer becomes "saturated" with radioactivity and is too dangerous even to return to the base. If this happens, then it is sent out over the ocean and directed down into the sea, at one of the deepest parts of the ocean. Thus the rate of replacement of these craft is fairly high. However, their cost of operation is extremely low, and their range and power supply are practically limitless. By their construction, no saucer of this type can land or come closer than a few feet to the ground; nor can one crash on the ground even if it should go out of control. An automatic destruction mechanism causes it to disintegrate in flight if necessary. Similarly, a device which for want of a better term shall call "reverse radar" prevents them from crashing into objects to which they fly near, such as airplanes. During flight, these saucers operate partly by remote guidance, and partly by an extremely complex system of automatic devices within the machine itself.

These saucers make very little noise in flight, because they ionize the air in front of them, and minimize air friction as they fly along. Because of their electrical nature, they glow in the dark, and when photographed in daylight they do not show a sharply defined outline. Because of the fact that they overload the atmosphere with electricity, they are the cause of many thunderstorms, and of much of the unusually perverse weather we have had during the past few years. They are usually flown over populated areas at night if possible, and "The Organization" is happiest when they are not seen often or from close range. However, the purpose they serve is so important that it is merely a "calculated risk" if the saucers occasionally cause an air accident or a mild panic-as in the summer of 1952, when the necessity of having saucers fly over Washington D.C. caused an unusually high amount of speculation as to their nature. But anything is preferable to allowing this radiation to go unchecked.

"The Organization" knows the panic that would follow if the public were to realize the fact that the atmosphere is dangerously contaminated. Perhaps damage too great to undo has already been done, or possibly this radiation is still out of control, and will continue to get worse until or unless some new and better method is invented to cope with it. I believe that the saddest thing of all is that all this has been going on: the pollution of the atmosphere and the attempted control of this pollution by the saucers, without the public knowing anything about it. This shows just how far the people have lost touch with the technical advances of our Nation. While the battle for our survival against radiation poisoning is going on secretly in the skies above us, we continue to maintain our Economy by building almost as many conventionally propelled aircraft as ever; those we all read about and see overhead every day. And the public is never the wiser!

Even the nation's top rocket experts seem to have been kept in the dark about saucers in the early days, until it became necessary for them to know about them. I said earlier in this article that the saucers were originally designed to make tests that would eventually lead to the construction of large rocket-shaped craft. Some of these larger craft have already been constructed. Willy Ley, one of the world's outstanding authorities on rockets, stated publicly on April 7, 1950, that his personal opinion is that the saucers are a United States military secret. But on April 22, 1956, the same Willy Ley stated that he is convinced that "nothing is being suppressed by the Air Force except the names and addresses of the multitudes reporting saucers." In other words, he no longer claims to believe that saucers are U.S. made. Why is it that, of recent years, every top scientist or engineer who has made a public statement of saucers either claims to believe they do not exist, or that they are extraterrestrial? Why do they not suggest or even consider the "Earth Theory" in public anymore? Are these men being sincere, or are they covering up something of vital importance to all of us?

In closing, I wish to point out that I do not claim to have discussed all flying saucers in this article. There are other unconventional craft being built by this country for other purposes. Some of these are saucer-shaped and some cigar-shaped, and quite a few are piloted. There are also unidentified flying objects, which have been seen for many, many years, and perhaps even for centuries. These latter may or may not include spaceships from other planets. What I have discussed in this article is the type of saucer which is the cause of all the secrecy. It is this type, and its purpose, that 'The Organization' does not want you to know about.

In short, this type is the 'key' to the saucer mystery.

Reaction by readers to the above article were unexpected, and definite. They not only disliked and disbelieved the article, but more and more expressed their belief that I was a secret AF of CIA agent, trying to lead them away from the truth.

Not wishing to back down from my article, and still not wishing to reveal just why I had written it, I continued to employ subterfuge as the editorial policy of **Saucer News** continued to emphasize what came to be widely referred to in the UFO press as **Moseley's Earth Theory**.

There probably is still a minor part of my Earth Theory which I developed over the years in **Saucer News** which may be of some value to UFO research. I am also convinced that the ideas to be found in the many articles on this subject represent only a small part of the total UFO mystery.

My confidence in the Earth Theory and my cynicism about hush-ups began to crumble one night on the Long John show. It started with a telephone call and ended in near panic.

4:30

HUSH-UP!

Some day I may actually ask Long John just what happened on his show that morning.

Probably it wouldn't be fair. I doubt if he would give me the answers anyhow. He probably knows, more than I and the other panel members know, what actually happened. But I doubt if he knows everything involved.

It almost seems that somewhere there is a shadowy Establishment, or Entrenchment, which would like to keep the saucer mystery, just as it is today—unsolved. But in its zeal this Establishment does not always handle things wisely. It is probably bogged down with red tape, with its own weight and incompetent representatives who do not understand psychology.

I think it slipped up on that particular morning.

Long John had been obviously enjoying the leg-pulling I had been taking as a result of the misspelling of my name and the boondoggled air force letter. One of the panel members, however, seemed to be taking this with a seriousness inappropriate to the mood of the discussion.

As a result the show once more got around to my possible involvement as a former member of the air force or as a secret government agent.

As we talked Long John had moved back from his microphone, turned his face aside, and was whispering into the telephone, as he often did when he conferred with the producer and others in the control room. Since this was such a routine action, I did not notice any particular facial reaction or mood he may have expressed during his conversation. I only know that he was on the intercom phone before he interrupted our conversation:

"I think, gentlemen," John abruptly told us, "it would be advisable at this point if we forget the air force letter. We'll just drop this completely."

One of the panel members objected to the decision and persisted in the same line of questioning.

"Would you do me a favor, Ben?" John's voice had taken a strange tone. He was either frightened, or angry. His fingers tensed where he held the next commercial. He was disguising his feelings but I could tell one thing: Long John was shaken.

The shocked panel member had turned to John.

"Let's drop the subject!"

There was such firmness in John's voice that the studio immediately became deathly quiet, except for the subliminal sound of the subject dropping like a ton of bricks.

Yonah was the first to collect his wits and change the subject. He asked Barker a question.

I was still stunned. I wondered what was going on. If I was certain of nothing else I knew that if the audio had conveyed the happening realistically to the listener that I would no longer be able to convince anybody that I was not an agent of some kind.

If somebody or some organization was stopping the questioning of myself, it certainly was without my own knowledge or participation. In fact, I had been rather enjoying playing the man of mystery.

I had even confused Capt. Edward J. Ruppelt himself, still without intention or saucers aforethought.

Shortly after his book had come out I visited him in California where he lived. I had learned of his whereabouts from a television producer and rang him up. He seemed affable and quite willing to talk with me. But my first impression of Ruppelt, aside from his intelligence and pleasant personality was the suspicion that he seemed to entertain of me and which he couldn't completely hide. I got the distinct impression that Ruppelt, himself, former head of Project Bluebook, and titular leader of the official Air Force party line, thought I was an agent who had come to checkup on him!

After a while Ruppelt must have at least partially abandoned this mistrust, for he opened up somewhat and I must say that I was amazed at what he told me.

Not that he gave me any secret information. I am now convinced that practically everything Ruppelt really knew about saucers was contained in his book.

THE ASTOUNDING UFO SECRETS OF JAMES W. MOSELEY

Since there was a great deal in the conversation which was either personal or off the record, let me get over this particular subject by saying that my main impression of Ruppelt was that he was an ardent saucer believer! Whether his book—one of the most sensible and definitive in its area ever published—was heavily edited, or whether he had the good sense to tone down his own beliefs, I don't know.

The most amazing thing about his enthusiasm was his great interest in contactees. After his initial mistrust of me abated, I spent most of our interview not asking him questions, but giving him data I had collected on the contactees and especially on the little men.

I was well equipped to brief Ruppelt on the "little men," for though they bordered on the "contactee" area which I disbelieved and mistrusted, the subject to me had always been a fascinating one. To me it seemed pretty logical that if, indeed, saucers were interplanetary, the creatures or people piloting them might be very unlike Earth people. In fact they likely would appear quite grotesque.

One of my most interesting cases on file involved a twelve-year-old boy who lived in Coldwater, Kansas, who maintained he saw a strange looking little man climb out of a flying saucer in a corn field.

"I was on our farm, sitting on the tractor," John Jacob Sqaim told an investigator for *Nexus*, "when suddenly I saw him, about twenty feet away. He stood right there, a little fellow about the size of a 5-year-old child. He had long, pointed ears and a pointed nose. He was sort of crouching, looking at me. Then he ran—or maybe *flew*—to the saucer."

Until then the boy hadn't seen the saucer, which was hidden behind a terrace. It was hanging about five feet from the ground. Then the little man jumped into a door and the saucer took off.

"It went awfully fast—so fast that compared to it, a jet would seem like a turtle."

The boy's father said that he questioned the boy closely and then called the sheriff, who advised the family to stay away from the scene, and found weird, pear-shaped footprints there. It was the sheriff's opinion that the boy might have been deluded as to seeing the saucer—but he could not explain the mysterious footprints.

Meanwhile, one saucer that didn't land, but made a dramatic enough story just being in the air, was reported in Lisbon, Portugal by a landowner named Cesar Feriera. This man had seen not a flying saucer, but a flying cup, complete with "two eight-foot giants clad in pocketless metallic suits."

A "little man" saucer landing scare pervaded France. In Quarouble a steelworker claimed that a small flying saucer paid him a visit and that two armless men in space helmets came out for a look around. When he ran out of his house for a closer look, a bright light seemed to paralyze him, and the strange machine made a clean getaway.

The steelworker, Maurice DeWilde, had been reading a book in his kitchen when his dog became aware of the visitors and began to bark. The Frenchman then peered out the window and saw a "black mass" on a nearby railway line. When he hurriedly flicked on his flashlight, he saw two little creatures about three feet tall.

The little men had wide shoulders, normal legs, but no arms; and each had something that looked like a space helmet on his head. When DeWilde ran toward them, a bright green light from the machine temporarily blinded him.

He described the saucer to police as shaped like a cake cover, about eighteen feet in diameter.

Suddenly the object rose, with a cloud of black smoke hissing from it. Police found marks where the saucer had landed.

As I took out a large envelope containing the first mailing from a foreign press clipping service to which I had recently subscribed, I could see that Ruppelt was impressed. I did not mention to him the large fee I had paid for the service, which indicated that the landing "flap" had certainly hit its peak in Europe, unequalled since the concentration during 1952 in this country!

From Belgium, Spain, Portugal, England, France, Norway and Austria the clipping service had dug up strange reports.

In Muenster, Germany, a movie projectionist, Franz Hoge, told the news agency DPA that he saw a saucer land and peculiarly-shaped creatures get out of it. They were only three and a half feet tall, and wore rubber-like clothing.

From Castelibranco, Portugal came the story of four men who saw two tall aluminum-clad figures emerge from a grounded saucer. The saucermen picked flowers, collected twigs and shrubs, as if gathering scientific information.

Not only were the odd beings scientific, but hospitable as well, for they invited, by means of gestures, the observers to come aboard their ship to look inside it. When their invitation was, somewhat understandably, declined, the creatures boarded their craft and took off vertically at unbelievable speed.

A mail carrier in the Belgium village of Hmy, spotted a saucer near the ground, and claimed to have seen two silhouettes, "roughly human in shape," aboard the machine.

THE ASTOUNDING UFO SECRETS OF JAMES W. MOSELEY

From Chatterlerault, France, came the story of Yves David, who said his arm was caressed by a little creature dressed in a space suit and who talked unintelligibly, paralyzed him with a green ray, and then ran off to his saucer.

In Bugeat, France, Antoine Mazaud had a similar experience, with a man described as "normal looking," who came up to him, kissed him, mumbled unintelligible words, and then retreated to his saucer (about 10 feet long and cigar shaped).

Also from France was a report by a Madame Leboeuf, of Drome, who said that a man in a "plastic outfit" come toward her and frightened her. As she ran in fright he took off vertically in his craft. The machine sounded like a musical top as it left, she reported.

One of the clippings, from Perpigan, France, told how a retired French custom official saw a saucer land and a tall man, dressed in a diver's suit, step out. The Frenchman, Damien Sigueres, described the saucer as a large red sphere. Suddenly the saucerian saw Sigueres' two dogs and hastily retreated into the machine. Another attitude was expressed by two other saucerians, who petted a Monsieur Garrau's dog. These two men were dressed in Khaki.

So far the creatures had either said nothing or used strange language, but in Perpigan, France, it seemed that the strange visitors had mastered at least a smattering of the language, and even employed terrestrial fuels in their machines. A railroad worker discovered a saucer pilot next to a Diesel oil tank, and asked the spaceman, who was either covered with hair or was wearing a long, hairy overcoat, what he wanted. Although the man's language was incomprehensible to the Frenchman, he distinctly picked out the word, "gasoil."

The story had it that the workman ran off to report the incident to the stationmaster—we don't know whether it was to get permission to sell the man some "gasoil" but suspect that it was due to fright—but before he had gone 100 yards, the strange machine took off and vanished.

In general, Frenchmen were taking the reports very seriously and near panic was said to have pervaded some provinces. It may have been just Gallic humor, but the mayor of the village of Chateau Neuf-du-Pape issued a decree forbidding flying saucers to land, and ordered the local constable to impound any which disobeyed. The decree stated that such strange aircraft "would be of a nature to disturb public order and the tranquility of the inhabitants," most certainly an understatement!

An innkeeper in Brittany placed an advertisement in his local paper, offering $35,000 to anyone who would bring him a Martian alive. I had no follow-up to this story, but presumed it was as unsuccessful as my own publicly announced $1,000 reward to anybody who could provide me with "concrete, material proof that flying saucers are visiting Earth from other planets."

Another saucerman managed to mumble something that at least sounded intelligent, to wit, "I'll be seeing you," to Jean Narcy, a road mender of Haute-Marne, France. The man was riding to work on his bicycle when he spotted a little whiskered man in a wheat field just under four feet tall. After saying this goodbye, the man got in his saucer and took off with a buzzing sound.

A Breton baker, a Monsieur Pierre-Lucas, said that a Martian had asked him for a light, but didn't remember what language he used.

But one of the weirdest Martians was the one who stopped Roger Barrault near the town of Lavous. The creature had brilliant eyes, an enormous mustache, wore rubbers and spoke Latin.

But that was not as marvelous as the sight a traveling salesman witnessed in the Cotes-du-Nord district: a deep rose colored flying saucer from which stepped a zebra-striped man. As he alighted, he changed color, chameleon-like, from yellow to green!

Another packet of clippings contained numerous French landing reports: In Vron two youths stumbled across a flying saucer as they returned from work. "Strange little men" were clustered around it, but as soon as the youths drew near, the little men hurried back inside and the saucer took off.

A "moon-shaped" machine, a new configuration in the French landings, touched down near Lusignac; at Poncey-sur-Lignon, a small village near Dijon, a saucer landed and left strange markings on the ground. The markings were examined by the entire village, and photographed. Another landing, at Diges, was witnessed by Gisele Finns, a fifteen-year-old farm girl, who said "the pilot looked just like men who live around here." Some children at Sainte Claude watched the landing of a saucer "of such a vivid color that it looked like the metal was burning up." They described the occupant as looking "like a giant lump of sugar."

Two inhabitants of Lezignan saw a disc thirty feet in diameter land in a field between the villages of Lagrasse and Aude. When they approached it, the machine flashed a blinding light on them, and made the usual getaway. In Megrit, a farmer named Henri Lehrisse saw a small machine only one yard in diameter in his courtyard. Inside were two human forms, which looked like children.

I had rather definitely come to a negative conclusion on the so-called "contactees," I told Ruppelt. As Long John would put it, I certainly didn't "buy" them.

Some of the little men sightings, I pointed out, were just as suspect. For example, one report had two Frenchmen seeing two strange little creatures standing next to a saucer-shaped machine. At first something about the clipping seemed to strike me, but it wasn't until I had read it several times that I discovered that, translated into English, the name of the man telling of the adventure was "Blind", the name of the man who allegedly saw the saucer translated was "Liar"; and the place where the incident occurred was "House of Liars."

Another Frenchman, a restaurant proprietor, reported that while motorcycling between the towns of Toulon and Heyeres, he saw a man who stepped out of a saucer, and asked him, "Are you a Martian;"—to which the man, dressed in overalls, replied, "No, I am French. Where am I?"

Although many of the 'little men" reports were obviously full of hot air, the multitude of them contained some logic.

Many of the little men seemed merely to be carrying out scientific investigations, such as gathering samples of soil, vegetation and so on. They seemed generally to avoid contact with "natives," as our own astronauts might, should they land on Mars and find intelligent creatures there—at least until they found that the Martians harbored no dangerous germs.

I told Ruppelt of my investigation of one similar incident, though it didn't involve a little man, but a monstrous looking "Head man" and despite the fact that I had to suggest it was a hoax to get permission to publish the picture I think it is a pretty good case, considering the caliber of the witnesses involved.

I still can't give the names of the witnesses; suffice it to say that they were members of a certain South American embassy returning to their own country for a vacation at home.

Five of these people told me that shortly out of Miami a gleaming disc shaped object approached their plane and flew alongside, at very close range. The pilot, in a shaky voice, got on the intercom and advised the passengers there was an unidentified flying object flying close to the port side, but to "not be alarmed," because that in the past such objects had not shown hostility.

"I don't want to try to get away from it for it's too close to our wing and I'm afraid to maneuver. I'm sure it will soon go away after looking at us for a while.

"Meanwhile our stewardesses will give you a cup of coffee to go with the flying saucer, if you like," he continued, apparently hoping that a bit of humor would ease the fear and curiosity of the passengers.

The five people were seated in the same area, directly opposite the saucer. People were straining to see the thing, and the stewardess firmly told them to remain seated and to fasten their seat belts.

169

"It was a cigar-shaped object, half as long as our plane," one of the men stated. "It had no visible antenna, landing gear or anything like that, and no windows, until a large port suddenly appeared as if it were fading in like a movie scene.

"Then peering at us from the port we saw a horrifying thing, Senor Moseley. It is impossible to describe, except as you might say it was a large head or brain with terrible tentacles."

I managed to talk with all five people, in separate interviews, and all of their accounts substantially agreed. One of the witnesses did the mentioned sketch.

These people apparently had no reason to perpetrate a hoax, and had good reason to request that I withhold their names.

The postscript to this story is also strange. After the cigar-shaped craft pulled away and vanished at great speed, the pilot mentioned he would make a non-scheduled stop in Ecuador, "to pick up a diplomat of high standing."

As soon as the plane had taxied to a stop, several men in American Air Force uniforms hurried to the cockpit and met the South American pilot, engaging him in animated conversation. He accompanied them into an area other than the passenger entrance to the airport.

Several ambulances had been driven up to the landing area. As soon as the passengers embarked, a man, dressed in what apparently was a protective suit to protect him from radiation, climbed into the cockpit and taxied the plane away. The passengers were taken to the VIP lounge, an official entered and read from a paper. His spiel went something like this, as well as the witnesses could remember:

"Welcome to the——Airlines office in Ecuador. We are pleased to have you stopping here. You will soon be departing on another aircraft, since we are not equipped to refuel the aircraft you arrived in.

"During your flight I am advised you had the unique experience of seeing an experimental Russian aircraft. They are very sorry about its unauthorized approach to the plane and have cabled their apologies. The pilot will be severely reprimanded."

Ruppelt told me he had never heard of the report, but appeared to be greatly interested in it. He pointed out, and logically, that a helmeted pilot, with goggles and oxygen apparatus which may not have been seen too clearly through the port, could have been misinterpreted by nervous passengers. They certainly had a right to be nervous, I agreed, during such a close approach of another aircraft, whether terrestrial or UFO. The porthole could have appeared suddenly, having been unseen due to reflections.

But the obvious concern over radiation made the story very interesting, he admitted, regardless of who or what the "headman" was.

Ruppelt insisted that I visit him the next time I was on the West Coast, where he had taken up residence. Unfortunately I did not have an opportunity to do so, for a year or so later the former Captain, though a very young man, died of a heart attack.

Many questions, which Ruppelt could no doubt answer, remain mysteries. The chief question is why his book was revised after I talked with him, and after it had already played out, as far as sales went. A huge edition was printed but few were sold. Had the original edition been too greatly *"pro saucer" for* the AF's stomach?

* * * * *

I have pieced together what actually happened that morning on the Long John Show from three sources: a tape recording of the broadcast; my own personal remembrances, reinforced by talking with Yonah; and Gray Barker's reporting of the matter in his column, "***Chasing the Flying Saucers***," in Ray Palmer's ***Flying Saucers*** magazine, December, 1959.

The tape recording at the point of the famous cutoff has the subject of hush-ups being argued hot and heavily. Long John is addressing Gray Barker:

JOHN: Did anyone ever hush YOU up?

BARKER: No, I. . . .

JOHN: Did you mention in one of your recent magazine articles about the possibility of hushing Long John, and was it written in one of the Palmer magazines that Long John will be hushed up or.. . . .

Gray Barker's column, mentioned above, picks up the narrative at this point.

Suddenly music filled the studio as Long John jumped up angrily. For some unknown reason we had been cut off the air, and recorded music had been substituted. John ran into the control room where we could see, but not hear, his excited discussion with the engineer. The producer of the show then entered the studio and said slowly to another official, "It's serious this time."

Neither I nor the panel members were let in on what was going on. In answer to a question by Moseley, Long John replied only with, "You've seen what you have seen. I don't know any more myself."

We drew the producer aside and tried to question him.

" 'All I can say is,' he told us, 'that a voice which I knew, and knew to represent proper authority, was on the phone, and the voice ordered me to give the phone to the engineer. Let me say this—that the voice represented enough authority to be able to order the engineer to cut the program off and fill with music.'

"Then John instructed the producer how to answer all calls, especially those from regular panel members who would be calling up to find out what had gone wrong.

" 'When they call, tell them that John hasn't been feeling well all morning, that he had a slight headache, and planned to end the show an hour early and play music during the remaining time. Say that the engineer made a mistake and cut the show too early, and that I'm giving them all kinds of hell over it.'

"Then Long John cut into the music and made an announcement, stating that the program had been interrupted because of reasons beyond his control. We could sense that the staff wanted us out of there, so we left the studio and went our separate ways, after a hurried conference in the lobby, trying to figure out what had happened."

In his magazine story, Barker probably had good reason to limit his reporting of what occurred at the doorway of the lobby. In clearing the story with Long John, he had been asked to report the matter truthfully but to avoid, if possible, reporting of the public reaction which followed.

A man who evidently was one of the elevator operators was assisting a night watchman in moving a heavy packing box against the main doorway. Outside a crowd of people had gathered; evidently listeners who had been up or driving in New York at that time. Probably imagining all sorts of things that might be happening to Long John, they had come to the studio to see what they could do and to engage in loud protest. Among the people were perhaps a half dozen reporters who held up notebooks on which they had scrawled **News, Tribune, Post** and so on. But the doors were being barricaded against everybody.

Dave Field, the producer, had followed us to the lobby and became our rescuer.

Years later, in 1964, the famous night of the power failure in New York, Barker and I again ran into Dave Field when, on a mutual dare, we would enter the same studio and walk up the labyrinthine stairways to the same 24th floor, using book matches for guidance.

On the night of the "hush-up" Dave led us through a ground-floor labyrinth to a freight entrance and told us to get home as fast as we could manage.

I got my car at the parking lot two blocks away. Ordinarily I would have driven back around the front entrance of the studio to see just what was going on then, but frankly all three of us, Yonah, Barker and myself, were scared.

THE ASTOUNDING UFO SECRETS OF JAMES W. MOSELEY

What dangerous line of discussion were we pursuing or leading into at the time of the cutoff? What had we said earlier on the show which had made the Silence Group jittery?

We dropped Yonah off in Brooklyn. Barker and I continued the discussion as I drove him to his uptown hotel. Barker grew silent and I knew he was thinking, trying to figure the situation.

"I'll get some sleep, and call you this afternoon. Maybe we can come up with something then," Barker told me as I let him out.

I turned the block and headed back down town, for I had suddenly decided to drive by the studio once again to see if the crowd had dispersed.

As I neared the location I met some police cars, their red lights still blinking; two of them were paddy wagons though I could not see inside them.

Silence reigned in front of the studio. One lone cop walked slowly by the doorway.

I circled the block and headed back through Times Square, on the way to the West Side Highway and home to Fort Lee, New Jersey.

The Crossroads-of-the-World had a haggard and eerie look. The neon had gone out and dawn was breaking. Pieces of newspaper, and other debris from the previous night, flew about, whipped up by a rising wind.

I wondered if everything was as unreal as this, if there had actually been a Long John Show. I switched on the radio. The music was still there, but it was fading.

"This is Long John again, we're going to wrap it up for another morning. I'm sorry that we ran into some difficulty, and I'll be back with you. . .again. . .tonight, I hope. . ."

A staggering drunk started to step off the sidewalk in front of my car, and I screeched to a stop. He fell, staggered to his feet, then walked in sidewise motion. The man, dishevelled, had an odd look, a strange look of youth just fading away. I looked again and saw long blonde hair, like that of a prophet, falling around his shoulders. The man, obviously one of the characters that frequent Times Square, was reminiscent of the Venusians we had discussed, and probably just as far out as were they.

I backed up, swerved and passed him. The near miss had shaken me. I was tired. I had slept little the night before the show, having stayed up late discussing saucers with Barker.

The George Washington Bridge loomed in the distance, shrouded in fog. The

173

radio blanked out; an awful buzzing came through, probably due to some local electrical interference. I turned it off. Maybe we were fooling around with a dangerous subject. Maybe Bender hadn't been hoaxed. Maybe my strange visitor, Bob had been more than a hoaxter or a government agent. Maybe I should drop UFO research.

Somehow, I mused, there was something to saucers that all of our theories and collecting of sighting accounts and investigations hadn't managed to cope with. There was very much still hidden. The saucer mystery seemed to be more vastly complex than one could ever imagine.

Then, suddenly, a penetrating understanding seemed to hit me and course through all my body. For a moment I had the real solution to the flying saucer mystery! Then the complex understanding faded as soon as it had filled my mind.

"But I still have a fact!" I almost shouted to myself.

Ray Palmer claimed to have such a fact. Like Ray, I felt that the possession of this fact would enable me to more thoroughly analyze reports and theories in the UFO field.

Then I knew that despite the many unknown quantities and potentially dangerous facets of deeply exploring the UFO mystery, I would go on, hot and heavy, pursuing the elusive discs. Whatever they were, I knew they could change the course of history.

In the meantime I would reveal my fact to nobody.

THE ASTOUNDING UFO SECRETS OF JAMES W. MOSELEY

SMiles Lewis and Jim Moseley

Jim Moseley Guests On The PsiOp Radio Talk Show:

The Transcript Of Jim's 2010 Appearance, As Interviewed

By SMiles Lewis and Mack White

SMiles: Stay tuned for our guest tonight, Jim Moseley of *Saucer Smear* magazine.

[Music]

Smiles: Welcome back. This is PsiOp-Radio, Sunday, May 23, 2010, already. I'm Smiles Lewis.

Mack: And I'm Mack White.

SMiles: We have a guest tonight who is someone who I was lucky enough to meet back in 1999 in San Antonio, Texas, when the National UFO Conference was being held there in our wonderful state. Then I got the pleasure of interacting with him again a year later at the Corpus Christi National UFO Conference, again in Texas. The National UFO Conference was destined to have three in a row in the same state, but for whatever reasons, the powers that be, something happened, a strange little horrible day called September 11th, and all that was not. This individual is somebody who has been making the investigative trail for the last several decades. He's, I'd like to say, a good friend of mine, and that is Jim Moseley. Jim, are you with us?

Jim: Yes, I'm here.

SMiles: Thank you so much for joining us tonight.

Mack: Hello, Jim.

SMiles: How's the weather down there in Key West, Florida?

Jim: Oh, very nice. I was expecting your call an hour later because your letter says nine to eleven, and it's eight.

SMiles: Well, that just goes to show that the public education worked its magic on me, and I didn't get the time zones correct. I'm sorry about that.

Jim: Well, I'm here.

SMiles: Well, we're glad to have you. One of the things that I look for when I look into people who are fascinated by the UFO topic is people who appreciate not just the science of trying to prove whatever UFOs might be but somebody who can appreciate the funnier side of things, and you definitely fit the bill with regards to that, don't you?

Jim: Well, my magazine, *Saucer Smear*, is not intended to be just a joke book or anything, but it has a humorous overtone. It reflects my personality, which is even though this is a serious subject, most of the people in the UFO field take themselves too seriously, and they need to lighten up or else, you know?

SMiles: Indeed. You're somebody who I think is incredibly valuable to American history and ufological history. At the same time, I know that you've taken your share of abuse over the years from people who take themselves too seriously and didn't always appreciate a little gentle ribbing now and again. Jim, you've been at this for many decades. What really was it that got you started on the path of investigating and writing about UFO's?

Jim: Well, I was always interested in the subject when I was a kid. The flying saucer era, so called, began in 1947. I guess I was about 16 then. I don't remember specifically the Kenneth Arnold sighting that started it, or at least I didn't hear it at the time that it happened. The thing that got me going really was in 1948, Captain Thomas Mantell. That was the pilot who was chasing whatever kind of UFO it may have been up to a very high altitude. Finally, something went wrong, and his plane went out of control and fell to the ground and disintegrated over a large area. Of course, he was killed.

Some were saying that he was blown up by aliens. The whole thing, I don't think, is totally solved yet. There are always disagreements that continue through the years, but I think the most likely answer is it was a Skyhook balloon that he was chasing. That was a classified project at the time, so they wouldn't admit that it was Skyhook. I don't think he was blown up by aliens, but it was a scary concept. I think that's what finally got me really going onto this subject.

SMiles: Well, and that launched you on a long trail. How did you then make that leap to being really a journalist covering the story? Had you had any background in writing at that point?

Jim: Well, yes and no. In school, sure, but no, I had not had any actual job or anything involving writing. What happened was that there was a man long ago forgotten named Ken Krippine who I met. He was a South American explorer supposedly and had written a whole lot of articles about lost treasures and what have you, which, by the way, is another thing I'm very interested in. Anyway, he told me that if I would go around the country and do the legwork for him and interview a whole bunch of people that had had saucer experiences and so forth, then he would use that material and we would co-author a book.

So in the fall of 1953, I had some time and money and I had a car, and I made about a 6-week trip from where I lived just outside of New York City all the way down through the southeast on out to California and then coming back sort of a central route. In the course of doing that, I must have interviewed about a hundred people who had been mentioned in the early books as having had a saucer sighting or a scientist who had made some pronouncement on the subject or military people who had done such a thing as making a pronouncement, pro or con.

I brought all this stuff back to Krippine. To make a long story short, there never was a book. We fell out, and one thing or another went wrong. Finally, many, many years later, almost 50 years later, I did come out with a book in 2002 called *Shockingly Close to the Truth: Confessions of a Grave-Robbing Ufologist,* which is a strange title, but it's a strange book. That was finally the book that I have written on the subject, the only major book that I've written. All along, I have this magazine called *Saucer Smear,* which comes out about every six weeks. I've been doing that for all these years, and I'm still doing it.

SMiles: It's a great newsletter. In doing that, through its many different incarnations, it's one of the longest running saucer UFO magazines out there. Correct?

Jim: Well, actually it is the oldest. There was one in England that would have been older had it continued. The man is still there, but he doesn't put out a zine anymore. If you take all the technicalities, I am led to believe that *Smear* is the oldest UFO magazine in the country or on the planet, I guess, begun in 1954.

SMiles: Well, we've provided links on our website, on the infernal Internet that Mr. Moseley refuses to use, where folks can find his snail mail address and can send off a love offering and get on his non-subscriber list to *Saucer Smear.* I highly recommend it. It is shockingly close to the truth. The book is still available. We've provided a link online where people can go and buy a copy of *Shockingly Close to the Truth: Confessions of a Grave-Robbing Ufologist.* I was recently going back through it and re-reading so many of the wonderful informative and entertaining sections that document all the many people in the flying saucer community – the field, as you say – that you had the wonderful opportunity to meet, from the contactees whose stories of contact with space brothers seem so mystical and hard to believe and some of which we know are out and out hoaxes. Tell us about some of your experiences with those people.

Jim: Well, how would I put it? There was a series of conventions years ago at Giant Rock California, which is out on the desert in southern California. I think the nearest real town is Twenty-Nine Palms. Then you go out beyond that, and you get into the desert. There was an alleged contactee named George Van Tassel that either bought or rented some property out there. Every year from the early 50s through the end of the 60s, I think, he held an annual convention. These were huge outdoor things. People would come with their campers and so forth and stay overnight or for the weekend and commune with nature and listen to entertaining speakers on all aspects of the UFO subject. Among the many people that went to these conventions were a handful of well-known contactees who are still remembered today. In fact, Nick Redfern has a new book out that you're probably familiar with, right?

SMiles: Yeah, *The Contactees*, actually we're going to have him on in a couple of weeks.

Jim: Yeah. I contributed to the book, and he interviewed me for it. I didn't know any of them terribly well because I was on a different wavelength. They were into pure belief and philosophy and sweetness and light and so on, which is okay, but it's not science. I was really trying to get to the bottom of the subject in a nuts and bolts sort of way in that time frame. I met them now and then at these conventions. George Adamski, the most famous of the bunch, I met I believe at Giant Rock, and also I had a long interview with him at his home digs, which was also in southern California.

Then I was on the radio in New York with him at least a couple of times a few years later. So I got to know him fairly well. It was an interesting aspect of the subject. It's interesting, too, that that type of thing has ceased. We have the grays and the abductions and all kinds of things now, but we don't have these benign space people who come looking very much like us and giving us messages of sweetness and light like these contactees allegedly had happen to them. It's a new era, and that kind of thing isn't happening anymore, and I'm not sure why.

SMiles: I remember demonologist, ufologist, Fortean, whatever you want to call him, John Keel, whom you also met back in the day. He was often talking about what he called the silent contactees. He felt that there were a lot of people who had had these really strange encounters but who never actually promoted themselves or even ever reported it to anybody and that there may in fact be this kind of mass of people who are experiencing contact. I think to some degree that's still true today, but you're right. There's no real movement. There's no real – like these conventions.

There are still always going to be New Age conventions where people are marketing crystals and alternative therapy, some of which I think are valid and interesting and important to be investigated. Often, as you say, so much involve philosophical belief systems. Besides the contactees, you also were meeting the movers and shakers who, like yourself, were trying to look for scientific evidence for these phenomena, including all these different organizations that sprouted up during the height of the flying saucer era. Can you tell us about the rise of these groups like NICAP and CUFOS?

Jim: Well, NICAP was started by someone named Townsend Brown, who was a shadowy figure about whom I know very little. That was, I think, in 1956. It was quickly taken over by Major Donald Keyhoe, who had already written articles and at least one book on the subject of flying saucers. They were trying to be strictly scientific. They abhorred the contactees and wouldn't have anything to do with them.

Funny enough, they also were not interested in the stories which were more believable, the stories of little men without any philosophy to impart to anyone but just little men and their craft that were seen in various places in Europe and less so in this country but in South America. In the early 50s, there were lots of stories like that. I always felt, well, NICAP was willing to let the saucer get close or even land, but if anybody got out of it, then that was the end of it, and they tossed the thing away.

What I'm saying is they had their parameters of what they were willing to consider or believe. The other big thing about them was that they thought that the Air Force had the key to the solution to the whole thing, and their main objective was to badger the Air Force into giving out more information. Of course, that kind of thinking continues. That's controversial in itself because in my opinion – I being a conservative – I don't think the government knows a whole lot more about real UFOs than we do. Certainly, they know something more about them but not enough to solve the mystery. Since Keyhoe got so fixated, you might say, on this one thing about the Air Force, some of his followers broke away and different things went wrong. Eventually, NICAP folded a few years later. Then we had the beginning of MUFON, which is the big thing for the last 30 years or so.

SMiles: Right, and to a lesser extent, organizations like CUFOS, the Center for UFO Studies, which seemed in some ways to have more of an air of scientific respectability.

THE ASTOUNDING UFO SECRETS OF JAMES W. MOSELEY

Jim: Oh, yes, yes.

SMiles: But they never quite attained, as you said, the size or scope of groups like MUFON, which at one time had thousands of subscribers. Nowadays, I think it's a very small percentage of that. You too, you've watched readership wax and wane over the years. Part of your involvement in the scene was starting the National UFO Conference.

Jim: Yes. I wasn't really the founder of it, but it began in 1964, and I became the head of it a few years later. The biggest thing that we ever did was in 1967 we had the largest indoor flying saucer convention that's ever been held, I think. That was at a hotel in New York City called The Commodore. We took over the grand ballroom, which held 2,000 people. I got many of the leading lights of the UFO field of that time to come as speakers, many of them for free because the thing was like a snowball. It got so big that some were willing to come just to be seen there, rather than try to charge me for coming. It was a wonderful thing, and we had a full house for four sessions at roughly 2,000 people each. It only broke even, unfortunately, for very complicated reasons. I think as a landmark in the UFO field, it still stands. On a much smaller scale, we continued to hold conventions, as you pointed out at the beginning of this segment.

SMiles: All right. Well, we'll hear more about that on the other side of these messages. Stay tuned. This is Psi-Op Radio.

[Music]

SMiles: Welcome back, everybody. This is SMiles Lewis.

Mack: And Mack White.

SMiles: We are talking to our guest tonight, James Moseley of *Saucer Smear*. You can send a love offering to *Saucer Smear* headquarters at PO Box 1709, Key West, Florida, 33041. You can see a sample of the newsletter there at www.martiansgohome.com/smear for those of you using the cursed Internet. Honestly, Moseley, at this point, Jim, I think it's great that you have refused to use the Internet. I am so completely addicted. It's how I get all of my information. I've got to get outside more.

Jim:
You know, when the Internet obviously was growing and was going to be the future of communication and so forth several years ago, at first I thought maybe it would go away. It became obvious that it wasn't going to do that. I am quite seriously and literally incompetent in certain ways, especially regarding technology. I mean, I can deal with very simple things but not anything complex. I could see that I would have a terrible time getting to use the Internet properly. Then there are the crashes and the people that deliberately screw up the operation of the thing, etc., etc., complexities upon complexities. I decided from the beginning that I'll just skip it and get by without it, rather than frustrate myself trying to learn it. Since I'm of the older generation, I do believe now I'll get out of this world eventually without ever having to deal with it.

Mack:
Well, sometimes it really doesn't seem to be worth the grief. That's been my experience. Between the viruses and...

Jim:
I don't hear as much now about personal computers crashing as I used to. Maybe they've gotten rid of some of the bugs or put up – what is it – firewalls, as they call it. I have no idea, but it seems to be operating better. Is that correct?

Mack:
Oh, I don't know.

SMiles:
It varies from day to day. It's a source of much frustration in my life. That's one of the things I like about *Saucer Smear* is it has that old school feel to it because it's being done old school. It has that feeling of being typed on a typewriter, and it's always got some fresh information. Thankfully, people send you printouts of things that they find on the Internet.

Jim:
Well, that's exactly it. I have one guy in particular. His name is Vince Ditchkus. I don't know if he'll eventually hear this show or not, but he is, strangely enough, a computer expert of sorts and works for the Marriott Hotel chain up outside of Washington D.C. He is just interested enough in this subject that he takes his spare time and I guess some of his time at work when he is not busy and just prints out endless saucer-related stuff from the net and sends me I guess a couple hundred pages of it every month, roughly speaking. I don't count the pages, but it's a lot of material. Most of it is, I have to say, garbage, but some of it is interesting and worth repeating. So I have the option

of using whatever portion of that stuff that I want to use. What I don't use I pass on to somebody else.

SMiles: Well, I thoroughly enjoy it and highly recommend it. Going back to contactees, I was looking back through the book and there were some very interesting things that I was reminded of. You've really tried to keep politics pretty much out of your presentation of the subject. Certainly, as you were alluding, the bright and cheery contactee movement kind of got soured and turned into the 70s, 80s, and 90s postmodern dark conspiracies and alien abduction kind of stuff and lots of conspiracies. You even admit to kind of getting wrapped up in what you described as a ufological Red Scare at one point.

Jim: Would that be in the early days?

SMiles: Yeah, during the McCarthy era, I'm gathering.

Jim: Yeah. Well, there are different versions of that. In general, I think the government being over sensitive to the communist menace during that era of the early 50s, they certainly were concerned that these alleged space people were talking about love and peace and world brotherhood and so forth, which is vaguely like the communist party line. So they became interested in learning more about these groups. I don't think they really tried to silence anybody, but they no doubt infiltrated the groups and wanted to make sure that there was no political hidden meaning or that there wasn't any communist infiltration into the groups and so forth.

SMiles: Well, and people like Vallée and others have pointed out that there were people that were part of the psychological warfare, military types that were infiltrating the groups and may have been pushing here and there for their own agenda. We've covered a lot of stuff on this show about counter-terrorism's involvement in certain things like the Paul Bennewitz affair and what not. You even in another portion of the book talk about kind of some of the – you describe W. D. Pelley as a fascist mystic and how George Hunt Williamson, one of the famous contactees got involved with him. You mention also the Stanford brothers. Of course, the Stanford brothers were active here in Austin, Texas or at least one of them, Ray Stanford, was with his Project Starlight International. These are all people you, I guess, met and interacted with.

Jim: Yeah. Is he still active out there?

SMiles: He's, I believe, up on the northeast now and pretty much using his psychic abilities to find amazing fossils. So he's kind of gone into the archeological arena.

Jim: Yeah, he's a very strange guy. I was on a radio show with him at least 20 years ago. You might remember Long John Nebel on New York radio.

SMiles: Oh, yeah.

Jim: Well, after Nebel died, his wife Candy Jones continued with a very similar program. Ray Stanford came on one time. This is a five-hour show from midnight to five a.m. In the course of time, Candy started asking Stanford questions about his supposed laboratory in Texas, actually, I guess. Very well financed and all kinds of machines and so forth that he had for investigating saucers. I suppose she was trying to find out where the money for all that came from. He became irate. I kid you not. Nobody else knows this but me because it was only the – what do you call it? – the engineer and myself and Candy and Stanford were the only people there. He jumped up out of his seat and said, "I'm not going to go on with this," and he stormed into the control room.

          He had signed some kind of a waiver or release before going on the air, and I don't quite know what that would've been because I was on many shows, and I never signed anything like that. Anyway, he wanted to get it back from the engineer. They physically fought in the control room until finally he got his hands on the release. Then he stormed off into the night. That's my only personal meeting with Ray Stanford.

SMiles: Well, I will say I was very entertained and enlightened by him one fine day, actually, about six months before the September 2001 National UFO Conference was supposed to occur, and got to pick his brain. Like you, he interacted with so many of these contactees. Of course, he was in amongst them and kind of a believer himself, both trying to do scientific research but having seemingly some kind of psychic gift that ended up going into the same things that these other George Hunt Williamson and other types – the channeling and more

New Age stuff. So yeah, he's an interesting character. I remember reading that in your book as well.

Besides Long John Nebel, you also interacted with a number of fairly noteworthy media personalities. You were on TV on that – I forget the performer's name. He had, I think, a dummy and he wore a circus outfit.

Jim: Oh, that's funny. I guess that is mentioned in the book, or maybe there's a picture from it or something. Terry Bennett, I think his name was. He wasn't very famous or anything. He had a kiddie show in New York, and it was televised on one of the lesser TV channels. I forget if it was the WWOR channel or another one. Anyhow, somehow, at the height of my fame, which was in the early 60's, I got onto his show. I think I was on three times, once a week for three weeks. He didn't have a studio audience of kids. He just had a stool for himself and a stool for the guest and a stool for this dummy, which was the key to the thing for the kiddies.

He interviewed me and was very good about giving out my address several times each time that I was on there. I literally got thousands of letters. I've never had an experience like that before. Quite a few of those people subscribed to *Saucer News*, and I made quite a lot of money out of it considering it was something that I absolutely did not expect and also the fact that it was a kiddie show. People told me, "Why on earth would you go on something like that?" I'm certainly glad that I did.

SMiles: Well, there's a picture from that in the book. That's, again, one of the things I love about this book, *Shockingly Close to the Truth,* is there are so many pictures of the people from this period of time, so many of the contactees, you and John Keel and you – kind of blurry – meeting Harry S. Truman and asking him a really important question.

Jim: Yeah. Do you want me to talk about that?

SMiles: Sure. Go ahead.

Jim: Well, we go back to that original trip I made in 1953 interviewing people that would have something to say about saucers. As I returned from California, I took a route through the center of the country, so to speak. I believe it was Independence, Missouri, that he was living in at that time. He was out of office as president for roughly a year then, but he still had work that he did of whatever sort.

I called up on a Saturday, I think, and he answered the phone himself. I told him that I was writing a book on flying saucers and I'd like to interview him. He said, "Well, come in Monday morning." So I did, and he was there. I think there was somebody else there in the inner room, someone I never saw. The outer room of the office was the one that you walked into when you came in through the door. I got him to sit down for just a couple of minutes with me and talk. I had the feeling that he wasn't particularly interested in the subject, and he wanted to make the whole thing as short as possible.

The memorable quote from that was when I asked him what he thought of flying saucers, he said, "I've never seen a purple cow. I never hope to see one." I think that's in the book. That's in the first of part of – I think it's an old nursery rhyme. Then it goes on: But this I know and know it now, I'd rather see than be one. Have you heard that?

SMiles: No, I don't think so. I don't think so.

Jim: Well, you didn't go to the right nursery. In other words, he knew that people would know what he was driving at. That was the best I could get out of him as to what he thought of flying saucers. There are rumors about MJ-12 and so forth that he knew a great deal about saucers and he knew about the Roswell crash and so no, I doubt that. That's all I could get out of him anyway.

SMiles: You mentioned Roswell. Have your views on that changed?

Mack: Yeah, what are your views about that?

Jim: Well, I've been to Roswell three times all together, I think 1996 and then 1997, which was the big 50th anniversary celebration, and then again in 2002. The Roswell saga is so long and complex that two hours wouldn't even scratch the surface. I really think it's totally overblown, and I really think that the probability is that it's an earth-made thing and very likely what the government claims it is, which is a Mogul balloon, which was set off from Holloman Air Force Base, I think, not too far away from Roswell.

These were secret at that time – top-secret balloons – because of their purpose, not because of what they were made out of. The purpose was to spy on the Russians and get sound vibrations from any atomic tests that they were making. That was the purpose of the series of balloon runs. One of them apparently landed on this ranch near Roswell, and the pieces were found and photographed and so on, and it goes on and on and on. People came along with stories about alien bodies, but none of them have been substantiated. Through the years, I think most of those stories, if not all, have been discredited.

To me, UFOs, whatever they are, are a fantastically interesting thing. We don't know what it represents, but it is something beyond our present technology and our present understanding. Why make it more sensational than it is? I think that's the trouble in the saucer field. So many people are exaggerating, making things up, misreading things. So that the things that are provable or at least probable are lost in the melee, and the noise out-noises the small kernel of truth that there is in the saucer mystery.

Mack: Do you think it's probable that there are visitors from outer space?

Jim: Well, there again I would've thought so for a number of years. Now together with many others, such as Vallée and John Keel and I would think several of the modern UFO writers, such as Redfern and Bishop and the fellow that just died recently, Mac Tonnies – who I think was a great intellectual in the field, and it's a shame that he died so young – but these people are looking for an answer in a supposedly unbiased way. They don't really think anymore that it's from another planet. It's just hard to explain, but there are many reasons to think that it's something in and of this earth. Whether it's from another dimension or what, I don't know. I don't think they're physical spaceships coming in from some other planet.

SMiles: Yeah. You refer to this as the 4D hypothesis, correct?

Jim: Yeah, 4D. You know, you can call it anything you want. Years ago, I used to – as one of the hopefully humorous things I did in *Saucer Smear* – I said there are people who say it's 3D, and there are people who say it's 4D, so let's call it the 3-1/2 D theory. I ran with that for a while. I don't know. Even the 3-1/2 D theory is I think more likely than physical visitors from another planet, not that it couldn't happen and not that it's not theoretically possible. The way these creatures act, just everything about them doesn't designate to me an intelligence that we can understand or any consistency or continuity.

Each one has a different message. Each one looks a little different from the other. All of the UFOs look somewhat different from each other. It's just a collage or whatever – or mollage, whatever word I'm groping for – of just different, somewhat similar occurrences, but there is no rational thread that runs through them and no message, I don't think, that's being given to us in a consistent way. So I think it's more in the realm of the paranormal.

SMiles: I agree very much with just about everything you said there. I too feel that they seem more Earthly in some sense, and that's one of the things I liked about Mac Tonnies' idea and his book that was published posthumously.

Jim: Yeah, I saw his book. I'm glad that we seem to agree with each other, but I just want to say I can't imagine either that they come physically in a 3D way from some part of the physical planet Earth. I don't think it's reasonable to think that something that extraordinary is going on... on the planet and maybe in a jungle or under the ice of the Arctic or something. I don't think that's a very good choice either, but I think he's on the right track.

SMiles: Yeah. All right. Well, this has been the first hour of PsiOp-Radio with our guest James Moseley. We'll be back for another hour of conversation and questioning. We'll open the phone lines, so get ready for the second hour after these messages. Stay tuned.

[Music]

SMiles: Welcome back. This is the second hour of PsiOp-Radio live from Austin, Texas. I'm SMiles Lewis.

Mack: And I'm Mack White.

SMiles: We are talking to saucer extraordinaire, Supreme Commander James Moseley. He is live from his saucer headquarters in Key West, Florida. You can find out more about...

188

THE ASTOUNDING UFO SECRETS OF JAMES W. MOSELEY

Jim: Miles?

SMiles: Yes.

Jim: Listen. I'm having a problem with a cough that I've had off and on for a while. If it comes back during this hour and I can't control it, then I'll just have to hang up, but I don't think that will happen. Okay?

SMiles: Okay. That's understandable. Thank you for the heads up.

Jim: Okay. I just thought I'd let you know.

SMiles: All right. In the previous hour, you did mention that one of the things vexing ufology – or ufoology, as you so affectionately call it – is the shenanigans and the craziness. At the same time, is it not accurate to say that you've certainly contributed your share to those shenanigans and the circus-like atmosphere on occasion?

Jim: Well, you might be referring to the R.E. Straith letter from I think 1957. This was a letter that Gray Barker and I – Barker being a long gone and forgotten ufologist of that era – he and I were close friends. One weekend we got together in Clarksburg, West Virginia, where he lived. He had some stationary that someone had supplied him with from the State Department and other government agencies, just blank stationary, which this other person had just picked up and taken away and mailed to Barker.

On that weekend he and I, sort of being a bit under the weather from excessive alcohol, wrote a letter. I can't give you the exact wording offhand, but I think the text is in my book, and it's been published many places. The gist of it was it was a letter from a man named R.E. Straith in the State Department to George Adamski, the contactee, saying more or less clearly that we of the State Department can't come forward officially and back your claims, but we do underneath the surface, so to speak, agree with you, and we do want to encourage you in your work and so on and so on.

This letter went to George Adamski and made him feel much more confident in what he was doing. Obviously, he must've known this was a hoax, or maybe he was so out of it that he thought this could be real. In any case, he publicized it a great deal, as one would expect. The government got angry. I forget if it was the State Department or the FBI who went out to see him and told him, "Look, George, this is a hoax. This letter is not genuine, and we are ordering you to stop distributing it the way you've been doing." Of course, that convinced him more than ever that it was real. Many people in the saucer field thought it was real.

In fact, there's a guy – I wish I could remember his name – but there's a George Adamski Foundation that still exists in California. There's a fellow who's the head of it who is a spokesman. It's not more than two or three years ago I had a couple of phone conversations with him. I think I finally convinced him that it was a hoax. I said, "What more can I do? I supplied all the details, and you still think it's a cover up." I guess I did really finally convince him. If somebody wants to believe something hard enough, it's awful hard to get them out of it. You know?

SMiles: That is so, so, so true. All right. Well, we'll be back for a long segment after these messages. Stay tuned. This is PsiOp-Radio. We're talking to James Moseley, and the phone lines are open.

[Music]

SMiles: All right. We are back. It's 8:08 p.m Central Standard Time, and you are listening to a live episode of PsiOp-Radio from Austin, Texas. We've got Jim Moseley on the line. The phone lines are open. Jim, we were talking about shenanigans, and you were talking about the Straith letter and how that really supercharged the conspiracy element within the UFO contactee movement. Earlier in the show you had mentioned your other pastime around the early days when you were starting the UFO newsletters. You were spending time out of the country. The subtitle of your book *Shockingly Close to the Truth* is *Confessions of a Grave-Robbing Ufologist.* Where were you robbing graves?

Jim: Well, that's another long, long story. Remember, people that are still listening from the very beginning of this, I mentioned a man named Ken Krippine who was an adventure writer. He was doing various things in Peru in South America. I won't say he was really treasure hunting, but he was writing about the subject and seemed to be treasure hunting. I got to know him and got interested in the subject, which perhaps anybody would. In 1955, I think it was, it was the first time I went down to Peru.

Making a very long story short, he and I eventually fell out, as I said. We did not do the saucer book together either. I had gotten the treasure bug. How can I tell you? There are two kinds of treasure legends in a place like Peru. One would be from the colonial period after the Spanish invaded the country and took over. Then there was the Catholic Church and all kinds of intrigues and so on and possible treasures here and there. Those are few and far between. There are legends and people looking for that kind of thing for years and years. Generally speaking, nobody finds anything.

Then you go before the Spanish conquest into the pre-history of Peru or Mexico or several other countries where there had been advanced civilizations before the white man ever got there and where the custom was to bury with the person whatever worldly goods they had during their life. If it was a chieftain, a ruler or whatever, it would likely be fine textiles and very intricate pottery and gold, things made of gold. So I got into that area of treasure hunting with a Peruvian partner who spoke English. We went up and down the coast of Peru. We didn't go everywhere, but we went to the easy places, relatively speaking.

It's amazing. It's not just that you can walk in somewhere and say, "Tell me where to dig, and I'll just take this stuff and leave." We did find a lot of stuff. Sometimes we had to share with other people involved and sometimes we didn't. It's a long, confusing story, but for several years I was doing that and quite successfully I would say.

SMiles: This, I guess, inevitably led to your operating the gallery?

Jim: Yeah, well, eventually. Many years later, in the 80's I think, for about 6 years here in Key West I had an antique gallery. In the long run, that didn't make money either. All the things I've tried in my life, they all sound like they should've made a lot of money, but none of them ever did. With the gallery, it was just that I wasn't on the main drag. It was too expensive to do enough advertising to get people to know where we were located. Also, the market for pre-Columbian art, which is the category that we're talking about, is rather limited. Of course, there's a lot of fakery, and the people are worried that you're selling fakes. So it didn't do too well, but yes, I did have a gallery for a while.

SMiles: Too much fakery, eh?

Jim: Well, yeah, a lot of fakery. My stuff was real. The "Straith Letter" was not real but the antiques I sold were real.

SMiles: But you did continue your fun with "discovering" saucer landing sites in Peru, eh?

Jim: Well, now, yes. What's the source of that? From my book?

SMiles: Yeah, there are photographs.

Jim: Oh, are there? Well, then it must have happened. Well, I made up a story. This was way back in the mid 50's before I became more mature and serious as I am now, hopefully. We claimed that a saucer had landed in a given place in the desert and left behind a charred circle where it had been. We got that into the tabloid newspaper of Lima, Peru, on the first page. The story was carried one day, maybe two days. It wasn't really true, but it got people interested in the subject. I guess my excuse for doing stuff like that was to keep the subject alive and to keep people interested. Whereas this may not be true, something else will be, and let's pay attention and see what we can find.

SMiles: Well, another photograph that you reproduce in the book is a seemingly "real" UFO photograph from Peru of what looks like a bullet with a trail of smoke flying through the air.

Jim: Oh, yeah.

SMiles: I remember seeing that in my early days of investigating UFOs. To see it in your book and find out that you had helped bring that to the public...

Jim: Yeah. Well, I had nothing to do with taking that. As far as I know, that is genuine. I never met the man that took it. It was given to me probably months or a year or two later by someone else. I really think that is a real photo. It's interesting because it looks like the exhaust is coming out the back like a rocket. If it's a rocket, then it isn't really what we would call a flying saucer, but it was an unidentified thing flying over the jungle. It's really very mysterious.

Mack: Isn't Peru supposed to be a hot spot for UFO activity?

Jim: Yeah, one of many. Well, I guess most of the countries in South America have at different times been hot spots. I get a lot of this stuff from the Internet also. Argentina and Chile and, funny enough, Puerto Rico, which is not in South America, but that's been a big thing for many years.

SMiles: Now, you ended up spending about three years cumulatively down in Peru?

Jim: Yeah. Well, I was back and forth. I never stayed more than a few months at a time. I was lucky enough to be able to do that. I had an apartment in New Jersey, and I had an office in Lima, and I flew back and forth about a dozen times over a period from 1955 to 1960 roughly.

SMiles: So I guess jumping back to the saucer scene, Gray Barker, he is a fascinating character. From what little there is to find out about him, he seems like a really interesting, warm fellow with a very similar take and love of the scene as yourself and this love of wanting to publish information on the subject, even though sometimes you may not actually believe in the stuff being published.

Jim: Right. Right.

SMiles: Can you tell our listeners more about Mr. Barker?

Jim: Oh, yeah. Incidentally, there is a new video out about him.

SMiles: Really?

Jim: I forget what stage it's at now. It either just came out and is available on the net or will be within a very short time. It's called *Shades of Gray,* and it's about his life. There was a previous video done about him and his works several years ago. That was never distributed. The new one is better than the former one. If your listeners can find a way to get hold of it, they should because it's really very interesting.

He was a fellow from West Virginia that was born into poverty and just a rural farm environment. Got an education and a degree from a local college and was going to be an English teacher at one point. What got him started in the offbeat was the Flatwoods Monster. I think that was 1952. He was one of the prime investigators of that. The Flatwoods Monster is assumed to have some connection to flying saucers, although one doesn't know for sure just what it was.

From there, he got interested in UFOs, and he started publishing a magazine for quite a number of years. Then in about 1956 he had a book, which actually sold quite well, called *They Knew Too Much About Flying Saucers,* telling somewhat exaggerated and so on versions of people in the UFO field that have been hushed up by the men-in-black or the government or who knows who for knowing too much and the fear being that the public would learn the truth, and the truth would be terrible. So that theme got him a lot of publicity. He carried on with his magazine, but in later years it was not as popular. By the time he died, he was in debt. He wasn't doing terribly well. He died in 1984. I knew him very well, and he was a very close friend of mine.

SMiles: Did he help run a local cinema? Am I remembering correctly that he helped run a local movie theater?

Jim: Yes. Well, that was his other business. He was a booker or whatever – not a bookie but a booker of movies for the drive-ins in West Virginia. Later on, he actually managed – well, I guess he owned it – a small drive-in theater in one of the little towns near Clarksburg. He was in the edges, you could say, of the movie business as well as the publishing business.

SMiles: Besides his own book, he published some works of others.

Jim: Oh, yes. I don't know how many. Over the years, he must've published 30 or 40 saucer books, mostly 8 and a half by 11 soft cover books that you've seen many times.

SMiles: He also marketed a sound recording, a vinyl record of one of the contactees' supposed Saturnian music.

Jim: Oh, yes. That's Howard Menger. Howard Menger was one of the contactees. Yes. I remember that. He did produce that, I think.

SMiles: Menger's a really interesting character as far as contactees because he later kind of switched his story.

Jim: Well, that's right. Menger at a given point changed his story some-what. He had been going on the Long John Nebel radio show for a year or two telling these details about his contacts with flying saucers and his, I believe, voyage to whichever other planet it was. Then what went wrong was Long John at one point obtained a television show in New York, which he had never had before. He was just on radio. So he took his best guests from the past, including Menger, and put them on this short-lived TV show. I think it was once a week, and it maybe lasted 10 or 20 weeks. I'm not sure.

When Menger got on that, he changed his story and said he wasn't sure what happened. It might have been that he was fooled by the government and that these were not space people. It was something else. I don't know all the details, but it was an entirely different story, and Long John was devastated because that is not what he wanted to hear. I guess Menger was in the doghouse after that.

SMiles: Well, that's interesting too because wasn't it Long John Nebel's wife – you were mentioning her earlier, Candy Jones – there was a whole crazy story...

Mack: She was an alleged mind control victim.

SMiles: Yeah.

Jim: Yeah. Well, I can kill that off very quickly. It's not inside information because I wrote it up with Karl Pflock a few years ago, and it's been published in the *Fortean Times*. Essentially, that whole thing was made up by a couple of writers. *The Control of Candy Jones* I think it's called.

SMiles: Yes.

Jim: Candy told me that herself. One or two of the other key figures told me in confidence. Of course, I blabbed it around but after <garbled> and after it didn't really make much difference. I mean that was just made from whole cloth, as they say.

Mack: Hmm. So we can discount that book, huh?

Jim: Yeah. Listen, Miles, while I have you here – or you have me – I'd like to talk a little bit more about the convention that you almost sponsored for the National UFO Conference and which at the very last minute was cancelled because of 9/11. I think that's one of the weirdest things that's ever happened to me in the saucer field.

SMiles: Really?

Jim: I'm sure I must have told you at some point. I was flying on an early morning flight. It must've been midweek of that week. It was three or four days. What am I trying to say? The convention was going to be that weekend, and 9/11 must've occurred on a Tuesday or Wednesday.

SMiles: It was Tuesday, yeah.

Jim: I was flying out to Austin to be there a few days ahead of time to help organize the convention. I was actually in the air flying from Key West to Miami when the first of the World Trade Center towers was blown up. After I got to the airport in Miami – obviously there was some confusion and so on going on – the second tower was blown up during that period. I was reluctant to accept the fact that all flights going anywhere were cancelled, and indeed they were. What they did was they took everybody's baggage and instead of just throwing it correctly in the various bins that corresponded to the various flights, they just sort of dumped them all on the pick-up baggage area without any care as to which flight was where. Through a miracle, really, I got my suitcase back by looking through all this stuff. I was able to get a motel room in Miami, and I stayed for a couple of days.

SMiles: You said the events of that September 2001 were the strangest thing that's ever happened to you in your experiencing of saucerdom. That's a surprise to me because I know you've had some strange experiences.

Jim: Well, I mean that was a surprise to everybody. You were going to start your convention on Friday, right?

SMiles: Right.

Jim: So it would've been two or three days after that. What happened was those two events were just too close together. There was no way that people could get there in time. I remember Jenny Randles, I think, from England, was one of the people that was supposed to come. Everybody had to cancel. It was just a period of confusion, and you did the only thing you could do, which was to cancel the convention.

SMiles: Yeah. In hindsight, I guess I realized later that about a third to half of the scheduled speakers were actually from Texas, so they all could've made it in, and it could've been some kind of limited thing. At the time, it didn't even occur to me. The consciousness of that time seemed entirely anathema to try to think about something as cosmic as UFOs. Yet it's ironic to me in a weird sort of way that the person we were going to honor that year was Robert Anton Wilson for lifetime achievement.

Jim: Oh, I didn't remember that. Yes.

SMiles: He is the self-processed leader of the Illuminati. Of course, there is that portion of the 9/11 Conspiracy community that thinks it was the New World Order Illuminati folks that were behind it. Whatever you think about the events of that tragic day, they certainly were a shock, and I didn't think it was really appropriate to try to go on after that.

Jim: Well, I really never actually met Wilson. It's funny. I heard him speak once in Maryland, but that was before I knew him by phone and letter. I heard him speak, but I didn't talk to him. After that, I can't say we became close, but he wrote in comments on just about every issue of *Smear* for a period of several years and a few times I talked to him on the phone. He was a very, very interesting, cool guy and had many interesting thoughts. I never quite got it straight. I think he – if I'm not wrong – entertained all of these conspiracy theories, but I have the feeling he didn't really believe any of them.

SMiles: Right. I tend to think of him as like so many of the people I respect most. They're able to suspend judgment. They're able to entertain a multiplicity of possibilities in an agnostic way. That's, again, one of the traits in you I see that I like so much. You mentioned him commenting on issues of *Saucer Smear*, and that's one of the things I like about *Saucer Smear* is you print people's responses.

Jim: Oh, absolutely. I don't generally get as many responses now as I did before the cursed net took over the world. It seems archaic to a lot of people to have to actually write a letter. The other thing that I find amusing really is I have two phone numbers right on the masthead of every issue. Those are my home phone numbers, and it rings right next to my bed here. I'm not hiding from anybody in any way. I hardly ever get a call about *Saucer Smear* because it doesn't occur to anybody to call. They would contact me on the net if they could, but they can't so that's it.

SMiles: It was weird also – anomalous – as far as the National UFO Conference goes that it would have been the third year in a row in the same state. Previous to that, you'd really always moved it around.

Jim: Well, I can tell you how that went. It's just like the last two or three were in the vicinity of Los Angeles. I just took whatever I could get. Sometimes a person that was holding one convention would recommend a friend, and more than likely the friend would be living in the same state. My M.O. as national chairman forever, etc., was to find somebody in whatever state that was willing to do this in the name of NUFOC and take the financial risk and book the speakers and do most of the work, and then I could come in as the great guru. Sometimes I got free passage – I got my plane ticket and room paid for – and sometimes I didn't.

I was always on the speaker's program, and it was just, quite frankly, an ego thing for me in a certain way. I enjoyed it. You would've been, yes, the third in a row in Texas because – I'm trying to remember the names of the other two – Dennis Stacy held one of them. Was her name Church something? There was another woman who held the other one.

SMiles: Yeah, from the Corpus Christi – Doris Upchurch?

Jim: Yeah. Yeah. So that's how somehow you got into it. Anyway, that was just mind-boggling, that whole thing. As I say again, I don't know what prize I should be given for this, but I was in the air as the first tower went down, and that's not something everybody can say or would want to say.

SMiles: Yeah. I don't know how closely you've followed the 9/11 Truth Move- ment, those that have been skeptical of the official story of the events of that day. It's actually been like watching the emergence of a whole new esoteric field of study. Whether you're interested in ghosts or UFOs or Bigfoot and cryptozoology, each of these tends to be its own kind of enclave, even though Forteans and anomalists like myself and my friends tend to appreciate them as a broad spectrum. Here's a very focused conspiracy subculture that's emerged much more rap- idly than the JFK culture but largely because of the Internet, the cursed Internet.

Jim: Well, do you think that there was a conspiracy in regard to 9/11?

SMiles: I'll phrase it this way: I believe a conspiracy theory that's different than the official conspiracy theory is more likely. In other words, I think we all know it was a conspiracy of some sort, whether it's the official story or some alternative. I would go with some alternative just because as I delved into it, there were so many anomalies and so much foreknowledge. It just boggles the mind. It really begs the is- sue of is it really as simple as just foreign policy blowback. How much do our political overlords actually do covert operations? In investi- gating UFOs, that's the thing I came up against over and over and over was cover-up and covert-ops. As Vallée and others have said, the possibility that while there is a true UFO phenomenon and prob- ably represents some sort of "alien other" consciousness, the mili- tary has seen the psychological warfare potential and covert-ops use for paranormal and UFO phenomena. Yeah, I think there was a con- spiracy that's different than the official one.

Jim: That's interesting. Now, I know that you're more into the conspiracy angle of all of this than I am. I tend to avoid believing in conspiracies because if you really get into that too deeply, I think you can drive yourself crazy. I don't know.

SMiles: Indeed. I think paranoia is something that needs to be balanced with pronoia. If you're going to think that people are out to get you, you might as well balance it with the idea that there's a conspiracy of people out to help you.

Jim: Yeah, that sounds like a good idea.

Mack: Sometimes there are people out to get you.

SMiles: You know, Mack was actually going to be one of the panel speakers at the National UFO Conference. We both have a keen interest in the paranormal and UFOs but also how they are manipulated. That's a lot of the focus of this show. I do think that there's some true UFO phenomena at the heart that seem to be, if we can weed out the chaff of human misperception and belief systems, I think there's a kernel of alienness there that could...

Jim: Well, see, the trouble is everybody – not everybody – but a lot of people would say what you just said or agree with what you just said. Then when you get into the fine points and the details, which stories are you going to throw out, and which ones are you going to believe? It gets awfully complicated.

SMiles: Yeah. It does.

Jim: I mean, you take MJ-12. I am totally convinced that all of that is nonsense, but I still wonder. The last I heard the MJ-12 documents run into over 2,000 pages. What maniac or maniacs would bother to do that much? The Straith letter was one happy evening for Gray Barker and me. This is a great amount of work over a period of time. A lot of these documents in the MJ-12 thing are pseudo-real in the sense that they've taken a real document and changed it just enough to make it fit in with what they want people to believe. So that's a lot of work. As I said, I don't accept that whole MJ-12 category, but you can argue it endlessly.

SMiles: Yeah. Jim, we have caller who has been holding for a little while. Let's go to our caller. Hello, caller. You're on the air.

Carl: Hi. My name is Carl.

SMiles: Hi, Carl.

Carl: I have a topic I want to bring up. I don't want to change the topic, but I want all of your listeners to be aware of this and Google it and do their own research. It's called brain scan technology, fMRI. I have the article from *Wired* magazine, www.wired.com. "The jury reaches decision in brain-scan test case." This is May 14, 2010. Now they have a nano version of it where they can send remote signals and read people's intentions in their minds using these devices. I don't know if you've done any research on it – "brain scan can read your intentions," that's from CBC, the Canadian Broadcasting Corporation. There are several other articles. Alexis Madrigal of "Wired Science," she wrote the article. I have a whole bunch of articles here. I've been locked up in Canada for three years...

Mack: Do you have a question for our guest?

Carl: I haven't brought my case up before, but LiberateCarl.com is my website.

SMiles: All right. Well, thank you caller. Yeah. Actually, the area of fMRI scans is something that we've covered for some time. Jim, I'm not sure if you're familiar with this technology.

Jim: No. It's out of my area. You run with it.

SMiles: Basically, the fMRI is one of these big scanners that they put you into to read the minutest electromagnetic aspects of activity in your brain. There has been, post 9/11, a lot of talk about DARPA, of the military, developing these for use in airports so that they can read your mind, read your intentions, and know if you have any ill intentions. Now, I recall actually back in 2000, Whitley Strieber, the famous horror science-fiction writer and claimed abductee, talked about using this as a way of testing to see if somebody is in fact a true abductee, because they might see things – basically, they're billing it as the new lie detector machine. This gets kind of far off-field from our subject, but it dovetails with these conspiracy theories and the actual research into mind control that we know is done. Thank you, caller, for that information. I'll look into that. That's interesting that it's been reduced in size. We'll be right back for our final segment after this. Stay tuned.

[Music]

SMiles: Welcome back, everybody. It's that sense of being surveilled. This is the final segment of tonight's edition of PsiOp-Radio. Our guest is Jim Moseley. He is the editor of *Saucer Smear: The Official Publication of the Saucer & Unexplained Celestial Events Research Society* and the author of *Shockingly Close to the Truth: Confessions of a Grave-Robbing Ufologist.*

Our last caller was bringing up this high-tech that is so scary and so much a part of the police state. In India, they're already using this as a new lie detector test. Basically, they show you an image. It might be, say, the knife that a murder was committed with, and they can tell whether you've seen it before or not. If you have, then clearly you're guilty. As I was saying, Whitley Strieber, an abductee, was suggesting as far back as 10 years ago that this could be a way of testing the validity or the reality of alien abductions.

It's an interesting idea because I'm all for trying to use science and technology to document these things. Jim, you were talking earlier about the contactees. I think, like Menger was suggesting, he may have been deceived. I think some contactees may have had a legitimate encounter with the "true" UFO phenomenon. Often, as in what became abductee cases, when we went from the contactees, close encounters, and occupants, and full blown bedroom visitation alien abductions, it seems like there's a lot of fertile ground there for something real but also some machinations of darker forcers. What do you think about that transformation from the contactees to the abductees? Do they have anything to do with UFOs?

Jim: Okay. You're talking now about the contactees or the abductees? Is that it?

SMiles: How do you see the abductees in terms of the UFO phenomenon?

Jim: I've given it a lot of thought, and I know we don't have much time left anyway, but my view is very simple. We've got to find a way – and I don't quite know yet what that way is – to learn whether these experiences are completely internal for whatever reason – hallucination, dream, whatever you want to call it. Are they completely internal, or are they caused by an outside source? Again, the outside source could be anything. That's the dividing line as far as I'm concerned.

If it's totally internal, then you should forget about it as far as research is concerned. If something, whatever it may be, from the outside is causing this – beaming it in, whatever it's doing – if that is truly the case and if that can be proven, whether or not it's aliens or something else, then we have something to sink our teeth into, and we should find out what this is.

SMiles: Indeed. I think we just have to come up with more creative ways of testing these potential hypotheses. There was a time when various UFO groups like MUFON and CUFOS, and CAUS – I forget what their acronym stands for (Citizens Against UFO Secrecy) – they were petitioning the government to release documents and so forth. They all got together to form a coalition to fund some abductee research where they had a little black box that was developed with various types of sensors that could be put in the bedroom of these abductees. Sadly, there doesn't seem to have been anything really significant found from that.

Jim: Well, it would seem to me that, one way or another, if you're going to monitor the home or the bedroom of an abductee 24 hours a day indefinitely and try to catch on film or whatever the entities that are causing this, you're never going to get anything. It doesn't work that way. Whatever it is, it does not work that way. You're going to waste your time and money. That's what I think.

SMiles: I tend to agree. It doesn't mean that I think the phenomenon is any less real. I think it doesn't seem to be amenable to laboratory tests like most paranormal phenomena, like psychic phenomena.

Jim: That's true. I wish we had another five hours, and I would tell you about my paranormal experiences, which are not frightening or exciting, but I enjoy telling them. Some other time I will.

SMiles: Well, any other things that you want to say to our audience before the time runs out?

Jim: Well, what is our time frame here?

SMiles: Oh, you've got about three minutes. Two minutes.

Jim: Oh, my goodness. Well, you've got to give me a clue. All I can say is this...

SMiles: What's cooking for the next issue?

Jim: Well, let me go on this instead. I think that the UFO mystery is a valid thing. Absolutely something very strange is going on. Probably not space visitors, but whatever it is, it is happening and has been happening probably for thousands of years. At least we know just the modern period is now about 60 years. I think it's intermeshed with the paranormal. Unfortunately, it's intermeshed with religion, which I'm not into. I'm afraid that is going to have to be part of it in some way, shape, or form when we reach an answer. I don't think we're going to get that answer for many years to come. Science has to be in on this too. Whatever it is, it has to be scientifically valid, even if we have to expand the scientific method in some way to include things that are not yet included.

It's not easy to solve, but it does exist. Finally, there is so much nonsense mixed in with whatever truth there is here, that that makes it all the harder and will cause more delay and more trouble to ever get a sensible, objective answer. If you have enough patience and enough interest, in the long run you can work toward a solution, and I think it's worth looking for.

SMiles: Truer words have rarely been spoken. Thank you so much, Jim, for joining us tonight.

Mack: Thanks for coming on the show.

Jim: All right, and I'm hanging up the phone.

SMiles: All right. You take care.

Mack: Goodnight.

THE ASTOUNDING UFO SECRETS OF JAMES W. MOSELEY

OUR LIVES ARE A BIT MORE GREY SINCE THE PASSING OF JWM

By Adam Gorightly

I had written for "Saucer Smear" on occasion, such as this little ditty from the mid-1990s that appeared in one of the issues. Jim seemed to think it was funny.

SANTILLI'S GREY

(Sung to the melody of "Chantilly Lace" by the Big Bopper)

Santilli's 'Grey', that fucked-up leg

Oval-like eyes, open wide

On its butt with a pooched-out gut

What a way to die!

There ain't nothin' in the world like a six-fingered girl

Who is all cut open, I wanna go elopin'

With this alien dame and her sawed-off brain.

Oh baby, that's a-what I like!!

A self-described "crackpot historian," Adam Gorightly is a writer, musician and sometimes podcaster. Find out more about Adam at www.adamgorightly.com

DEPARTMENT OF STATE
WASHINGTON

Prof. George Adamski
Star Route,
Valley Center
California

My Dear Professor:

For the time being, let us consider this a personal letter
and not to be construed as an official communication of the
Department. I speak on behalf of only a part of our people
here in regard to the controversial matter of the UFO, but I
might add that my group has been outspoken in its criticism
of official policy.

We have also criticized the self-assumed role of our Air Force
in usurping the role of chief investigating agency on the UFO.
Your own experiences will lead you to know already that the
Department has done its own research and has been able to arrive
at a number of sound conclusions. It will no doubt please you
to know that the Department has on file a great deal of con-
firmatory evidence bearing out your own claims, which, as both
of us must realize, are controversial, and have been disputed
generally.

While certainly the Department cannot publicly confirm your
experiences, it can, I believe, with propriety, encourage your
work and your communication of what you sincerely believe should
be told to our American public.

In the event you are in Washington, I do hope that you will
stop by for an informal talk. I expect to be away from Washington
during the most of February, but should return by the last week
in that month.

Sincerely,

R. E. Straith
Cultural Exchange Committee

RES/me

206

Mr. ███████ also discussed this matter with Colonel L. R. Forney of MID. Colonel Forney indicated that it was his attitude that inasmuch as it has been established that the flying disks are not the result of any Army or Navy experiments, the matter is of interest to the FBI. He stated that he was of the opinion that the Bureau, if at all possible, should accede to General Schulgen's request.

7-15

(J. Edgar Hoover)

I would do it but before agreing to it we must insist upon full access to discs recovered. For instance in the La. case the Army grabbed it & would not let us have it for cursory examination

- 2 -

H.

Memo from FBI agent Ladd and handwritten reply from FBI Director J. Edgar Hoover regarding recovery of crashed disc.

THE ASTOUNDING UFO SECRETS OF JAMES W. MOSELEY

FREE BONUS DVD SHOT EXCLUSIVELY
FOR THE CONSPIRACY JOURNAL
Tim Beckley Interviews The Legendary Country Singer, Stuntman, Actor,
Johnny Sands On His Las Vegas Alien Encounter And Subsequent MIB Experience

---

AS FEATURED ON AN EPISODE OF THE HISTORY CHANNEL'S
UFO HUNTERS MEN IN BLACK –THE UFO SILENCERS

On this UFO Hunters episode Sands reveals the details of his bewildering contact with the dreaded MIB who have repeatedly warned eyewitnesses to remain silent about what they saw – OR ELSE! Also on the set was CJ editor/publisher Tim Beckley who displayed for the first time in front of a national audience a dramatic photograph of an authentic MIB he took back in the 1960s after a fellow researcher and his wife were repeatedly stalked by one of these "agents of terror and doom." Will Smith and Hollywood made a fictionalized version revolving around the MIB, but the outcome was a silly take off on the real drama that is much more mysterious and sinister.

After the History Channel shoot at the Grand Canyon Caverns, Sands and Beckley returned to their hotel suite for a one on one in-depth interview.

GET A FREE COPY WHEN YOU ORDER
THE CURSE OF THE MEN IN BLACK and/or UFO SILENCERS.

Order Book and bonus DVD from the author (autographed upon request)
Timothy Beckley, Box 753, New Brunswick, NJ 08903
Credit Cards 732 602-3407
Free newsletter and catalogs www.ConspiracyJournal. Com

THE ASTOUNDING UFO SECRETS OF JAMES W. MOSELEY

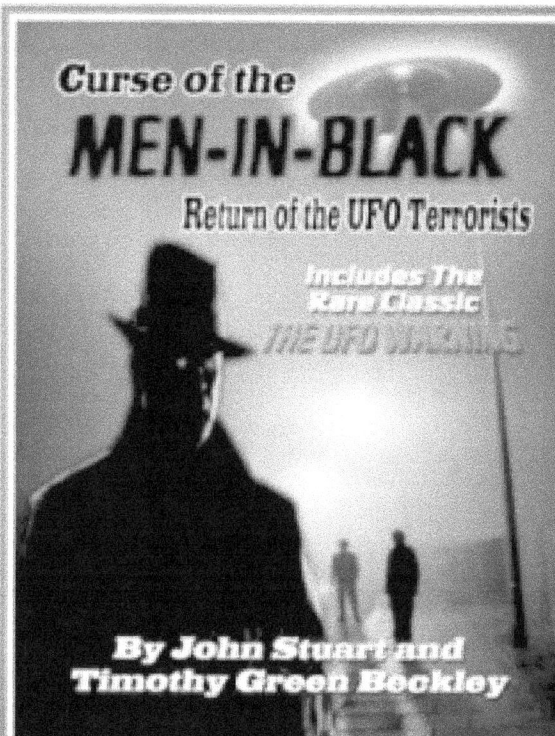

THE ASTOUNDING UFO SECRETS OF JAMES W. MOSELEY

JWM's buddy Gray - did he ghost write this book? — Barker proudly displays promotional material for his 1956 best seller. They Knew Too Much About Flying Saucers spawned the Men In Black pop culture that has lasted to this day. Hollywood has gotten into the act with three major motion pictures on the UFO silencers.

Is this a real Man In Black photographed outside the Jersey City apartment of Saucer News staffers Jim and Mary Robinson? Taken by Moseley and Beckley, Jim thought there was a "logical explanation " for the presence of this supposed MIB, while Tim harbors a less skeptical attitude.

APPENDIX 1: FINAL ISSUE OF "SAUCER SMEAR"

DEDICATED TO THE HIGHEST PRINCIPLES OF UFOLOGICAL
JOURNALISM

SAUCER SMEAR

Volume 59, No. 9
Oct. 20th, 2012
(Whole Number 455)

TELEPHONES:
305-294-2270
294-1873

MAILING ADDRESS:
P.O. Box 1709
Key West, Fl.33041

CONTRIBUTING EDITORS:
Vince Ditchkus
Dr. Chris Roth
Dr. Tim Brigham
Curt Collins

EMAIL:
saucer_
smear@
yahoo.com

EDITOR:
James W. Moseley

OPERATOR! YOU SAY YOU CAN HEAR THAT NOISE? GOOD! I WANT TO REPORT A UFO!!

RRRRRRRRRRRRRR

OFFICIAL PUBLICATION OF THE SAUCER & UNEXPLAINED CELESTIAL EVENTS RESEARCH SOCIETY

Here are a few extracts from a Net article by JOHN HARVEY called "Why Don't Scientists Take Ufology Seriously?" The article mainly concerns MUFON, of which your editor is a somewhat proud member:

"One of the most common complaints made by ufologists is that their work is not taken seriously by scientists, even though they claim to use scientific methods in their investigations...I will illustrate the point I am trying to make by making a critical examination of a fairly typical issue of the MUFON UFO Journal, a monthly magazine published by the Mutual UFO Network.

"The reason for picking on this journal is the statement which appears in each issue: 'MUFON's mission is the scientific study of UFOs for the benefit of humanity'. I have chosen the September 2012 issue, and I have read through it to see if its editor and contributing writers are adopting an appropriately scientific approach.

"The first indication that all is not well comes with the Director's Message by David MacDonald. It is mainly concerned with the announcement that MUFON has acquired many of the files compiled by Leonard Stringfield (1920-1994). MacDonald looked through a very small amount of this material and found accounts of beatings by Federal Marshalls, FBI documents showing death threats and intimidation, 'safe houses' set up by MUFON to protect Len from attack, and descriptions of how he was moved from hotel room to hotel room (to avoid the CIA, FBI, Federal Marshalls, etc.) at more than one MUFON symposium.

"It certainly looks as if some of this material could provide plenty of useful material for producers of slapstick comedy films, as it seems so delightfully absurd. However, MacDonald found it to be 'enlightening, inspirational, vindicating and humbling... and also frightening if not downright terrifying...'"

(Editor's Note: It is absurd to believe that the Dark Forces would act so very badly, especially as Stringfield always admitted that he could prove nothing. On the other hand, ufologists enjoy feeling paranoid, because it makes them believe that they know something very important.)

Continuing the quote from Harvey: "...In another investigation, by Norman Gagnon, details are given of a small group of people who noticed a string of ten orange lights silently ascending over a lake and disappearing into the clouds. The sighting is considered important enough to feature on the front page of the Journal, even though the obvious explanation is simply that they were fire balloons, and I would guess that they were possibly released during the celebration of a child's tenth birthday...

"Stanton Friedman's monthly article is better than usual, providing some interesting background information about some ufological characters. He is skeptical about the fellow who calls himself Chase Brandon, who claims to be an

LEONARD STRINGFIELD

APPENDIX 1: FINAL ISSUE OF "SAUCER SMEAR"

(2)

ex-CIA man who states that the Roswell crash really involved an alien craft, but he is suspected of making up the story to plug his new science fiction novel. Friedman notes the odd fact that the producer of his 1979 DVD 'UFOs Are Real' was named Brandon Chase!

"Friedman is indeed a modest, self-effacing person. When he heard in 1973 that Robert Emenegger was making a documentary on UFOs, he phoned him and asked him how he could make a UFO documentary without involving him...

"The basic difficulty with ufology is that it is a non-subject. By this I mean that a sighting of an unusual atmospheric optical or electrical phenomenon and a report of an alleged abduction by aliens are two quite different things, as there is no causal connection between them. Most solved UFO cases have many different and unrelated causes. Some are sightings of real objects or phenomena and others are subjective experiences...Solving interesting UFO cases involves separating facts from lies and misinterpretation, and ending up with a coherent account of what did or did not happen. MUFON, along with most other UFO organizations, does not seem to be capable of this task."

TWO VERY UNUSUAL SIGHTINGS FROM THE "GOLDEN AGE"(?) OF UFOLOGY:

Somehow it turns out that there is a lot more Negative stuff in this issue of "Smear" than usual. We want to try to balance this with two "classic" but little-remembered UFO events that occurred many years ago.

These are among the dozens of first-hand accounts we gathered on our unique drive to California and back in late 1953. (We still have about 150 pages of single-spaced typewritten pages of detailed notes.)

The first of these two sightings, which was presented in one of Major Keyhoe's early UFO books, was told to us in person by a man named William Squires, who lived on a farm near Pittsburg, Kansas, and worked at a radio station near there. He was by no means an educated man, but he told his story clearly and coherently. As often happens, he had no additional witnesses with him; but he also had no known reason to lie.

At about 5:30 in the morning of August 25th, 1952, Squires was driving to work, when he saw an unknown object hovering near the ground over a field not far from the road. It was shaped like two oblong dinner plates placed on top of each other. It appeared to be about 100 feet long and one third as wide, and there were three or four windows. Through these windows he believed he could see "shadowy forms" moving about within the craft. There were bright blue lights shining out of these windows, which kept changing from one shade of blue to another.

As soon as Squires stopped his car and got out to take a better look, the object shot upwards and was out of sight in 15 to 20 seconds.

The saucer made a sputtering sort of sound, and unlike any other UFO we have ever heard about, it had many, many small propellers around the whole perimeter, spaced as close together as possible. However, these seemed to be only for stability, and were not the real source of power, in his opinion...

On this same western trip, we also interviewed a man at the very opposite end of the educational spectrum. His name was Dr. Clyde W. Tombaugh, and he was the scientist credited with the discovery of the planet Pluto, back about 1930. (Some time after Tombaugh's death, Pluto was downgraded to a "planetoid", as several other relatively small sky objects about the same size as Pluto had been discovered by then.)

One evening in August of 1949, Tombaugh and his wife were sitting outdoors at their home in Las Cruces, N.M. At about 11 p.m. on a very clear night, while watching the stars with the naked eye, they saw a UFO at the zenith. It went quickly to a point 35 to 40 degrees above the horizon, where it dimmed out gradually and disappeared in a very few seconds.

Our notes don't tell us the object's apparent size, but it must have been fairly close to them, as they could see a row of about ten rectangular lights on it, arranged in a symmetrical manner (like windows??)...

On a slightly different subject - our very next interview on that western trip was with Dr. E.C. Slipher, another famous astronomer of that era, who worked at the well-known Lowell Observatory near Flagstaff, Arizona.

Slipher, in regard to the controversial "canals" of Mars, told us that he was of the opinion that they are artificial, made long ago by a now-extinct intelligent race, rather than being natural markings such as river beds, etc. This just goes to show how orthodox scientific opinion has changed over the years. Our present robot on Mars is not seeing or looking for artificial canals of any sort!...

● PERSONAL HEALTH NOTE: All is about the same. ●

212

APPENDIX 1: FINAL ISSUE OF "SAUCER SMEAR"

(2)

HERE'S SOME MORE ANTI-ROSWELL "NONSENSE" (?)

Here we go again!

There is in the public domain a genuine and formerly Secret Air Force document dated January 2nd, 1952, which seems to close the door to the possibility that an ET craft had crashed at Roswell (or anywhere else in the U.S.) up until that time.

It is headlined "WMD" ("Weapons of Mass Destruction"?). It was written by Air Force General Garland to General Samford, who was then Chief of USAF Intelligence.

It begins: "MEMORANDUM...

"SUBJECT: (SECRET) Contemplated Action to Dtermine the Nature and Origin of the Phenomena Connected with the Reports of Unusual Flying Objects.

"(1) The continued reports of unusual flying objects requires positive action to determine the nature and origin of this phenomena. The action taken thus far has been designed to track down and evaluate reports from casual observers throughout the country. Thus far this action produced results of doubtful value and the inconsistencies inherent in the nature of the reports has given neither positive nor negative proof of the claims.

"(2) It is logical to relate the reported sightings to the known development of aircraft, jet propulsion, rockets and range extension capabilities in Germany and the U.S.S.R...

"(4) In view of the facts outlined above, it is considered mandatory that the Air Force take positive action at once, to definitely determine the nature and, if possible, the origin of the reported unusual flying objects..."

The whole rather long memo is a discussion limited to possible Russian aerial capabilities. Nowhere is there any mention whatever of the possibility that these unknown objects are or might be extraterrestrial. The Air Force just did not think that way, in those days. Note also the wording "unusual flying objects" rather than the now commonly-accepted "unidentified flying objects".

In 1952 there was no Freedom of Information Act, so there was no reason to think that these generals were lying (or covering-up) to each other because they feared the memo might someday be made public.

Some people have said that since the memo is classified "Secret" rather than "Top Secret", these generals were lying to each other because they knew that co-workers not cleared for "Top Secret" information would read it - even though the public would probably never see it. We simply can't accept this point of view.

For what it's worth - the late Karl Pflock (formerly with the CIA) believed in the authenticity and truthfulness of this memo, even though he did believe in the existence of interplanetary UFOs. He did not believe in Roswell, however. His handwritten comments are on our copy of the memo.

Readers' comments are cheerfully invited. We will mail a copy of the full "WMD" text to anyone who sends us a two dollar Donation. (The purpose of the charge is to weed out trifflers)....

BIGFOOT HOAXER ENDS UP AS "ROADKILL":

In late August a 44-year-old man living in Kalispell, Montana, apparently tried to pull a peculiar Bigfoot hoax, and ended up losing his life for it. He was walking on a local highway one night, and was hit by two different cars!

This man, named Randy Tenley, was hard for motorists to see, because he was wearing something called a ghillie suit, defined as "a type of three-dimensional camouflage, sometimes worn by military snipers". These outfits are available online and at hunting shops.

His companions told police that Tenley was out there on the highway in this strange suit, trying to incite a Bigfoot sighting. The implication is that he was drunk at the time.

....Incidentally, in our late-life madness, we now believe that Bigfoot, if he exists, must be paranormal in some way. Why? Because all living creatures die, and no Bigfoot remains have ever been found. There has, however, occasionally been unidentified shit....

Martians
sink Yellow
Submarine

Invisible
man close
to reality

Graham & Telegraph, 11 Aug 2004

Monkey man found
guilty of supplying
cannabis

Halifax Sun. Gazette 5 Feb 2002

213

APPENDIX 1: FINAL ISSUE OF "SAUCER SMEAR"

THE "PHILADELPHIA EXPERIMENT" REVISITED :

One of the most fantastic legends of our times, though not directly related to UFOs at all, is the story of the "Philadelphia Experiment". An interesting rehash of this mystery appeared on the Net very recently, written by someone named Keith Veronese. We learned much new info., though many important details already known to us have been left out for some reason.

The article mentions movies on this subject that came out in the mid-1980s. However, these were preceded by a paperback book written about 1980 by William Moore and Charles Berlitz. Incidentally, these are the same two gentlemen who wrote the original "Roswell Incident" book in about the same year. Of the two, the Roswell narrative was <u>far</u> the more believable!

Both of these books were actually written by Moore alone. He teamed up with Berlitz, a much better-known writer ("The Bermuda Triangle", etc.) in order to get the book published easily. These two men, both of whom we knew quite well, eventually fought bitterly over royalties, and ended up hating each other. They never wrote any more books together. Berlitz is long deceased, but Moore went on to give us "MJ-12" and other intriguing UFO-related mysteries. He now lives in Florida in semi-retirement.

Anyhow - Veronese tells us that the Philadelphia Experiment syndrome actually consisted of two separate and quite different events, both in the year 1943. They both involved a Navy Destroyer escort called the USS Eldridge, according to the lore.

This is the legend! In the first experiment, an alleged method of electrical field manipulation allowed the USS Eldridge to be rendered <u>invisible</u>, on July 22, 1943, in the Philadelphia Naval Shipyard.

The second rumored experiment was the <u>teleportation</u> and small-scale <u>time</u> <u>travel</u> (with the ship sent a few seconds into the past) of the USS Eldridge from the Philadelphia Naval Shipyard to the corresponding shipyard in Norfolk, Virginia. This supposedly occurred on October 28th, 1943. This extraordinary event was said to have been seen by sailors on board a nearby troop transport vessel called the SS Andrew Furuseth. There were horrible tales of mangled seamen and sailors driven mad or stuck within the metal of the Eldridge. There was, of course, no proof whatsoever.

According to Veronese, careful research shows that neither of these ships was even <u>in</u> the Philadelphia Naval Shipyard on either of the dates in question!

The source of these strange stories seems to have been a very unusual man from a small town in Pennsylvania named Carl Meredith Allen, who changed his name to Carlos Miguel Allende. He was probably a retired seaman living on a (mental!) disability income, who for some reason spent most of his time living in cheap hotels along the Mexican border. He claimed to have been on board the SS Andrew Furuseth at the time of the second experiment, and to have seen its terrible effects.

Now the story gets weirder, if that's possible. Allende somehow got into a correspondence with a professional writer named Morris K. Jessup, who published four UFO books during the 1950s. Jessup eventually committed suicide for reasons unrelated to any of this. We knew him slightly, and though he seems to have exaggerated his educational background, we believe that he was a sincere and serious researcher.

Jessup's first and most successful book was called "The Case for the UFO". Somehow, in a manner we don't precisely remember, there came to be a spin-off of sorts, which was called The Vero Edition of "The Case for the UFO". This was published somewhat mysteriously by a small outfit in Texas that somehow had ties with the U.S. Navy. For some reason it was not widely distributed.

This edition was just like the original one, except that many pseudo-scientific comments were made in the margins, written in three different handwritings. These writers often argued with each other about obscure scientific points.

Eventually Carlos Allende admitted in writing that his story of first-hand knowledge of the second Philadelphia Experiment was untrue. He also is said to have admitted that all three of the handwritings in the Vero Edition were <u>his</u>! Weird indeed.

The truth about the Philadelphia Experiment(s) seems to be this: In the early 1940s, the Navy did conduct experiments to make naval vessels "invisible" in the Philadelphia Naval Shipyard, but in a different manner and with completely different desired results. Germany was using magnetic mines that would latch onto the metal hulls of ships as they came near. In these U.S. experiments, researchers ran an electric current through hundreds

APPENDIX 1: FINAL ISSUE OF "SAUCER SMEAR"

of yards of electrical cable around the hull of
a ship, to see if they could make the ship "invisible" to underwater and surface mines. In theory, this system would make the ships "invisible"
to the magnetic properties of the mines - NOT invisible to the human eyeball!

Apparently these experiments were not successful and were discontinued, but we are not sure
about this.

Getting back to Carlos Allende - never was
there a more colorful fellow associated with the
UFO field. He was "mad as a hatter" in our opinion, but he spoke beautifully in a cultured, deep
voice and a fake Mexican accent that he had somehow acquired.

Allende never appeared at UFO conventions or
made formal statements of any kind, but over the
years, when not living on the Mexican border, he
visited a few UFO researchers around the country.
Among these was the APRO organization, and also our
close friend Gray Barker.

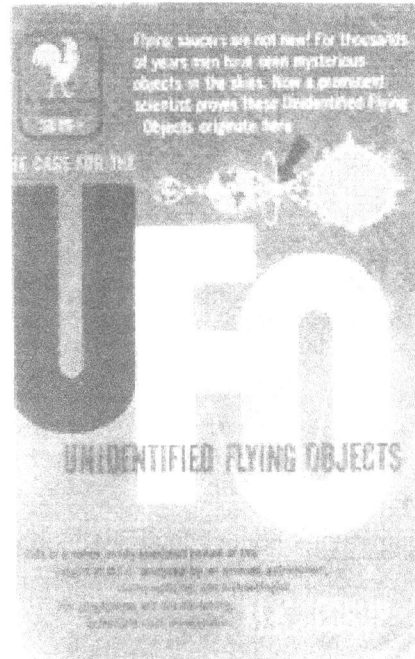

We used to occasionally drive from our home
in New Jersey to Clarksburg, West Virginia, to commune with Barker. One weekend, Allende appeared
from out of nowhere, uninvited and unexpected. We
took him out to dinner and paid one night at a lo-
cal motel, so that he could join us for a long evening of talk, which Barker recorded and
later sold through his Saucerian magazine.

Barker also sold copies of the uncopyrighted Vero Edition for the then unheard of
price of $25 each. This was a collector's item, and it sold well.

Your editor's only contribution to the Allende visitation was to pay for the dinner
and motel. At Barker's apartment we said very little and drank heavily while listening to
Allende's endless pseudo-scientific rant.

In 1999, fifteen surviving members of the USS Eldridge crew held a final reunion in
Atlantic City, with these veterans bemoaning the decades of strangeness surrounding the
vessel they had served on.

William Moore, co-author of "The Philadelphia Experiment", is still on our esteemed
mailing list; and we would be glad to hear from him or anyone else with worthwhile comments
on the above...

This item is postponed from our last issue.

Last September Ereditato (right) announced
that Opera, an Italian physics experiment,
had clocked neutrinos moving faster than
the speed of light. Six months later, after
discovering that a loose cable had skewed
their data, he and Autiero (left) resigned.
Did they announce the findings too early?
Yes. But to their credit, they invited other
physicists to try to prove them wrong. Plus,
when was the last time the public cared so
much about the theory of relativity?

"She's lookin' good, Vern!"

Hints of God particle found

GENEVA: Science collides with faith in the God particle. After two experiments using the Large Hadron Collider, the world's biggest atom smasher, scientists at CERN physicists say they have glimpses at the Higgs boson subatomic particle. The last missing link in understanding the universe.

© METRO WORLD NEWS

"It would be extremely kind of the Higgs boson to be here. It's too early [to say for sure]."

FABIOLA GIANOTTI, SCIENTIST AT LHC

APPENDIX 1: FINAL ISSUE OF "SAUCER SMEAR"

LETTERS TO YE OLDE EDITOR and

QUOTES FROM YE OLDE INTERNET

Herein famed ufologist/Fortean NICK REDFERN sends us some comments on criticism we made about him in our July 15th issue - having to do with alleged MIB interference on radio shows where he discussed - well, MIBs.

Further along, we quote part of Nick's recent Net rant about the sad state of ufology. Here we _agree_ with him completely.

"Many thanks for the latest issues of 'Smear' and your letters. I have gotten way behind on correspondence, so I'm finally catching up now.

"I don't dispute the possibility that the weird and repeated interference on the radio shows when I was promoting my book 'The Real Men in Black' _could_ have been studio based. But the reason I don't think that was the case is because it wasn't just a case of interference here and there. In one instance, it fucked up the show for like eight or nine minutes - and it was only a thirty minute show to start with!

"And with the 'Coast to Coast' interview, there were problems with _two_ landlines _and_ my cell phone!

"It doesn't, of course, prove any sort of MIB connection, but I still find the whole thing interesting."

From the Net: "THE FUTURE OF UFOLOGY":

"...The reality is that 65 years after our Holy Lord and Master (Sir Kenneth of Arnoldshire) saw whatever it was that he saw on that fateful June 24, 1947 day, Ufology has been static and unchanging. It has endorsed and firmly embraced the ETH (Extraterrestrial Hypothesis) not as the belief system which it actually is, but as a likely fact. And Ufology insists on doing so in stubborn, mule-like fashion. In that sense, Ufology has become a religion. And organized religion is all about upholding unproven old belief systems and presenting them as hard fact, despite deep, ongoing changes in society, trends and culture. Just like Ufology...

"What this stubborn attitude demonstrates is (A) a fear of change, (B) a fear of having been on the wrong tract for decades, and (C) a fear of the unknown. Yes, mainstream old-time Ufology lives in fear. It should be living in a state of _strength_. And it should be a strength born of a willingness to address _everything_, not just the stuff that some conference organizer thinks will attract the biggest audience... Ufology commits an even bigger crime as it coasts aimlessly along, like an empty ship on the ocean waves. It avoids the alternative theories _knowingly_ and fully aware of the long-term and possibly disastrous consequences that a one-sided biased approach may very well provoke for the UFO field...

"Ufology needs to expand its collective mind. It needs to be revamped. Other than collecting reports in massive amounts, _nothing_ tangible and provable in terms of the true nature of the phenomenon has been achieved! We need proof and undeniable evidence, not more reports. Ufology, as it has existed for decades, has consistently failed to provide that proof, as a result of largely following the ETH and nothing else....UFOLOGY HAS FAILED!

"SEMI-MYSTERIOUS KNOCKINGS, DAY AND NIGHT AT YOUR APARTMENT DOOR? MORE THAN LIKELY, NOTHING TO WORRY ABOUT. BUT THEN AS YOU KNOW, OR SHOULD KNOW, KEY WEST IS ONE OF THE MOST HAUNTED LOCATIONS IN THE U.S.A. THE RESTLESS SPIRITS OF KEY WEST BEGAN TO AWAKEN WHEN THE SUN DROPS BELOW THE GULF'S HORIZON. THERE ARE TALES BY FAMOUS WRITERS ABOUT PIRATES, RUM-RUNNERS AND THE GHOST STORIES IN KEY WEST ARE ENDLESS, CREEPY AND OFTEN FRIGHTENING. SO BE CAREFUL MY FRIEND."

Hang in there.

MILLER JOHNSON

APPENDIX 1: FINAL ISSUE OF "SAUCER SMEAR"

Our esteemed contributing editor CURT COLLINS writes as follows:

"The latest issue of 'Smear' was a good one. I liked the Mothman cartoon and commentary, and also the coverage of the Valentich case. I'm in total support of you revisiting classic cases. The older cases tend to have more interesting features, particularly the involvement of military participants and investigators. We may not be able to know what the UFOs were, but at least there is a formal record to work with. Also, reading about the cases as presented by you is always interesting, and I like hearing your opinions and how you put things into the larger picture.

"My favorite bit was your coverage of the Flatwoods intergalactic war, where you talk about Dwight Connelly's plea for ufologists to 'hang together'. That sounds so much like the arrangement the Contactees had, where they didn't dispute each other's contradictory stories...Stanton Friedman seems content to 'hang together', except when someone peddles a story that goes against his grain.

"Your continuing coverage of the MUFON promotion scandal was good. They have hit a new low, hawking their conference like a carnival exhibit. On reflection, that may be a good model for them - they just convert to a rolling tent show and hire carnival freaks!...

"The UFO presentation at the National Atomic Testing Museum has come and gone, without the disclosure that some were longing for...Apparently long-retired Col. Coleman was on the verge of some kind of disclosure and backed off at the last minute. Is he taking lessons on teasing from MUFON's MacDonald?...'"

We met Col. Coleman at the Pentagon many years ago. He had had a UFO sighting of his own, and was a writer of science-fiction. He seemed like a really cool guy. Did he really have something truly important he wanted to tell the crowd? We will never know for sure.-Editor.

Here are a few extracts from another sadly Negative Net item, by RICH REYNOLDS. It is called "The Soul-Killing UFO Obsession - or Is It an Addiction":

"It is so blatant, the addiction - the obsession - that some people have with and about the UFO topic - not UFOs, but the topic of UFOs...That marriages, jobs, and lives have been interrupted or set aside by some men & women in the pursuit of the ephemeral UFO phenomenon is palpable and disheartening (to the rational among us)....

"For example - Gene Steinberg, the Paracast guy, has been under an economic siege of some magnitude, as his many months of pleas for donations from the UFO community indicate. But yet, Mr. Steinberg will not relinquish his interest in UFOs (per his Paracast endeavors) to get a job, any job, to assuage his financial plight. UFOs, as he and his family seemingly go under, remain his primary pursuit, not a job or even a bank robbery. He's devoted to UFOs come hell or high water..."

Anthony Bragalia continues to rant on the Net about his solution to the famed Socorro landing in N.M. in 1964. He believes it was a hoax by students at the N.M. Institute of Technology. Dreaded skeptic TIM PRINTY agrees with pro-UFO researchers that Bragalia's evidence is inadequate at best. Printy, of SUNlite fame, writes us as follows:

"...Bragalia has refused to release the entire transcript of his interview with Prof. Stirling Colgate of N.M.I.T, which makes me wonder about how much 'selective editing' was done by him. In an e-mail to me, Bragalia stated that he has the names of the hoaxers but never would release them to me or anybody else, because he was trying to protect the reputations of these men. He added that the principals would never reveal how they actually did it or attempt to give a demonstration of how it was done...Bragalia also stated that I was pig-headed for not recognizing this was a hoax, and that in his heart (and his mother's grave!) he knows it was a hoax.
"...I think Bragalia tends to play Captain Ahab too much, and appears to be obsessed...
"I have also reread Kevin Randle's public letter about Don Schmitt, back in an old issue of 'Smear'. Back in 1995, Randle basically stated that Schmitt was a liar, a lazy researcher, and could not be trusted. As of 2011, Schmitt is now a respected researcher and can be trusted! Now you imply that Schmitt has some 'new evidence' about Roswell, but is not sharing it with the 'dream team'. My guess is that he probably could not get Randle to buy into his 'new evidence', which may have something to do with Frank Kimbler's research, which is nothing to get excited about, from what I have seen..."

APPENDIX 1: FINAL ISSUE OF "SAUCER SMEAR"

79 PEMBROKE CRESCENT
FREDERICTON, NEW BRUNSWICK, CANADA E3B 2V1
506-457-0232 FAX 506-450-3832 Email : fsphys@rogers.com

Subject: False claims in Saucer Smear 59:8   Sept. 27, 2012

STANTON FRIEDMAN writes:

I am curious as to who is supplying you with wrong information about UFOs and about me as shown in the latest SS. How can you claim I am "a hard core "True Believer?" Such a person would do his research by proclamation, not investigation as I do. Anybody who reads my books or listens to my interviews knows I reference and present evidence. True believers, such as the debunkers, don't reference sources, data, facts. They make claims. I am just reviewing a book by Dr. John Gribbin "Alone in the Universe: Why our Planet is Unique". He makes all kinds of claims without providing evidence or sources ... sort of a younger Phil Klass.

You say "as usual, he bills himself as a Nuclear Physicist, although he has not practiced that profession for well over 40 years". Poppycock! That would mean since 1972. Source please? I gather you are not aware that I worked as a nuclear physicist on the commissioning of the Point Lepreau Nuclear Generating Station here in New Brunswick in the early 1980s? I did a report "State of the Art Survey , Commercial Utilization of Power Planet Waste Heat " for the Canadian Electrical Association January 1985. I published a study "State of the Art Survey: Electron and Particle Beam Devices and Their Impact on Electrical Energy" January 1986 also for the Canadian Electrical Association (250 References.) I published a study for the Research Division of the Canada Mortgage and Housing Corporation "Radon Exposure in Fredericton Area Houses and Wells" , 1988.(Radon is a radioactive gas of interest to us nuclear physicists). In June 1989 I published a report for the Innovation Centre of New Brunswick entitled "Future New Brunswick Technology Scenarios". I gave presentations at two meetings of the European Society for Nuclear Methods in Agriculture in the 1980s in Piacenza, Italy, and Warsaw, Poland, on seed stimulation and food irradiation and also spoke at an International Meeting in Washington D.C. I should also mention that I am still a member of the American Nuclear Society and the American Physical Society and the American Institute of Aeronautics and Astronautics.

With regard to the Flatwoods Monster case, let me contrast my position with yours. I have visited the actual site of the event twice and have met with the primary witnesses and reviewed a lot of evidence. The evidence and investigation convinced me that Frank was spot on. What convinced you as a hard core disbeliever that he wasn't? If you would read the press articles about the orders to shoot down UFOs, if they didn't land when instructed to do so, you would see that they were not talking about Soviet or other planes. They were talking about UFOs. I have personally heard of seven cases in which pilots went up to chase UFOs and never returned. Frank has listed 200 cases right out of the New York Times of fatal military plane crashes between 1951-1956. Five of the pilots had flown over 100 combat missions in Korea came back to the USA, had a fatal crash. There with MiGs in Korea but none in the USA. Hard core disbeliever Joe Nickell says Flatwoods Monster was a 6' owl!! In short Jim, try to get your facts straight as we nuclear physicists do.

Most cordially,

Stanton T. Friedman   Hard Core nuclear physicist, lecturer, author

Editor's Note: We respect Stan Friedman as a friend and a legitimate scholar. Obviously, we were not completely aware of his continuing work in physics. HOWEVER, to seriously believe that our AF has actually shot down one or more ET UFOs or any such thing, is beyond reason! Surely we would have heard a lot about it by now, and not have to rely on Feschino's totally unproven speculations. - Stan, you are a "True Believer", and you are rooted in the 1950s (not even the '60s!) We believe in the possibility of ET visitations, but our guess is that we earthlings are dealing with various complex aspects of what we call (for lack of a more precise term) the paranormal. Time will tell, but neither of us has   all that much time left!

POST OFFICE BOX 753
NEW BRUNSWICK, NJ 08903

www.ingramcontent.com/pod-product-compliance
Lightning Source LLC
Chambersburg PA
CBHW080459110426
42742CB00017B/2944